Faith and Feminism in Pakistan

"This sophisticated, sharp analysis of women's activism in Pakistan, brings home the crucial relevance of secular women's movement and working-class women's activism, under religious militancy. An essential read for those interested in better understanding the many dimensions of the sensitive subject, women's political actions in Muslim contexts."

Haideh Moghissi, York University, Toronto, author of the award-winning *Feminism and Islamic Fundamentalism* (OUP)

"Through a critical feminist theorization of the relationship between Islam and feminism in Pakistan, Afiya Zia takes on the provocative questions of 'Are secular politics, aims and sensibilities impossible, undesirable and impracticable for Muslims and Islamic states? Should Muslim women be exempted from feminist attempts at liberation from patriarchy and its various expressions, which include Islamic laws and customs as they are practiced in the present time?' Her compelling response to these questions incites us brilliantly to read the religious challenges facing feminist studies and women's movements beyond Pakistan. This book is a layered analysis of the retreat of secular and liberal feminist spaces while it also critiques the limits of liberal secularism."

Shahrzad Mojab, University of Toronto, co-author of *Revolutionary Learning: Marxism, Feminism and Knowledge*

"Every once in a while there comes a book that is guaranteed to make its readers sit up and take note of the power of its argument, the clarity of its expression and the sheer audacity of its claims. This is that book. Indispensable for any understanding of the pernicious effects of an Islamically informed faith-based politics on women in Pakistan, it puts paid to the idea that such politics could ever serve as the engine of feminine agency. This is a rare and much-needed corrective against the present sweep of insidious currents hostile to the promise of a secular future for Pakistan and its women."

Farzana Shaikh, author of *Making Sense of Pakistan*

"In this book Afiya Zia brings into play all her skills in incisive analysis and her ability to go to the heart of the matter without fear or reservations, for which she has built a solid reputation over the many years of advocacy of women's rights. *Faith and Feminism in Pakistan* should not fail to shorten the journey to salvation of not only Pakistan's Muslim women but also of women in all Muslim majority countries."
I. A. Rehman, Human Rights Commission of Pakistan; recipient of the Ramon Magsaysay Award and the Nuremberg International Human Rights Award

"This is a superb and much overdue study of the history of feminism in Pakistan and its involvement in the question of Islam in state and society. Afiya Zia brings a keen analytic eye to the task, without sentimentalizing any of the actors or ideas concerned. But her own lifelong involvement in the feminist movement in the country adds a richness of texture to her discussion. This is a brave new contribution to the extensive discussion of Islam and gender across the disciplines, insisting that we view the women's rights movement as a legitimate part of contemporary Muslim societies. It will make waves in the academic world and in politics, and rightly so."
Aamir R. Mufti is Professor of Comparative Literature, University of California, Los Angeles and author of *Forget English! Orientalisms and World Literatures* (Harvard University Press)

"Pakistani women have been at the forefront of struggles for democracy and secular human rights. From her vantage point as member of the women's movement, Afiya has documented the multiple challenges that we have faced as women activists during the 'War on Terror'. Those who want to understand the tensions between faith and feminism in Pakistan should read her account in this book."
Asma Jahangir is a lawyer, co-founder and chair of the Human Rights Commission of Pakistan. She has served as the United Nations Special Rapporteur on freedom of religion and is recipient of the Hilal-i-Imtiaz, Right Livelihood and Ramon Magsaysay Awards

For Aadil and Emad

Faith and Feminism in Pakistan

RELIGIOUS AGENCY OR SECULAR AUTONOMY?

sussex
ACADEMIC
PRESS
Brighton • Portland • Toronto

2 4 6 8 10 9 7 5 3 1

First published 2018, in Great Britain by
SUSSEX ACADEMIC PRESS
PO Box 139
Eastbourne BN24 9BP

Distributed in the United States by
SUSSEX ACADEMIC PRESS
ISBS Publisher Services
920 NE 58th Ave #300, Portland, OR 97213

British Library Cataloguing in Publication Data
A CIP catalogue record for this book is available from the British Library.

Library of Congress Cataloging-in-Publication Data
Names: Zia, Afiya Shehrbano, author.
Title: Faith and feminism in Pakistan : religious agency or secular autonomy? / Afiya S. Zia.
Description: Brighton : Sussex Academic Press, 2018. | Includes bibliographical references and index.
Identifiers: LCCN 2017043011 | ISBN 9781845199166 (hardback : alkaline paper)
Subjects: LCSH: Feminism—Pakistan. | Secularism—Pakistan. | Islam and secularism—Pakistan. | Feminism—Religious aspects—Islam.
Classification: LCC HQ1745.5 .Z53 2018 | DDC 305.42095491—dc23
LC record available at https://lccn.loc.gov/2017043011

Typeset and designed by Sussex Academic Press, Brighton & Eastbourne.
Printed by TJ International, Padstow, Cornwall.

Contents

Acknowledgements

The kindest support to my person and feminist politics has been a mother who has nurtured and encouraged me and defended my pursuits through life and now does the same for my sons. Without her, I could not have made any professional progress or contributed to any political or scholarly cause. Thank you, Purveen, for literally everything. Both my grandmothers were amazing pioneers in their respective ways and I'm privileged to have spent time with my *naani* as she aged with wisdom and in the most graceful way a person could. My non-biological mothers and sisters have been invaluable allies and provide a loving haven since childhood: Anna (Afroze), Jaana (Farzana), Sarah Burki, Faryal Khan, Ambreen Marghoob, Batul Rizvi, Naila apa, Alia Fawad, Emma Ali and Sadia Mahmud are strong, independent, beautiful women who inspire me all the time.

There is the extended family of matriarchs of the women's movement in Pakistan who are (thankfully) too many to list, but Anis Haroon, Nasreen Azhar, Uzma Noorani, Rubina Saigol, Hina Jilani, Hilda Saeed, Kausar S. Khan, Nuzhat Kidvai, Fauzia Qureshi, Sheema Kirmani, Rukshanda Naz, Shaheen Sardar Ali, Mariam Bibi, and (the late) Razia Bhatti, as well as all the other dynamic women who are members of the Women's Action Forum, have taught me the most important lessons of the unending feminist struggle for a more just and equal Pakistan. They encouraged me to debate and disagree as an equal. I am thrilled by the energy and spunk of the young women who are committed to feminist activism, including Amar Sindhu, Farieha Aziz, Qurat, Naghma, Malka, Rahima, Seema, Shirin, Natasha Noorani and many, many others. Feminists such as Saba Gul Khattak and Farzana Bari, Irum and Farah Zia inspire me for their accomplishments and integrity and have been unwavering in their support and loyalty. Sisters, such as Ayesha Tammy Haq, who make ripples in a male-dominated society and Nazish Brohi, who make me laugh at myself, are my sounding boards and occupational oases. There is no way to quantify the value of Bushra's and Sumera's labour in my home. I owe them a lifetime of gratitude for their dual and triple labour and care-giving services and hope that my and their own children will recognise, value and respect their autonomy as working women.

Young women and men from minority groups who struggle for their lives and rights in big cities, forgotten ghettos, small towns and obscure tribal areas draw my admiration and shame simultaneously, on a daily basis.

As a feminist, I have been lucky for the support from a selection of brilliant men. S. Akbar Zaidi has been the invaluable mentor, friend and critic that everyone should be lucky to have. His teaching, guidance and critiques have improved the minds of many young scholars and his own work has contributed to enriching the social sciences in Pakistan. He may just be the last of cutting-edge socialists in Pakistan who has not compromised his political views or fallen victim to a politics of appeasement and convenience. Human rights defender, I.A. Rehman is another man who has been fighting for rights for longer than anyone I know and yet, is still ahead of his time and stands tall amongst a new generation of activists who feel they have seen and heard it all. He will always remain my go-to man for human rights advice and learning. Salman Akram Raja is one of Pakistan's most brilliant minds and his instinctive insights have often landed us on the wrong side of acceptable opinion, but at least we have occupied that space together. Stephen Hall is the most radical and committed thinker that I know in the Western world and I value his quirkiness and his complete disregard for fame, recognition or worldly achievement. If Pakistan had more lawyers, politicians and statesmen like Aitzaz Ahsan, it would be able to convert some of its revolutionary and progressive potential. I am grateful for Aitzaz's and Khaled Ahmed and Arif Hasan's generous words of encouragement, always. I admire the skilled outliers within government, such as Afzal Latif who works tirelessly with a kind of defeatist determination that claims change will not happen within state structures but continues to try and make it happen anyway. Activists, comrades and thinkers such as, Farooq Sulehria, Asad Jamal, Omar Waraich, Ali Arqam, Owais Tohid, Shahid Fiaz, Muhammed Hanif, Ammar Rashid, Fahd Ali, and some of the younger men and women from the Awami Workers Party hold promise for the promotion of feminist causes in Pakistan. I hope they are able to do so, for the sake of my and their sons and daughters.

My brilliant and beautiful sons, Aadil and Emad, are my closest friends, sharpest challengers and most compassionate and fun companions. Without their spark and independence and the help of their father, I could not have studied or politicked through motherhood. I am especially thankful to my own father, Hussan Zia who has always supported and invested in my academic pursuits in equal measure to what he did for my brother. A special thanks to my uncle, Farooq Feroze Khan, baby brother, Saad Zia, and the brotherhood provided by Fahad and Faisal Farooq, Zain Ghazali, Ahmed Rana, and Dr. Nadir Ali Syed for their love but mostly their ability to make me laugh till it hurts. Childhood friendships that continue to sustain me today include the bonds I share with Shabnum, Sadiqa, Kamila, Hyder Ahmed, Ghouse Akbar, Nadir Shah, Ameen Jan, and Nasser Aziz.

For her contribution to Marxist feminism and personal encouragement and guidance, I am deeply grateful to Shahrzad Mojab. She will always be more friend than advisor or colleague. The same is true of dynamic and inspiring scholars, Deniz Kandiyoti, Haideh Moghissi, Huma-Ahmed Ghosh, and activists such as Meredith Tax. I am also appreciative of the readings and comments by these scholars on earlier versions of this work, as well as those by Kiran Mirchandani and Ania Loomba.

A section of the analysis of the fate of Lady Health Workers in Swat and polio campaigns in the country have been reproduced in Chapter 3 with the kind permission of openDemocracy (50.50) where it first appeared. Thanks to Jane Gabriel and Deniz Kandiyoti for their encouragement and feedback on all my contributions to this important independent online global media forum. I am thankful to Anthony Grahame, Editorial Director at Sussex Academic Press, for his intuitive grasp of the subject of this book and his decisive willingness to publish it.

I am deeply respectful of the women artists of Pakistan and their defiant insistence on advancing the living and performing arts under the most challenging and difficult circumstances. A special thanks to the generous artist and friend, Naiza H. Khan for providing an image for the book's cover. I have always admired the politics behind her "Henna Hands" series. Thanks also to Sameera Raja and Maliha Noorani for their research, advice and explanations about feminist art in Pakistan.

Global spectators often ask women of the south – as if it is an aberration or in expectation of an exotic anecdote – what led them to become activists in their contexts and what inspires them to document the struggles for rights against patriarchy and militarised, religious and cultural norms. This has always struck me as an odd query because I grew up in a Pakistan, South- and wider Asian region that was always in dissent and where women spearheaded pro-democracy movements and forged regional linkages for the common cause of feminist transformation, equality and the redistribution of wealth and power. Given our long herstory of bravery and many successes, and the fact that so many more continue to swell our ranks, I wonder if the inquiry lingers because of the way the spotlight remains on women as subjects of patriarchy and global imperialism and now, on their interior subjectivities and pious agency, and not enough light has been shed on the achievements, changes, challenges, grit and the survival strategies that independently define many resolute and audacious Pakistani women.

The list of intrepid women and girls who have resisted patriarchy in all its expressions and asserted their right to be counted and valued is fortunately, too long to include here. The dream is that over successive generations more will survive, thrive and be determined to tell their own stories of courage, resistance and autonomy.

The Cover Illustrations

The two images on the cover are from the Henna Hands series (2002) by award-winning Pakistani artist, Naiza Khan. Naiza "dislocated" this work from the gallery and recreated the images made with henna pigment on the walls of colonial buildings in a *mohalla* (neighborhood) near the Cantonment Railway Station of Karachi. The site hosts a mixed community of Parsis, Muslims, Christians and Hindus. Most of the residents are slowly being evicted from their homes to make way for demolition and rebuilding of the area. Naiza explains the fate of these images in the *dhobi* (laundry)-site, where the implied march of three women was all but scratched out soon after it was put up: "The residue remains as part of the wall, marking a different sort of web with graffiti, *paan* (beetle nut) stains and party political slogans. In another location, the work remained for some time, children enjoying it, women angered by the blatant use of the woman's body, arguing to see it replaced by a man's body. The images have slowly been erased, scratched, in part preserved, and integrated with the writing on the wall." Naiza Khan explains that in the process of relocating the images from the private to the public, the body became a 'site' for inscription in which it gained and lent new meaning to the notions of the symbolic and the physical.

Introduction

Secular Possibilities

Pakistan is one of the last three countries[1] where the preventable poliomyelitis disease is still endemic. In a sharp rise from previous years, some 306 cases were registered in 2014 (National Emergency Action Plan for Polio Eradication (NEAP) 2016–2017, Government of Pakistan), and the World Health Organisation had temporarily imposed travel/visa restrictions and toyed with the idea of imposing sanctions if polio continued to spread. The majority of cases are found to originate in Pakistan's northern tribal areas, which are less populated but where religious militants have actively resisted the vaccination programme, terming it an un-Islamic practice and believing it to be an international conspiracy to sterilise Muslims. In 2012, over a dozen health workers, many of them women, were assassinated across the country while they were administering polio vaccines to children in poorer communities. Almost twice the number of security personnel designated to protect the vaccinators have been killed subsequently. Some polio vaccinators have been attacked with improvised explosive devices while some women health workers have been kidnapped and killed for their role in administering door-to-door vaccines.

Following the assassinations of their colleagues in 2012, and as part of their protest campaign demanding protection in the future, several members of the Lady Health Workers Programme[2] were seen burning government posters that carried images of prominent male clerics and born-again sportsmen who endorsed the vaccine. When I asked some of these Lady Health Workers why they had objected so indignantly to such rare support from the religious community on progressive programmes such as vaccinations against disease, they replied,

> This is a mockery and false pretense. It is an attempt to grab the moral ground and worth of our practical contributions towards vaccinating Pakistani children against all diseases. Why should we allow these clergymen to become the false faces of such an important job? They are simply doing so for political mileage. They are men. Which women will let these men into their houses for vaccinating their chil-

dren? Historically, these clerics have been the cause of suspicion and refusals of such vaccinations and contraception, spreading false ideas that these are dangerous for Muslims. If they repent their earlier ways, they should do so in the mosques. Leave us to do our practical job, which has nothing to do with religion or faith. It's a medical requirement and it's shameful that we are behind all other progressive countries when it is entirely preventable. We know. We have the blood of our sisters to show who has paid for such misinformation and deliberate falsity. (Bushra Arain, 2013)[3]

Are secular politics, aims and sensibilities impossible, undesirable and impracticable for Muslims and Islamic states? Should Muslim women be exempted from feminist attempts at liberation from patriarchy and its various expressions, which include Islamic laws and customs as they are practised in the present time? Considerable literature[4] on the entanglements of Islam and secularism has been produced in the post-9/11 decade and a large proportion of it deals with the "Woman Question". Nearly all of it offers targeted critiques of "the secular" and "Western feminism", as well as an unpacking of the racialising backlash that informed the occupation of Afghanistan and policies in other Muslim countries, under the shield of the "War on Terror" (WoT). Implicit in much of the critical works on Islam and secularism is the suggestion that it is Western secular feminism that is the motivating driver and permanent collaborator – in partnership with other feminists, secularists and human rights activists in Muslim countries – that solely sustains the West's actual and metaphorical "war on Islam and Muslims".

Such literature avoids, ignores or downplays the role, growth and agency of religious militancy and conservatism and its growing influence, encroachment and practical (often, bloody and violent) usurpation of all secular space and expressions in Muslim contexts. It also excludes mention of the historical benefits or contemporary viability of secular politics and expressions that predate the "WoT" in countries such as Pakistan. Neither does such scholarship acknowledge the resilience and continuity of such secular resistance and desire for secular space in such contexts. Most damaging of all, the benefits that are possible and demonstrable through such secular politics have been deliberately subsumed and replaced, even inverted, by such scholars who found Western academic settings and publishing houses conducive to literature that attempted to explain Islam and its alterity in the post-9/11 period. What was sacrificed in the process was the consideration that women and minorities in Muslim contexts very often participate, actively seek the benefits from and, form the direct leadership of secular resistance to Islamist politics, whether pitted against the state or private sector Islamist franchises.

This book attempts to trace the interplay of Islam and feminism in Pakistan in order to recall the debates and successes of secular and modernist feminism that predate 9/11 and continue today. The bias of the research lies in the more detailed attention I call towards working women's movements that are secular in nature. My argument is that these deserve as much, if not more research attention than the disproportionate reception and reification of religious actors in international circles, including in the Western academy. The concern over the anthropological recovery of Muslim women's non-liberal agency is that it encourages a kind of Muslim exceptionalism while diffusing the politics of faith-based empowerment, and is justified through a concentrated critique and rejection of universalism, secularism and Enlightenment-based rights

The work also traces the incredible loss in progress made by the feminist movement due to Islamist politics, conservatism and opportunism as employed by the state, religious groups and parties, but also the lack of meaningful support from many liberal men and women who are fearful of a backlash from Islamists, or are genuinely ambivalent about Islamic norms and perspectives. Necessarily, what is challenged here is the broader narrative found in the scholarship that is critical of feminism in Pakistan and which attempts to negate, delegitimise or seeks to soften the radical edges of activism that directly and unapologetically confronts and exposes the misogyny and hate-crimes enacted or inspired by faith-based politics. My attempt here is to recover the processes and examples of non-theocratic and secular engagements and movements and to highlight their viability, contributions and possibilities towards the progress of women's rights in Pakistan.

Waves of Influence

The trajectory of feminist and/or modern academic interest in Muslim women's experiences and political activism is a fairly recent one, spanning just the past three to four decades. Over this period, the scholarship produced has widened its reach and galvanised much attention. The reception and influence of such scholarship on the women's movements in Pakistan may be divided into three broad 'waves'.[5]

The first wave was marked by the infiltration of international feminist scholarship published in the 1980s on the relationship between women, Islam and feminism and which became available and relevant for feminist interest in Pakistan. The relevance of such scholarship was that it emerged in the form of several path-breaking studies and theorising by feminist scholars (usually from Muslim contexts or consciousness) working in the field of the social sciences, law, and/or involved in the feminist recovery of what can be broadly described as, Harem Literature.[6] Apart from scholars, feminist activists around the world were also "writing their bodies" and on their multiple experiences of being Muslim, feminists and citizens in contexts that were experiencing Islamic resurgences. The growing interest in the relationship between Islam, women and feminism had an impact on the Pakistani women's movement, but largely as consumers rather than contributors to the growing body of such theory building.

Caught in the midst of a state campaign of Islamisation in the 1980s led by military dictator General Zia ul Haq (1977–88), Pakistani women bore the harshest brunt and backlash of a religio-military dictatorship.[7] During this time, Pakistani feminists and women activists mostly expressed resistance on the streets rather than in academia. Despite the legitimate constraints, as well as the non-academic slump that the urban women's movement yielded to in the following decade, this early period of Pakistani feminist encounters with "Men, Money, *Mullahs*[8] and the Military" is perhaps the richest in terms of feminist literature produced in the country. The phrase was an informal slogan coined and used during street demonstrations by the women of Women's Action Forum (WAF), identifying the common and complicit obstacles to their demands for equal rights for women. WAF is a women's rights organisation founded in 1981 and which has a presence in several cities in Pakistan. It is a non-partisan, non-hierarchical, non-funded, secular organisation. It lobbies on all aspects of women's rights and related issues, irrespective of political affiliations, belief system, or ethnicity. It was the lead organisation that during the military dictatorship of General Zia ul Haq, took to the streets in protest against the promulgation of discriminatory Islamic laws.

The second wave may be connected to the advancement of postcolonial studies in India, particularly the critical project of Subaltern Studies. This epistemological interest that emerged in the 1970s and grew strong during the 1980s signaled a deep analytical questioning of the failure of modernity – for India, in any case. A focus on the liberatory potential of an alternative, pre-modernist, cultural and community politics, "with an insurrectionary bent," led to the investment of hope in the assertion of "an alternative mode of power and authority" by the "subordinate forces" of the community (Bannerji

2000, 908). Critiques of postcolonial modernity also opened the doors for a surge of criticism of Western bourgeois feminist hegemonies, as found in the works of Chandra Mohanty (1988), Uma Narayan (1988), Inderpal Grewal and Caren Kaplan (eds.) (1994), to name a few. Postcolonial theories by the subalternists encouraged several South Asians (including feminists mentioned above) to extend their critique of postcolonial and modernist notions of liberation to that of "Western feminism". In particular, the "presumptiveness" of secular feminism in non-Western contexts has been a point of debate. It sparked and deepened feminist interests, contests and regional debates in South Asia, over issues of cultural relativity/specificity and the worth of national versus universalist agendas and liberal versus traditional strategies.

During the 1990s, many feminists in Pakistan were influenced by such debates and were simultaneously confronted by masculinist criticism of feminism as a foreign import that led to alienation within the broader class struggle. Feminists then began to translate and bridge the relevance of universal feminist agendas with local, indigenous struggles. The collective work of this generation of feminists is often characterised as modernist feminism. One branch of such interest morphed into what was later categorised as Islamic feminism – an against-the-grain reading of the Sharia and Quran – that has sometimes led to an instrumentalisation of Islam toward development and humanitarian programmes.

Islamic feminism sometimes overlaps and gets analytically lumped with modernist feminist research collectives and networks, which advocate legal reform and organise resistance to Islamist threats to women's progress, such as the Women Living Under Muslim Laws (WLUML) network, which is an international solidarity association formed in France in 1985. WLUML monitors laws affecting women in Muslim communities, publicises injustices and links activists and academics in an ambitious Muslim personal law reform project. However, there is a distinction between the political positions and geopolitical impulses informing these two streams (Islamic and modernist Muslim feminisms), although their nexus is such that it often masks this distinction. The consequences have been under-examined and under-discussed in the context of Pakistan.

Subalternist scholars in India looked to recover the historiography of the subcontinent through the eyes of the bottom-most classes while rejecting the potential of liberal democratic politics as the appropriate tool for true decolonisation (including, of the bourgeois imaginary). Simultaneously, religio-nationalists in Pakistan were dismantling and redesigning their own nationalist discourse. Buoyed by the state patronage they enjoyed under the Islamic regime of military dictator, General Zia ul Haq, Islamist political parties, despite repeatedly failing abysmally at gaining any electoral success, gained unprecedented access and control over state structures and ideological policies. Pivotal to their redefinition of the state and vital for their search for a legitimising religious and cultural identity was the notion of the "unfinished project" or what Chatterjee (1990) discussed with reference to India, the "nationalist resolution of the woman question" but in this case, for the Islamic Republic of Pakistan.

The overlap in the above academic and political formulations of identities in India and Pakistan respectively – though not epistemologically connected by any means – may be read through Partha Chatterjee's argument that links the subaltern, community and religion. Chatterjee recognises religion as "a constitutive force in a subaltern consciousness" and so concludes that the closer the local elites are to religion the more 'subaltern' they are (original cited in Bannerji 2000, 909). Bannerji points out that Chatterjee makes a case for the Gandhian subaltern leadership in India that was defiant of "universal codes of justice and rel[ied] on the culture and authority of a religious-ideological community to have differential forms of conduct" (cited in Bannerji 2000, 909). Chatterjee argues that the Gandhian project, under the latter's genuine subaltern leadership failed only because Gandhi's traditionalist communitarianism was hijacked or polluted by the ideological imperatives of modernity for state formation. Such "partial rehabilitation" of the colonised elite by Subalternist scholars is the main impetus of Himani Bannerji's Marxist-feminist critique of the latter as contributing supporters of an illiberal, cultural nationalism (Bannerji 2000, 909).

In Pakistan, the notional rupture of tradition from modernity or indeed, the spotlight on such a binary was not developed under the vocabulary of nationalism as it was in India. In 1947, freedom and a modern nation state had been won from both the British colonisers and Hindu majority India. The anxiety for religio-nationalists was not so much on preserving traditions and rejecting modernity but far more so, over the need to religiously baptise the perceived secular nature of the Pakistani state in the early, post-Partition years under its founder, Muhammad Ali Jinnah. It was only much later under the Islamic regime of General Zia ul Haq, that the issue of competing postcolonial religious identities met an uneasy and forced reconciliation, when the Islamist political leadership allied with the military-led state and managed to placate this anxiety through the passing of the Islamic laws of the *Hudood* Ordinances (1979) and other Islamic policies. Not too interested in class politics or the subaltern, Islamists' politics in

Pakistan over the 1980s and 1990s was satisfied with simply focusing on pan-Islamism and the potential of women as symbols of an Islamic citizenry for the Islamic Republic of Pakistan.

The last and most recent wave may be seen in a body of post-9/11 scholarship that is critical of Enlightenment ideals, modernity and secularism, and is invested in uncovering the "complex subjectivities" of Islamists. Predominantly produced by diasporic anthropologists, the politics of much of this body of work is postsecular and postfeminist in its bent. This collective[9] seems to be interested in recovering retro-Islamist possibilities for Pakistan and arguing for a postsecularist future (Aziz 2005; 2011; Cheema and Abdul-Rahman 2008–2009; Bano 2010; Cheema and Akbar 2010; Mushtaq 2010; Quraishi 2011; Iqtidar 2011; Jamal 2013).[10] The interest extends to Islamist women[11]and often posits them as agentive even in their docility and whose progress must not be assessed against Western feminist goals and struggles (Mahmood 2005).

I use "retro", rather than revivalist, to distinguish this recent scholarship from the earlier Islamic revivalist and modernist feminist scholarship. The latter, which attempted to recover the historical continuity of feminist consciousness amongst Muslim women, was interested in evaluating the patriarchal obstacles that early feminists faced in Muslim societies and whose contributions had been either discounted, or "Hidden from History" (Rowbotham 1975; Mernissi 1997; Moghadam 2000). In contrast, retro-Islamist scholarship does not read so much as a socialist or a feminist project but seems more of an anthropological interest to convalesce a reinvented identity of the "agentive" Muslim/Islamist woman through a critique of Enlightenment ideals and liberal universalism and by challenging what is considered to be an imposition of universal, liberal, secular, human and women's rights laws, values, principles or programmes in Muslim contexts.

Postsecular, Retro-Islamist Recoveries

Distinct from the earlier modernist and/or secular feminist task mentioned above, the current retrospective scholarship on Islamist women seeks to reconstruct narrowly defined religious identities by delegitimising the alternative strands of non faith-based identities as, colonial legacies or Western imports. This scholarship is historically framed within a post-9/11 context, which saw an academic revivalism of what came to be considered the "overlooked dimension" of religion in international relations and academia in general (Winter 2013, 151).

Bronwyn Winter (2013) confirms the connections made in this book with reference to the waves of scholarly influence on Pakistani feminism when she suggests that

> once the relevance of culture . . . had been "discovered" (thanks, in great part, to feminist and postcolonial scholars), one could consider religion, which is so closely imbricated with culture, historically, symbolically, socially, even materially, to be the next logical area of focus in any case, but 9/11 surely hurried along the process. (151)

The scholarship produced by those Pakistani women who I categorise as post-9/11 postsecularists is discussed with reference to their works which privileges and sometimes advocates a religious citizenship as a viable alternative to liberal feminism. The pejorative reference to "liberal" in much of this literature is usually used as a colloquial dismissal of those who would associate with progressive movements. Mistakenly, such criticism associates all those who would consider themselves to be progressive liberals as also, secular. Hence why I refer to the project of scholars who are critical of those who are called "liberal-secular" Pakistanis as a postsecularist one – quite different from Habermas' framing of the postsecular as a condition where "*both* religious *and* secular mentalities must "take seriously *each other's* contributions to controversial themes in the public sphere" which must remain ideologically neutral" (original cited in Winter 2013, 147).

Many of the postsecularist scholars discussed in the chapter to follow insist that they are simply reviving and interrogating a different way of being by show-casing the interiorised subjectivities of Islamists (particularly, Islamist and pietist Muslim women). Yet, this project runs the risk of rehabilitating what are in Pakistan certainly, Islamist men's patriarchal and nationalist agendas. Such scholarly efforts dovetail with the broader masculinist, Islamist demands that seek to purge all rights-based initiatives and movements of Western and particularly, feminist, liberal and secular influences. In particular, it is women's and minority rights that are targeted for being pollutant, Western, secular and complicit with neo-imperialist designs.

Even amongst those who would consider their own politics to be left-progressive, there are mocking criticisms reserved for those perceived to harbour "secular dreams" in post-9/11 Pakistan (Akhtar 2016). In keeping with the historical gender blindsiding that several men from left political groups have tended to treat Pakistani feminist movements, Akhtar (2016) makes the misplaced sweeping charge to prove his point about secular aspirations being an alienated and elitist dream:

> Throughout the Zia period, the elite, as Hasan incisively and meticulously documents, was content to reside and thrive within its walled ghettoes, abandoning both public space and practical politics. In doing so, it effectively abandoned the struggle for cultural hegemony. (648)

Such historically inexact accounts attempt to erase or negate the crucial contributions of the urban professional women activists (often of the elite or privileged classes) who spearheaded street demonstrations, demanded a secular state, and were equal members of the Movement for the Restoration of Democracy throughout the Zia period. As part of their public protests they were certainly critical of non-democratic and patriarchal Islamic politics and the limitations these placed on women's progress despite the fact that they were not directly, either personally or as a class, affected by the persecutorial policies of Islamisation. Such criticism also tends to target those involved in social movements or Non-Governmental Organisations (NGOs) that attempt to counter the cocktail of neo-conservatism and the impetus it receives from religious reasoning. The accusation is that these rights activists pander to the agendas of political neo-liberalism and even invite imperialist interventions and subjugate Muslim men at the expense and under the pretext of their own parochial agenda of freedoms.

Against the anthropological recovery of the Islamist Woman as representative of an imagined organic, indigenous and subaltern (suppressed classes) identity and all the other critical literature, I track the viability and contributions of a number of identifiably working women's secular movements in Pakistan. These I define as those struggles and campaigns that are free of theological underpinnings, motivations, slogans, and props and which have not been informed by religious debates, take no recourse from faith and are often targets of Islamist conservatism and militancy.

The purpose of outlining all these recent debates that have defined the interplay of faith and feminism in Pakistan is to recover the worth, value, contributions and viability of secular feminism in Pakistan both historically and with reference to the future, too. A secular standpoint has supported, broadly speaking, a liberal minimalist agenda of equality for all, while other expressions have been far more radical. The progressive women's movement has always acknowledged and debated the strategic worth of religion in their struggle for equal rights and this debate has never been conclusively settled. A more accurate description of urban progressive feminism in Pakistan would be that of a critical feminism rather than a liberal one, where the characterisation of critical feminism is said to be of a "combined activism and skepticism [which] also favors a contextual focus on concrete issues rather than generating utopian ideals" (Gruber 2013, 1386). However, the backlash of Islamic policies, laws and religious militancy even prior to the "WoT" has certainly overpowered and even negated and vilified the contributions and possibilities of secular and even, liberal feminisms in the country. The challenge has not come simply from Islamists of varying political bent but as mentioned above, from a new generation of post-9/11 scholars who conjoin and then dismiss the liberal/secular characteristics of the women's and human rights movements in Pakistan (Chapters 1 and 6). There is not much in terms of specifics in the criticism of the strategies of these rights activists and no mention of their successes or contributions but the objections are largely theoretical and presumptive, rather than demonstrative or context specific.

This book documents the historical worth and political contributions of the Pakistani feminist activism of which I have been a part for the last 25 years. The main debates are outlined regarding the interplay of faith and feminism with a focus on the main sources of the challenges pitted against Pakistani rights-based activists. Various limitations are also discussed – those of religious agency but also the limits of liberal activism, radical agency and capital. While every angle and aspect of Islamist women and their performativity seems to have become the doctoral subject of numerous post-9/11 Ph.D.s from Western academia, the possibilities and political consequences of secular movements have been less explored or ignored.

Methodology

A word on methodology is important here, for the tension that has marked feminist debates over and between (the privileging of) theory and/or activism, the political and personal and the academy and field is a very live one in Pakistan, too. In our case, feminist and human rights activism has been richly archived but under-theorised. This has meant that there are a wealth of case studies and documented histories of meetings, political statements, positions and debates amongst activists. Most of these testify to the varieties and evolution of ideological stands and differences, as well as resolutions and alliances that have marked these movements. Unfortunately, very few of these have been transcribed and so, much of the criticism that has subsequently targeted these movements has quite literally managed to sweep and dominate the international academy. This is simply because there is little written literature that can be referred to in order to offer a historical corrective in response.

Part of the reason for the emphasis on the post-9/11 postsecular scholarship is to reclaim the diversity, resourcefulness and influence of modern feminist activism in Pakistan that has been erased in this recent body of work. It is also to underscore the feminist movement's contributive role in stemming the swell of religious conservatism in the 1980s and 1990s. The same cannot be claimed today, since the narrative of women's rights activism has been successfully challenged from several directions simultaneously. Internal factions, NGO-isation[12] (Bari et al. 2001), stagnation of strategies, lack of new membership and dwindling participation, as well as competitive modes of anti-secular Islamist activism and market compulsions have overwhelmed the earlier feminist agendas. Yet the groups of the 1980s still hold political sway and legitimacy that none of the other, web-based, amorphous activist groups of recent years do. Such legitimacy is recognised not just by Western/international or state actors but Islamists and conservatives, too.

To recover some of the landscape of the liberal and secular leanings that have informed feminist politics, I have relied on personal observations and a variety of studies that span the last two decades. As a member of the urban women's rights/human rights groups and observer of the work of development organisations, I have had critical access to their workings and also had the opportunity of maintaining a working relationship with several government institutions. Through access to their records and by relying on the narratives that have informed the women's rights movement dating from 1989, this book draws upon personal experience but also on fragments of NGO literature, consultancy reports, development and university workshops, private study group discussions and direct talks with the founders and experienced leaders of these movements, as well as government officials. Necessarily, international feminist and critical theory around the recent debates of the religious and the secular inform the volume throughout.

The voice of women included in the case studies in this book has been represented through the channels of feminist activism. Many Lady Health Workers, nurses, factory workers, professional women in the public and private sector approach the Women's Action Forum for referral and support over their personal, political, legal and financial issues. Rather than relying on formal pre-set interviews, many of the observations included here are based on conversations with these women in their communities or when they have reached out to me in my personal capacity. These have been included here with their explicit permission. The specific case studies that I have collected and included are sourced from the existing work of research-activists who have shared their own findings with me and which are not necessarily available in published form.

This subjective method parallels the ethnographic methodology relied on by the new anthropology that is preoccupied with Islam and Islamists, which is critiqued herein. Some of the criticism that scholars in the Pakistani context face is over empiricism and demand for proof over what is sometimes said to be vague references to, for example, the impact of Islamist groups and their reactionary politics. This is a difficult and vast project to compress into one that is more committed to discussing the opposition but also, *ineffectuality* of Islamist politics for women's equal rights compared to that of liberal/secular possibilities. It is not in the scope of this project to provide empirical proof over how organised Islamist groups may have contributed towards impeding women's equal rights. However, such proof is cited, such as: Islamists' prevention of women from voting; their lobbying against reform of blatantly discriminatory laws against women and minorities; their direct opposition to policies and laws that guarantee freedom of expression or mobility; their campaigns of censorship and vigilantism. Islamists have even made concerted attempts to subvert the Constitution through the efforts to pass laws such as the *Hisba* (Accountability) law. In some cases, they have been outright supportive of, or at best, reticent about the murderous impact of radical religious militancy on women's and human rights in general.

It is pertinent to note that the reference to Islamist politics as politically regressive is not disputed – not even by conservatives in Pakistan. What is a common refrain amongst many, including some rights activists, is instead that Islam itself is not discriminatory in nature but rather, it is those who deploy the politics of religion that do so due to profane motives. Such politics are openly criticised – both in the media and popular culture. In Pakistan's academy and at community levels, criticising Islamist politics is far more difficult precisely because the Islamists who have come to dominate these institutions over the past few decades do not tolerate such criticism or challenges.

Another methodological challenge to feminist scholarship in Pakistan is over the question of representation. Some scholars writing in the frame of a post-9/11 politics and who are defensive about Islam and Islamists have been sharply critical of how political activism is not the determinant of epistemological privilege and that scholarly nuance is important. More recently, some have gone as far as to cast the accusation against select women's rights activists in Muslim contexts and implied that these feminists are serving as "native informants" (Toor 2012, 157). This anxiety is shared and resonates with masculine nationalist fears and feminists have faced these all through the post-colonial era. However, what is new in these current allegations is that they come from Muslim women scholars and/or, those of South Asian/Middle East North Africa origin. Based in Western academies or organisations, they seem to be missing the underlying irony in their attempted impeachment of "native" liberal-secular feminists. While jostling for a legitimate space and recognition for their own hybrid identities as *literal* and *paid* native informants in their occupations, it is simply ironic that these emissaries of South Asian/Middle Eastern/Islamic studies in Western academia should use the term in a pejorative manner for researchers and activists in native contexts (see Chapter 6).

When compared to the insistence for empirical proof mentioned above, such allegations and demands successfully sandwich scholar-activists in Muslim-majority contexts in a double bind. Further, too many feminists in countries like Pakistan, who straddle the discipline of scholarly research and developmental consultancy work know how easy it is to slide one set of findings across to the other and manufacture a product that can service both – academic purposes, as well as consultancy reports. This is not a comment on the ethics of this practice, simply an observation that reliance and insistence on empirical proof as a tool of validity may not be quite as impermeable as we romanticise it to be. Ethnography is a very contested methodology in the first place and to prescribe criteria over who applies it more authentically seems to be aggravating, rather than bridging the divide between feminist activism and theorising.

Some critics who argue that feminist readings are too narrow and who propose that "we" must be more inclusive as "we" work towards some imagined hybridity, urge a dilution of the political binaries and oppositional positions that have come to define rights-based movements. Most, if not all of the time, such advice is usually addressed to a liberal/secular (English language) readership rather than any faith-based audience. So, many of the arguments and debates, despite the stated intent of aiming to overcome binaries and divides are really about academic discussion between and amongst liberal intellectuals. The methodology herein consciously includes and relies on the experiential and political with reference to the movements and activism of the women's movement in Pakistan, with due emphasis and reliance on a cross-section of critical theories. For all the reasons outlined above, this work necessarily challenges recent scholarly interventions on the issue of faith and feminism, particularly with reference to Islamists and the Muslim context. While making the case for liberal and secular rights-based activism, I am all too mindful of the limitations of the latter and discuss these too, albeit, from the point of view that these have not been liberal or secular enough.

It is important to acknowledge the lack of reference materials, adequate libraries or academic work in Pakistan. This means that aspiring scholars and interested researchers have to rely on access to theoretical resources that are both expensive and often beyond physical reach. This is a serious limitation in terms of the production of published works but does not mean by any criteria (particularly feminist ones) that these researcher-activist-scholars are not producing theory or contributing to feminist epistemology. This book includes and references extensively the reports, papers and case studies that document the socio-political landscape of women's experiences in Pakistan but which tend not to get published and are simply not available to a wider audience. Recognising the worth of the analysis carried in these studies, these are referenced in some detail and relied on as independent observations that corroborate my case and which call for investing confidence in secular feminist resistance over and against faith-based politics and potential (particularly in the Conclusion). This may also serve the further interest of readers.

The 'waves' described above make circuitous and concentric sweeps around the body politic of feminist and faith-based political expressions in Pakistan. Debates, movements and strategies have become more visible and public as more women are becoming politically engaged and even competitive in their race to influence national and international discourse. While there is no formal forum, feminist journal or documentation of such exchanges and engagements, it is usually across individual cases, predominantly of violence against women, that such divergence of ideologies, thought and debate become most noticeable. Women's voices aided by the new media and through cultural and mainstream political expressions, have become important interlocutions in what was previously a male-dominated discursive field of nationalism, religion and identity-formation in Pakistan.

Chapter Organisation

The influence, impact and interplay of women's faith-based politics and feminisms in Pakistan are discussed over seven chapters.

Chapter 1 on "Islam, Feminism and Secular Resistance" summarises some of the main debates and strategies that informed the leading urban women's group, the Women's Action Forum (WAF) in the 1990s, over positionality and the judiciousness of working within the Islamic framework or retaining a secular alignment. It lists the risks and effects of Islamic feminism as a proposal as well as the implications of the project of working for women's rights within the framework of Islam – for Pakistan, in particular. It also identifies a body of post-9/11 Pakistani postsecularist scholarship that looks to recuperate the cultural relevance of religion (Islam) through a retrospective look at the "unresolved project" or nationalist resolution of the "Islamist woman question." Some examples of the anthropological scholarship on Islam and women produced over the last decade by Pakistani scholars (mostly women, nearly all diasporic) are discussed summarily.

Chapter 2, "The Postsecular Turn and Muslim Women's Agency," unpacks the influential work on Muslim women's pietist agency by Pakistani émigré, Saba Mahmood, in order to demonstrate its impact on the postsecular turn that her thesis has encouraged in academia and the new pedagogy on Muslim women. It has also encouraged a surge of new criticism cast against liberal and/or secular feminisms in Muslim contexts such as, Pakistan.

Chapter 3, "Beyond Faith and Agency," follows on the heels of the discussion of Muslim women's docile agency and presents the contrasting case study of the material and dynamic nationwide health advocacy undertaken by the Lady Health Workers (LHWs) who are recruited through a government programme. With their primary focus on rural maternal health services, the LHWs have played a critical role in reducing maternal and infant mortality and expanding the national vaccination policy through outreach. The process of empowerment, mobility and autonomy of these women are discussed. In contrast to the examples of religious agency offered by Mahmood, the activism of the LHWs is directed against the patriarchal codes of communities and often in defiance of faith-based obstacles and resistance to their work. Such secular resistance and working-class consciousness that motivates these women to strike for their right to regularisation of jobs and minimum wage is an important exemplar of secular autonomy and demonstrates by contrast the limits of religious agency towards the possibility of achieving equal rights for Pakistani women.

Chapter 4 offers some examples that demonstrate "The Limits of Religious Agency in Pakistan." It discusses the (re) construction of the "agentive" Islamist woman across the sites of religious nationalisms, Islamic extremism and popular culture in Pakistan. Three cases are discussed here, which may confirm the newly founded and celebrated "agency" of Muslim women. However, rather than strengthening the autonomy and independent interests of the Pakistani woman, it is demonstrated that "agency" works in collusion with and convergence and endorsement of the masculinised and increasingly hegemonic agendas of a narrowly defined Islamism and nationalism.

Chapter 5, "The Limits of Capital," catalogues several variants of the relationship between consumer capitalism and Islam in Pakistan and points out the consequences of the commodification of gendered religious identities. It questions the confidence entrusted in the way Islamists are embracing capitalist modes as proof that the Islamist imaginary has moved "beyond the state" (Iqtidar 2012). It argues that such hopes do not trace how the shift of Islamist consumer interest would mean that its members now qualify as the new, "Islamic Bourgeoisie". One of the self-critical discussions that concerned many feminists in the 1990s was the escalating "NGO-isation" of the women's movement. For several years now, I have been tracking how development organisations have been reengineering their projects to include faith-based strategies in their programmes, in order to avail themselves of the pool of funds reserved for such an approach to development in Pakistan. I call this increasing penchant for the strategic use of religion as a tool of gender empowerment and for the promotion of human rights, "donor-driven Islam." This chapter discusses the less examined and broader social influence and impact of this strategy of embedding progressive Islam under the guise of interpreting and servicing gender justice or, in offering this as a proposal for an indigenous resolution of discriminatory practices.

Chapter 6, "The Limits and Possibilities of Liberal Activism," is a critical discussion of the often limited and futile methods and strategies of liberal resistance to Islamic conservatism and religious extremism in Pakistan over the last decade. It discusses the increasing apolitical confusion and dependence on popular culture as a mode of resistance amongst "lifestyle liberal" activists. The futility of such strategies at a time when the veil has been deployed as a political signifier for Islamist women is contrasted against the attempts to prop fashion as a political decoy. The chapter also unpacks the diasporic scholarly criticism of Pakistani feminist activism against religious militancy. These academic and political allegations undermine the legitimacy of human rights defenders (and especially liberal/secular feminists), who are already misrepresented as anti-nationalists and Islamophobic by Islamists and in many cases, the state itself.

The concluding Chapter 7, "Beyond Faith and Fatalism," documents the consequences of pietist agency in the context of the Taliban invasion of northern Pakistan and analyses two streams of working women's (secular) movements in Pakistan. These movements peaked during and despite the decade dominated by Islamist politics, terrorism and counter-terrorism imaginaries; where the mobility of women was deeply hindered; where working-class populations were direct targets of religious and state violence alike, and their political aspirations and daily livelihoods repeatedly thwarted by foreign and domestic (economic) policies. It was also, paradoxically, the period when the most progressive affirmative action policies and conscious efforts towards women's empowerment were sponsored by what was euphemistically called, a "liberal dictatorship" under General Pervez Musharraf (1999–2008). The movements that chose to follow a secular mode and informed themselves with a liberal impetus, with no recourse to religious agency, are documented.

A final "Conclusion" makes the case for encouraging the expansion of secular spaces and political expressions for women's progress in Pakistan.

1

Islam, Feminism and Secular Resistance

The task here is to recall some of the political debates around Islam and feminism over the 1980s and 1990s, and discuss their relevance for Pakistan's urban-based women's rights groups in particular, the Women's Action Forum (WAF). It contextualises the strategic choice made by WAF to adopt a secular alignment while highlighting the risks and effects of Islamic feminism as a proposal. It discusses the implications of the project of working for women's rights within the framework of Islam for Pakistan.

A body of recent Pakistani scholarship shaped and responsive to the events of 9/11 and developed in Western academies is discussed here. These works are heavily influenced by postcolonial studies and are invested in recuperating the cultural relevance of religion (Islam) as a form of rights-based discourse and anti-imperialist resistance. Some of these are invested in a retrospective look at the "unresolved project" or nationalist resolution – of the "Islamist woman question". Most retro-Islamist Pakistani scholars producing such works are anthropologists, who reference the imaginary and cultural but not political practices of Islamist groups through academic inquiry. Another major omission in such works is the refusal to document the positive effects of modern, liberal, emancipatory or secular struggles and their yields for women, minorities and lower classes.

Islamic and Secular Feminisms

Much of the (now) fairly voluminous scholarship on women in Muslims societies may be categorised as a predominantly 'corrective' effort, especially in response to the monolithic stereotypes about the oppressive nature of Islam and assumed passivity of Muslim women (Joseph 2013).[1] A major portion of the early scholarly literature in this regard attempts to recover the contributions of Muslim women to national movements, social reform and literary writings. This encyclopedic literature also calls attention to the ethnic and political diversities and complexities of their lives with reference to Islam and local, cultural patriarchies.[2] Such anthropological literature began to acquire an activist bent and momentum in the wake of the grip of religious revivalism that spread in the 1980s in Muslim majority countries. In particular, this body of work reflected the expectations held by Muslim women who became invested in widespread legal changes aimed at improving women's status and rights. The central argument of much of this restorative scholarship on Muslim women's identities followed the revolution in Iran in 1979 and challenged the idea that "Islam" is a singular factor or primary determinant of Muslim women's status and well-being. Even from unlikely sources, such as studies by the American Central Intelligence Agency, it has been recognised that in its trajectory, Islam itself has been caught up in and "colored by, the specific histories and socioeconomic circumstances that shape the lives of Muslim women" (Offenhauer 2005).

Many of the historic, academic and strategic re-engagements with religion have yielded ongoing reinterpretations, with the aim of disentangling outmoded cultural ideas and patriarchal practices from what are considered to be the authentic Quranic norms and divine messages of revelation. Some of these efforts have graduated into professional, heavily funded research projects, out-reach and exchange programmes, legal aid services, international conferences and projects, lobbying networks and publications in/for Muslim contexts. Valentine M. Moghadam (2005) highlights the contributions of two of the larger and more organised Muslim women's networks, Women Living Under Muslim Laws (WLUML, which has its South Asia headquarters in Pakistan)[3] and Sisters in Islam.[4] However, there are many others across the Middle East, as well as now, in Europe and the United States.[5] International representation at regional and United Nations (UN) fora has sustained the recognition and continuity of such textual analyses and field-research – not just across the Middle East and North African, South and East Asian regions but in fact, many such projects are housed in Islamic Studies (or other) departments at Anglo-American academia, or headquartered in research institutes or donor agencies in European countries. No comparative independent study or activist group of such international claim may be cited as originating from or sustained within Muslim contexts themselves.

Islamic Feminism

More recently, there has emerged a proposal that is popularly referred to as "Islamic feminism". Islamic feminism can be described as essentially a postmodernist, diasporic scholarly project that does not recognise any single (male) interpretation or dominant narrative of Islam (Moghissi 1999; Mojab 2001; Badran 2011; Mir-Hosseini 2011). Instead, Islamic feminist epistemology claims an interest in research that includes multiple voices and historical debates in its endeavour to locate women's rights within an Islamic discourse. Ziba Mir-Hosseini (2011) dates this form of feminism – that takes it legitimacy from Islam – to 1979 and attributes its rise to a result of two catalysts. The first is the adoption of the United Nations Convention on the Elimination of all forms of Discrimination Against Women (CEDAW), which provided a point of reference, vocabulary and tools to resist and challenge patriarchy for women all over the world, including those in Muslim countries. The second force is the rise of Islamists who invoked Islam and Sharia in order to reverse secularisation of Muslim contexts and oppose women's rights, particularly in Iran. Mir-Hosseini argues that by the early 1990s, the conflict between these opposed forces of feminism and Islamism resulted in the emergence of a new gender discourse that came to be called "Islamic feminism" which identified a specific feminist standpoint as well as its target of resistance. Historically, however, it was only considerably later that this concept as a feminist imaginary attracted attention beyond Iran.

Shahrzad Mojab (2001) and Haideh Moghissi (1999) recount the emergence of this imaginary from a different perspective. Mojab recalls how "a group of feminists, mostly secular academics living in the West, has in recent years used the term 'Islamic feminism' to refer to Islamic alternatives to Western feminisms [who] treat Islam as the only authentic, indigenous road to gender equality and justice" (Mojab 2001, 130). Mojab confirms that the term is used to refer to the activism of a few Iranian women who seek the compatibility of Islam and feminism through lobbying for legal reform within the framework of the Islamic Republic but she notes that these Muslim activists themselves do not use the term.[6] Moghissi (1999) has suggested that Islamic feminism has been inspired from a sense of profound defeatism.[7]

In fact, Mir-Hosseini herself acknowledges that this term has been deeply contested in Iran and even during the Fourth United Nations World Conference on Women in Beijing (1995) there were disagreements by those activists who rejected either the Islamic or feminist part

of the term. Mir-Hosseini does argue though, that in the a.
the 11th September 2001 attacks in the US and the poli
ensuing so-called War on Terror, both feminism and Isla.
reductive and even discredited concepts by virtue of their a.
with the politics of human rights laws and Sharia-calling
respectively. Mir-Hosseini (2011) does state that she has been troubled
by the term "Islamic Feminism" herself (71). To the extent that feminism has always been a contested term and politics, even in the
pre-9/11 or "WoT" era, one is not sure of the accuracy of the observation that the scale of suspicion regarding feminism in Muslim
contexts has significantly worsened in recent times. Certainly, liberal
and secular feminisms in Muslim contexts have come under considerable more scrutiny and criticism by postsecularists, as well as those
feminists who support some Sharia compliant alternative to Western
feminisms or human rights discourses.

Margot Badran, historian and gender studies specialist who focuses
on the Middle East and Islamic societies argues that "unlike secular
feminism's emergence in the form of a *social movement*, Islamic feminism burst on the global scene in the late twentieth century in the form
of a *discourse* – a trenchant religiously framed discourse of gender
equality" (Badran 2011, 81). This is an important point because this
difference (activist/academic) has split feminists in Muslim contexts
over the worth, priorities and deployment of a strategic gendered politics that is based on faith. It has also complicated the lens through
which feminist identities in Islamic republics are viewed and read by
"Western eyes" (which includes not just "white feminist" ones but also
diasporic judgements).

The subsequent anthropological interest generated around the
movement of Islamic feminism has also engaged the attention of the
neo-liberal social development sector. In part, this interest came in the
form of Western governmental response to the global resurgence of
religio-political violence in the form of Islamic militancy, as it came to
be defined in the post-9/11 era. The combination of scholarly interest
and funded support for Islamic feminism has impacted feminism in
general and secular feminism, specifically. Mir-Hosseini notes that, "it
is interesting that some of those now classed as key 'Islamic feminist'
thinkers or advocates are among those who once found 'Islam' and
'feminism' irreconcilable" (2011, 71). She names Fatima Mernissi and
Haleh Afshar as prominent examples of those who held that "patriarchy was inherent to Islam" (Mir-Hosseini 2011, 72) but in their later
writings they abandoned this position without explaining their intellectual trajectories. Mir-Hosseini finds this silence significant, as "it
speaks of the ambivalence that many women, whether Muslim or non-

Muslim, feel towards certain aspects of their identities. The silence has both strategic and epistemological consequences" (72). This book documents how this silence has been broken by a whole host of cacophonous voices that have turned accusatory in tone against those who are critical of religious patriarchy in Muslim contexts.

The absence of a political base for any movement would mean that such an enterprise becomes limited to an academic exercise. Even for Islamic feminism to have a sustained influence on state policy, such agendas would have to address the material concerns of the citizens. In other words, in the absence of political appeal and anchorage for this movement within Muslim states, the chances are that this will remain a theoretical exercise limited primarily to the diaspora.[8] The efforts of Islamic feminism also need to go beyond the interest and activism around Muslim Family Laws, which is almost exclusively its current focus. In any case, in so far as both Islamism and feminism are political perspectives, Islamic feminism at an international level seems to be attempting to redefine both. It is my observation that in the process, the feminist agenda is getting diluted while the Islamic factor in this hybridised identity is increasingly accommodating patriarchal possibilities. Conservative Muslim commentators often take advantage of the Islamic feminism agenda to reference all the rights that Muslim women are granted in Islam – however, they stop short on agreeing that these are unconditionally equal.

More recently, Badran (2011) has argued that the trajectory from secular feminism to Islamic feminism in Muslim contexts has led it to become far more "communally based [...] and globally anchored" (78). In her view, the previous synergy between secular and Islamic feminisms is threatened not so much from conservative male quarters but she points out to the communalism "being fed from within the world of feminism" (83). Badran holds up the example of the organisation of *Musawah*, a transnational organisation created and run by and for Muslim women and which focuses on reforming Muslim Family Laws. Badran's argument is that secular feminism in Muslim contexts (citing Egypt, as an example) used to be a holistic feminism, which incorporated the rights of Muslim and non-Muslims alike. The politics that informed this feminism proceeded organically from the national base and was led by politicised activists to access the world of international feminism, usually through Non-Governmental Organisations. However, in Badran's view, the new Muslim holistic feminism, as a product of scholar-activists and based on theoretical structure, is led by professional women and public intellectuals who are also sometimes NGO workers, but well-connected, cosmopolitan and income-earning professionals.

Unlike secular feminists, these Muslim holistic/Islamic feminists are also well-received by governments and international fora seeking to show-case a supposed commitment or tokenism and even appease-ment policies towards "progressive" or "moderate" Islamic politics. In this regard, it is worth questioning whose interest Islamic feminism serves. More relevant is Badran's concern over whether it is only Muslim women's communal needs that are going to be the new area of feminist politics and funding and if so, whether secular feminism has a future. The collective discourse of the various combinations of feminist engagements with Islam, outlined above, may challenge patri-archal religion in theory but there seems to be no clarity as to the nature of the relationship of such a discourse with the modern Islamic state, its laws or politics. Indeed, recent scholarship seems disinter-ested in Muslim women's sexual, property or material-based rights or indeed, the relationship between Muslim men and women with refer-ence to violence, marriage or livelihoods.

The concern over the potential of the emergent school of Islamic feminism is that the strategy used by the earlier progressive women's movement in Pakistan is being repeated – reminiscent of the 1980s when women attempted to fight patriarchal fundamentalism within an equally patriarchal Islamic discourse. This empowerment within the Islamic framework has released a neo-Islamic political feminism as a side-effect. Today, this limited form of political empowerment has captured the imagination of young women in a more symbolic way that sometimes offers moments of political confrontation but mostly follows a route of stealth and accommodation with patriarchy. The fruition of a new, radicalised religio-political feminism dominating Pakistan's political future is highly possible.[9]

Secular Feminism

All feminists in Muslim societies do not share an "Enlightenment" or progressive interpretive view of Islam. Instead, many have pointed out and challenged the contiguous and more specific connections between religious and cultural patriarchies. They have commented on how Islam has often worked as a sealant of the overall patriarchal discourses in their contextual experiences. Such insights led several feminist activists in Muslim contexts to adopt a variety of stances and strategies in relation to patriarchal practices and in relation to religion. In some research literature, secular feminism in Muslim contexts is contrasted to Islamic feminism's positive approach to religion and is described therefore, as the "negative or Westoxified camp" (Offenhauer 2005, 15). Secular scholar-activists are more unqualified in their condemnation of misogyny in the name of Islam, arguing that defensiveness about women's conditions under Islam lapses into dangerous apologetics. From the point of view of this "negative camp", women's interests are best pursued in secular terms and in the name of combating universal human rights violations.

Secular feminists in Muslim contexts advocate secular activism and look at the interplay of structural and legal factors in order to explain women's status. These may range from advocacy for the reform of Islamic laws and faith-based policies towards secular principles and equality of all – particularly, women and minorities – to the total repeal of such laws and an adherence to international human rights tenets instead. It may also include the demand for a dismantling of clerical structures, authorities and institutions to be replaced by democratic ones in place. The state is often called upon by secular feminists to observe neutrality with regard to all religions and creeds and to guarantee freedom of worship and (non) practice of faith in public and private spheres under the given constitutional framework as it may be.

Ghada Karmi's work (1996) has attempted to examine the source of patriarchy within Islam and questions the role of religion in maintaining a patriarchal structure. Karmi's approach can be classified as secularist in that she is among those who see Islamic reform as necessary, but not as the only step required to change women's political and social situation. Karmi questions the conventional wisdom that Islam originally improved the status of women compared to the very few rights in a pre-Islamic world, and considers whether the patriarchal system that promotes the superiority of men and demeans the status of women in Arab countries is derived from or legitimised by Islamic law itself. Based on the literature of the pre-Islamic period, Karmi posits that women were better off in terms of personal legal status and independence than after the advent of Islam when rules of subjugation of women were introduced. In her opinion, women are infantilised in the Quran as they are to be provided for economically, their testimony not given the weight of men's and in reference to their status with regard to divorce, custody and polygamy – all of which favour men. In secularist feminist opinion, it is futile to pursue the standard pieties that some adherents to Islam repeat in order to justify inequalities. Instead, real reform is needed especially in the field of family law, such as that in Tunisia when polygamy was abolished. Karmi suggests that the solution to the conflicting issues on women could be found in a more objective study of the Quran in its historical and social context. The Quranic precepts must be seen as a function of social dynamics rather than used as a fixed text legitimising rigid patriarchal claims.

In the post-9/11 era, the normativity of liberal and/or secular politics, sensibilities and false expectations regarding Muslim women's autonomy and freedoms and the perceived attempts to displace their ethical desires have been challenged. The notion of imposed secularism leads some scholars to "jettison" the "'secularization as modernization' thesis" (Reilly 2011, 10) and even leads other scholars engaged in normative political theory to concede greater space to religious-based arguments and for a greater role for religion in the public sphere of civil society. 'Presumptive' liberal feminist expectations have become deeply contested sites and global secular feminist alliances and associated campaigns have become prey to conspiracies of an interventionist imperialist gender politics. European governmentality too, has been contested for "aiming to transform Muslim gender norms according to a particular liberal-secular script" (Amir-Moazami et al. 2011, 4).

Islam and Feminism in Pakistan

Two early voices that stood out in such debates at the international level included those of US-based Pakistani scholars, Asma Barlas and Riffat Hassan. Both have undertaken projects to debunk male (mis)use of linguistics and interpretation of Islamic scripture. Barlas, in *"Believing Women" in Islam* (2002) challenges what she calls "patriarchal exegesis" (xi) of the Quran and aims to "recover the scriptural basis of sexual equality in Islam and thereby to defend Islam against the claim . . . .that it is a religious patriarchy that "professes models of hierarchical relationships and sexual inequality . . . " (203). Riffat Hassan is one of the early feminist theologians who challenged patriarchal interpretations of Muslim women's rights as read in the Quran.[10] Dr. Hassan has also served as advisor to President-General Musharraf (1999–2008) on women's issues to further his purported project to spread "Enlightened Moderation" in Pakistan (see A.S. Zia 2009b).

On the other hand, Pakistani legal scholar and women's rights activist, Professor Shaheen Sardar Ali (2006) has written extensively on the link between religious and customary processes in the marginalisation of women. She takes a departure from the above scholarly views and argues that "the ethical voice of the *Quran* is said to be egalitarian and nondiscriminatory" but at the same time, "it concedes to resourceful, adult Muslim men, as the privileged members of society, responsibility to care for (and exercise authority over), women, children, orphans, and the needy" (12). Ali concludes that the *Quran*, therefore, "also contains verses validating the creation and reinforcement of hierarchies based on gender and resources" (12).

In Pakistan, much of the social scientific literature on women in the 1990s was produced by the non-profit developmental organisations and the more widely cited work is by Khawar Mumtaz and Farida Shaheed (1987). This work, and those published by the ASR Resource Centre,[11] grappled with the feminist engagements with religion, particularly during the period of Islamisation under General Zia ul Haq (1977–1988). Tahmina Rashid (2006) categorises two main groups who debate the interplay of religion and women's rights in Pakistan. She places Farida Shaheed and Khawar Mumtaz among those seeking to recognise the appeal of religion for lower- and lower-middle class women and Asma Jahangir, Hina Jilani, Fauzia Gardezi, Nighat S. Khan and Afiya S. Zia as representatives of "upper and upper middle class feminists" who state that women's rights fall into the realm of secular human rights (Rashid 2006). Although this is a broad categorisation (and not accurate on class representation), it is a fair reflection of the diversity within the liberal women's movement and the different understandings and approaches that inform a secular organisation, such as the Women's Action Forum, of which all the women named by Rashid are members. As argued later in the book, the myth of a liberal/secular imaginary as one restricted to upper middle class feminists or movements is countered by recent working women's movements from a more diverse class composition. This invites us to rethink the worth of such limited academic classifications and associative politics.

Currently, there is no identifiable Islamic feminist movement in Pakistan, although there are individuals within collectives who may be politically drawn to the concept. This is true of some feminists too, who may identify with or participate in secular activism and would resist any willful or political Islamisation of state and society but do not advocate for voiding a faith-based approach to women's personal empowerment. The self-proclaimed secular women's movement in Pakistan does not resist Islam, just an Islamic state. If anything, one of the critiques of the Women's Action Forum has been that despite taking such a radical political stand as demanding a secular state, many members diluted this by accommodating Islamic feminist approaches in their professional work (A.S. Zia 2009a). According to the critique, this has compromised the secular feminist project and allowed Islamist forces to strengthen their activism without any real secular political resistance, particularly at societal levels.

WAF Goes Secular

In order to understand the implications of such projects with regard to political movements and especially the women's movement in Pakistan, a brief her-story of the movement should be recounted here. The first wave of the women's movement is often identified in connection with nationalist struggles against colonialism (like many other countries) in the middle of the twentieth century and with the struggle for the independence of Pakistan in 1947. The concern of activists in the immediate post-independence reforms (apart from repatriation of abandoned or 'lost' women), become focussed on family laws, divorce rights, anti-polygamy and basic rights to services (Zafar 1991).

However, the second wave of the 1980s and 1990s pivoted around a dynamic and sustained struggle against the military dictatorship of General Zia ul Haq (1977–88), who made women direct targets of a misogynist state under his purported Islamisation project. The women's movement is acknowledged as perhaps the strongest challenger of this very politically and socially oppressive historical period. This is well documented (Mumtaz and Shaheed 1987; Jalal 1991; Iqbal 1992; Bhasin et al. 1994). It was the Women's Action Forum (WAF), formed in 1981, which acted as the lead urban-based alliance or forum to struggle against the imposition of discriminatory Islamic laws. WAF remains an important marker of the main debates that remain unresolved in the movement today. Rather than documenting the history of WAF, it is more pertinent to refer to the experiences and trials that this organisation faces, as an exemplar of the kinds of intertwined challenges that persist in Pakistan with regard to feminism, Islam and identity politics. The post-revolutionary positions that women find themselves in the aftermath of the Arab uprisings (Arab Spring) of 2011, clearly signal that there are common challenges that the women's movements in many Muslim countries are facing with regard to the intersection of feminism and Islamism.

In its initial years, as the organisation that spearheaded the pro-democracy movement against a military dictator and his imposition of Islamic laws, WAF decided to employ the strategy of using progressive interpretations of Islam to counter patriarchal state religion. They succeeded to some extent and even got the unlikely support of women from right wing Islamic groups/parties. On the question of violence against women, members from right wing and/or religious political parties participated in protests against state indifference but would distance themselves from WAF in their demand against Islamic laws (the *Hudood* Ordinances)[12] and the larger project of 'Islamisation'. Islamisation gave unprecedented (and undemocratic) access to religious parties, groups and individual theocrats to state offices and enabled them to define policies and seal many such rules with religious stamps, so as to render them immutable. Since General Zia ul Haq was considered a "US-sponsored dictator", it is argued that the Islamists' influential role and the construct of militant or armed Islamists (the *mujahideen*) to fight the (godless) Soviets in Afghanistan during his regime, was all part of the same imperialist agenda. However, the societal impact of Islamisation cannot be attributed exclusively to imperialist, geo-political impulses and consequences and neither does it explain the boost and resonance of religious with local/customary patriarchies, which translated easily into state laws and policies. A narrow reading which attributes all these developments to imperialist geo-political policies of the US also undermines the willful embrace of the private and public power and benefits accrued through Islamisation for Muslim Pakistani men.

A policy of Islamist ˋexceptionalism dominated the 1980s such as when Islamist student groups were exempted from the ban on all student unions. This in turn allowed students to act as extensions of Islamist political parties and exercise recruitment and vigilante politics while embedded in universities. Therefore, it cannot be ignored that the deliberate and conscious usurpation of Islam by the state was a political decision, not just an imperialist imposition. The idea that Islamisation in the 1980s was some evolutionary, natural social force emerging as a form of anti-imperialist resistance is a reinvention by postsecularist scholars. To ignore the role of religious actors and the militant directions of their religio-nationalist projects since the 1980s is historical oversight, at best. Neither can the revolution in neighbouring Iran in 1979, and its influence over a Pakistani state led by a military dictator committed to Islamising the country be ignored.

Based on the limitations of their experiences of working within the progressive Islamic framework, WAF made a conscious decision to take on the identity of a secular organisation to mark their resistance to the Zia ul Haq Islamisation campaign. The internal debate over the adoption of a secular identity in WAF was reflective of their views of what the nature of the State should be. It was also a deliberately subversive position marking the demand for diversity and equality in status for women and minorities and for guaranteeing neutrality in state offices and in policies within that particular historical context. In a sense, the resistance of women's groups to Zia ul Haq's Islamisation of the State and society may be compared to the French concept of secularism (*laïcité*), as a process of disengagement and struggle pitted against the church. *Laïcité* claims a moral independence from religion and religious authority and grounds its morality in the concept of liberty. This is not to suggest that Pakistani secularists refer to this model of secularism or appeal to some Treaty of Westphalia imaginary. Nor do secularists in Pakistan consciously follow the concept of *laïcité* in its original, radical form. In fact, many Pakistani feminists have been critical of the shortcomings of *laïcité* after the banning of the *niqab* or face veil by the French republic in 2004. However, the notion that secularism is about controlling and managing religion (by the Republic and with reference to the public sphere) is relevant to the Pakistani state and its repeat instrumentalisation of Islam since its independence in 1947. More specifically, the struggle of the Movement for the Restoration of Democracy and the women's movement in the 1980s grounded their claim for those democratic and moral guidelines that pre-dated the following unconstitutional process of Islamisation as sanctified by Zia ul Haq.

In other words, Zia ul Haq set up the Pakistani state as a "Church" and the struggle of the women's movement was pitted against this theocratic, state-driven attempt to reverse women's achievements and rights in order to showcase the State's Islamic credentials. Towards this, the women's movement turned its direction from a liberal, equal-rights framing to a quintessentially and additionally, secular resistance project. Usually, the touchstone reference for 'Pakistani *laïcité*' has been the 1973 Constitution, which many believe upheld the principles of a secular state (albeit compromised/negotiated in subsequent amendments). However, the concept of managing religions was not a matter of discussion at the time and the notion of separation of church and state is not technically viable in the absence of a state church. But, non-democratic theocratic institutions such as the Council of Islamic Ideology (CII), as well as the introduction of Islamic laws (*Hudood* Ordinances 1979) and the empowerment of a handpicked state clergy were consistently challenged.[13]

In their individual or other organisational capacities, some WAF members do engage or lobby with the Council of Islamic Ideology (CII) over laws regarding women. De facto, therefore, the CII is a recognised authority and de jure it is a Constitutional body. The same is true of the Federal Shariat Court (FSC) (although this remains simply an appellate body) and practically all Islamic laws passed under Zia's regime have been enshrined as part of the Constitution. Clearly, the secular feminists negotiate, accommodate and straddle the reality of Islamisation and its consequential legal implications, political policies and social effects, with the aim of resisting their use as drivers of patriarchy in the country. This does not mean that they do not simultaneously and effectively challenge and expose the failures and collusion of liberal-secular (male) politics with similar rigour.

In chronicling the women's movement, Pakistan's secular feminists such as Shahla Zia (1998) have argued that "the women's movement in Pakistan did not emerge suddenly out of nowhere in reaction to General Zia ul Haq's 'Islamisation' measures, nor is it based merely on events that transpired after the creation of Pakistan" (373). Shahla Zia argues that while women's successes have not been spectacular, their cumulative effect is quite substantial. The documentation of these "successes" has been more difficult considering Zia's observation that "the critics of the women's movement abound" (372). As a feminist and human rights lawyer, she took exception to some of these critics and identified the range of obstructions in the cause of pursuing women's rights. She included in her list obscurantists, as well as sympathetic politicians, who only espoused women's causes while in opposition but not when in power. In her critique, Shahla Zia (1998) addresses those "women scholars, many of whom live outside of the country away from the conflicts and tumults which confront the move-ment, who criticise its 'conceptual' framework, without any real perception of the situation on the ground" (373). Zia suggests that "perhaps what all these 'supportive' critics have in common is that they manage to absolve themselves of the guilt of their own inaction by placing the blame for all the failures on the women's movement" (373). Based on her own experiences in the movement, Zia considers attempts to invoke rights within the religious framework to be a limiting strategy, and advocates for a "secularisation of the laws . . . as the only means of attaining any continuing measure of success" (409). Her criticism was in many ways prescient yet unexpected from the new fronts from where it has been launched in the post-9/11 period. The recent challenges to the liberal/secular women's movement in the form of accusations of complicity with imperialism and "anti-Muslim politics", depends on an erasure of the historical contributions of this movement. Secondly, such criticism ignores the material dimen-sions or indeed, interdependent relationship between imperialism, nationalism and local patriarchies.

Postsecular Flirtations in WAF

In 1991, when WAF took a radical departure from its liberal feminist history and declared itself to be an organisation committed to a secular Pakistan, there was an overarching clarity in its vision to resist the increasing theocratisation of the Pakistani state. WAF's struggle was to retain the country's original secular constitution and political incli-nation.[14] The decision included urban based, "Western-educated" women but also rural women's nationalist-political organisations such as *Sindhiani Tehreeq*. The history of secular women's rights movements in Pakistan is often misrepresented in current literature as being purely bourgeois and urban and invested only in the cause of liberal rights that would work towards their own interests. Although there was little or no serious discussion in Pakistani feminist circles about secularism or liberalism in terms of its colonial baggage, there were always debates about the need to evolve an "indigenous" feminist discourse. By the time of the UN International Conference on Human Rights in 1993, many of these debates coalesced at the Asian regional level and peaked into a passionate discussion over Western universalism versus culturally relevant human rights. Necessarily, faith-based approaches in Muslim contexts looked to construct an alternative human rights discourse steeped in "Islamically appropriate" rights. Such debates encouraged several women's research and activist groups to further pursue projects based on the idea of the strategic worth of using the religious (Islamic) framework as a tool for negotiating and advancing women's right. This in turn, saw the introduction and growth of Muslim feminist consciousness – both funded and political – in Pakistan, Malaysia, Algeria and several other countries. Some of these groups were knitted together under networks such as Women Living Under Muslim Laws and other such transnational, Muslim women's rights groups. Many of these served a critical strategic worth, if limited measurable success, particularly in innovative interpretation of Islamic texts, especially with reference to Islamic jurisprudence.

Arguably, this approach of working within the Islamic framework has diluted and ultimately weakened secular feminism and relinquished considerable space for the recent Islamist political backlash witnessed in Pakistan, in general. It has had more serious implications for the women's movement specifically. These streams of cultural and religious feminist consciousness and their inclusiveness in development and rights-based movements swim dangerously close to the kind of cultural particularism that other feminists had warned would distance the women's rights discourse from the broader universalist paradigm of freedoms.

Tahmina Rashid's research on Pakistani women's rights in 2006 attempted to categorise the various strands within the women's movement. She broadly identifies these as four schools that include traditionalists, modernists, socialists and secularists. But by 2008, this categorisation was already outdated. The new scholarship and terminology developed over the last few years suggests that apart from traditionalist or modernist feminists, Islamist women became a new category of interest and political promise within Muslim majority contexts. These Islamist and pietist women may or may not question or challenge patriarchy per se, and may very well embrace and represent conservatism, particularly with regard to gender roles and status. Some may purport to refute Western values and actively reject any form of liberalism or universal rights for Muslim women, arguing instead for exceptionalism in the form of exclusively Islamic rights only for women.

Even before 9/11, the earlier incongruities with reference to Pakistani feminist politics on the question of Islam had already began to unravel. Even after the endorsement of a secular political identity in 1991 by WAF, instead of secular feminism gaining ground, one found that many members of WAF started getting involved in setting up organisations and funded projects that sought to deploy empowerment strategies within cultural Islam. They suggested this would counter the fundamentalist challenge posed by political Islam. Several members wished to draw a distinction, arguing that many women found it personally empowering to draw upon religious rites and locate themselves within piety movements and that this could challenge patriarchal religious politics. It is relevant that WAF split on this issue regarding differences in opinion on the strategic use of religion and political affiliation (Mumtaz and Shaheed 1987).

Organisations such as Shirkat Gah in Pakistan, which hosts one chapter of the transnational network, Women Living Under Muslim Laws (WLUML),[15] works towards eliminating religious and cultural impediments through field research, strategies and programmes while advocating for the pursuit of justice and equality for Muslim women. Shirkat Gah's research has focused extensively on women's religious, cultural and legal identities and on how Islam features as a conduit in their routine lives. They have attempted to demystify, translate and bridge Western feminist theory with local, indigenous culture via religious reclamation, as a relevant way of promoting women's rights (Shaheed 2002). This organisation was one of the first NGOs to work on women's concerns. It is headed by some prominent rights activists who despite their secular credentials, continue to spearhead heavily-funded, large-scale social development projects with titles such as "Women's Empowerment in the Muslim Context" (WEMC).[16] The project's rationale and approach reveals some of the contradictions discussed above.

Interestingly, it used to be the Islamic state that was the target of critique within the modernist feminist women's movement but projects such as the WEMC and others framed in the post-9/11 era cast the entire "Muslim context" as a developmental category unto itself. The WEMC framework document that describes the project makes sweeping claims such as "the Muslim context actively disempowers women" but goes on to say there are lessons therefore, even for those who live in non-Muslim contexts (Wee and Shaheed 2008, 6). Then why call it "the Muslim context" at all? This is a good example of the kind of exceptionalising of Muslims observed by modernist feminists that the postsecularist scholars discussed in this book also deploy. The framework observes that women "use culture and religion . . . to reshape disadvantageous power relations" (Wee and Shaheed 2008, 8) but avoids referencing the more controversial practices of the veil or polygamy which are also strategic props claimed by Islamist women as deployed to negotiate and reshape relations. The central weakness of the empowerment thesis, as defined in the WEMC project, is that it does not acknowledge that empowerment is a process that can be experienced by women of the rearguard too. The project thesis argues that Islamists view women's struggles as alien to the Muslim context. On the contrary, many religio-political groups are increasingly accepting of women's empowerment in Islam as a useful tool to counter accusations of being regressive and anti-woman. However, several religio-political groups and the postsecularist/retro-Islamist scholars share their acknowledgement and concern over the agency of believing Muslim women (within the Islamic socio-legal ethos) but consider secularists to be adversaries to the Islamisation-as-empowerment process.

Acknowledging these complexities would mean having to identify these and taking a political stand in confronting them rather than side-stepping and just empowering women through NGO-style training and awareness, in a vacuum. This separation between development and political activism allows NGOs to "empower" without challenging the patriarchal obstacles directly, or taking the risk of running programmes outside of the religious discourse. This WEMC project was implemented in 2008, when Pakistan was at the peak of an Islamist surge that was claiming human casualties at an alarming rate, challenging the state military and mounting a political and social battle by way of bombing schools and conducting public hangings of women. In the background of such an insurgency, such projects and approaches to development assistance seemed insignificant, misplaced and contrary to the reality of what constitute challenges within a "Muslim context". This overlapping consensus between some modernists and the postsecularists over Muslim exclusivism suggests that Muslim contexts require a specialised approach to rights and development. In this instance, modernist feminists are complicit and contributing towards the process of instrumentalisation of Islam in development.

Several aid assistance organisations have already inculcated such Muslim exceptionalism under the guise of cultural particularism or religious sensitivity. While such (self) ghettoisation concerns some feminists because it privileges a material and social patriarchal discourse, it is celebrated by its supporters because women adherents embrace it. Similarly, the idea that domestic religious rituals such as *darses* (pietist study groups) and *khatams* (funeral prayers) are spiritually and personally empowering practices, need deeper examination. The question also then applies to *madrasas* (religious seminaries) for girls, which scholars like Bano (2010a) argue, are also empowering young women. However, when such pietist practices or faith-based education and symbols (such as the veil) convert into activism or political agency, then what position is recommended for the progressive women's movement? The political fallout of conceding ground up to a point and marking it off by saying "empowerment is alright but just up to this point" after which it is "bad empowerment", is an unconvincing position.

On the eve of the events of 9/11 and under a military dictatorship, Pakistan witnessed the growth of the *Al-Huda* phenomena. This refers to the efforts of Dr. Farhat Hashmi, the founder of an academy for women in Pakistan to re-learn Islam in a "modern" way. Hashmi has set up some 200 schools across communities all over Pakistan and travels and lectures all around the world. She has been challenged by feminists and fundamentalist groups alike. Theologian Dr. Riffat Hassan (2002) has insisted that Hashmi is no more modernist than feminist or liberal but instead, very markedly right-wing. Hashmi defends her own enterprise as non-political and some retro-Islamist scholars support this claim (Mushtaq 2010), while in other analysis this is seen as a nascent socio-political movement (Ahmad 2009). After the events of 9/11, this debate spilled into the academic realm and retro-Islamist scholarship emerged as a response or project that would enable a more palatable acceptance of the legitimacy of political Islam in order to counter Islamophobia in the West. This scholarship is being produced by a broad spectrum of urban, upper class scholars, many of who study or teach in Anglo-American academia and who form the Pakistani diaspora. Several other scholars interested in such retrospective inquiry are found in some private sector universities of Pakistan, particularly the Lahore University of Management Sciences.

Summary

The terrain of the various streams of debates and identities that have emerged over the last few decades with reference to women and Islam in Pakistan have been set out, with some focus on Islamic feminism. It traces the effects of the strategies of working for women's rights within an Islamic framework, and the argument presented is that this fault-line within the secular feminist school in Pakistan has encouraged the instrumentalising of Islam for women's empowerment. In the process of such a compromised approach, not only have feminists lost ground in promoting secular options but also Islamist women's politics has appropriated this strategy to promote an anti-feminist and conservative agenda. Some examples of this scholarship and analysis and effects of these processes are discussed in the chapters ahead.

CHAPTER 2

The Postsecular Turn and Muslim Women's Agency

This chapter unpacks the now popularised notion of Muslim women's pietist agency as theorised by Pakistani émigré and US-based academic, Saba Mahmood (2005). As an academic proposal and challenge to feminist theory, Mahmood argues for a need to move beyond the binary of resistance and subordination to understand the complex ways in which Muslim women express their agency. This proposition has been of tremendous value, particularly for many Muslim women scholars and researchers who subscribe to and reference her theory to explain and recover Muslim women's docile agency. However, the implications need to be questioned, and discussion will focus on the influences and applicability of such postsecular theory for Muslim contexts such as Pakistan, not just in political and pragmatic terms but also, by way of its usefulness to understand gender relations or those between women, the Islamic state, and capital.

The academic and political challenges for secular feminist activism in the post-9/11 era will be scrutinised, and the main criticism and challenges posed by Pakistani postsecular scholarship against liberal/secular feminisms, as found in the works of Sadaf Aziz (2005), Amina Jamal (2013), Humeira Iqtidar (2011) and, Masooda Bano (2010a), will be examined. A series of recently passed legislation in Pakistan contravenes the postsecularist proposition that universal human rights laws are redundant for Muslim contexts where Islamic provisions and juridical traditions would resonate more.

Muslim Women's Agency

In the post-9/11 period, several fairly expensive courses began to be offered at various academic institutions in Anglo-American academic institutions, devoted to understanding the diverse streams of Islam and political Islam.[1] This has been a lucrative enterprise, given that there are so many Muslim countries in so many different continents, each with their own histories, experiences of colonisation, language, and with their own peculiar schools of Islamic thinking and practice and politics. Often, these studies morph into large research and development projects (see Chapter 5). Projects need money and several well-funded research projects are now sponsored by international development agencies and by Western governments in order to "understand Muslims". This has encouraged the emergence of new and "authentic" experts on Islam, who often became employed by think-tanks while others become spokespeople, to promote the cause for a peaceful or softer side of a progressive Islam. Even rehabilitated jihadists have been incorporated into not only Anglo-American government bodies or think tanks but also transnational human rights organisations, such as Amnesty International. The trend includes a noticeable keenness for the institutionalisation for inter-faith dialogue tasked to integrate the place of faith in governmental foreign and international developmental policies (see Chapter 5).

Specific to the post-9/11 counter-terrorism preoccupation with gender and sexuality, there has been some scathing criticism of the penchant of transnational feminisms and even liberal feminisms, for their perceived affiliation with neo-conservative agendas, and co-optability by imperialist wars and free market savagery (Abu-Lughod 2002; 2013; Butler 2003; Mahmood 2005; Scott 2008; Nesiah 2013). Brown (2011) and Puar (2007) have looked at how feminism and queer terms may be appropriated by conservative projects for racist, imperialist ends, while Butler (2003) argues that women's sexual freedom has become an instrument for waging "cultural assaults on Islam that reaffirm US sovereign violence" (3). It is important to point out here though, that this is a simultaneous and two-way benefit. Islamists too, use the same tool (women's sexual freedom) to launch cultural assaults on the West and to reaffirm the sovereignty of (an imagined) Muslim *Ummah* (global community, represented by male clerics) through a commitment to protect society and women from their own collective sexualities.

The source and nature of a new challenge to liberal and secular feminisms is different from the earlier critiques of feminisms in Muslim contexts in two significant ways. First, this post-9/11 critical scholarship on feminism has emerged pre-eminently from the humanities in Western academia and in the case of Pakistan, has been spearheaded by several women scholars (largely diasporic to their native contexts). Secondly, it has attempted to epistemologically sever or delink liberal/secular feminism from the Muslim context in order to argue for the recovery of a postsecularist, postfeminist and certainly, non-liberal re-consideration of Muslim women's subjectivities, experiences and even rights. The central challenge to liberal/secular feminism in the post-9/11 period has concerned the wisdom of associating these political sites with freedoms, autonomy and agency for women, particularly in relation to Muslim women's rights. Much of this inquiry has come by way of the work of US-based anthropologists and academics, Saba Mahmood (2002, 2005) and Lila Abu-Lughod (2002, 2013). Unlike earlier feminist anthropology on Muslim women that explored the complexity of gender relations during and under global Islamic revivalist or fundamentalist religious movements, Mahmood reconceptualises pietist women's agency in the context of contemporary Egypt (Mahmood 2005). Her work seeks to vault the structural binaries of subordination and resistance and proposes a detachment of (Muslim women's) agency from the goals of liberal and feminist politics.

The influence of Mahmood's theory of agency is apparent in a tract of recent Anglo-American anthropological studies on Muslim women in various contexts. Mufti (2013) notes that

> in this sense, the new ethnography of Islam – and Saba Mahmood's The Politics of Piety is now hugely influential and even canonical in this regard – is in active agreement with Islamism itself when the latter thinks of itself in revivalist terms as a return to the true tradition of Islam. (12)

Several studies that have been inspired by this venerated text begin with a customary disclaimer acknowledging and cautioning against reading Mahmood's specific ethnographic study of a women's piety movement in Egypt as a general model of Muslim women's piety. Despite that the majority of such anthropological works then reference, borrow, extend and model Mahmood's theory of the docile Muslim female agent as an alternative discourse to (liberal) feminist aspirations in general. The reframers of Muslim subjectivities argue that

> [Saba] Mahmood's work, in particular, has encouraged scholars to consider how we are to understand and conceptualize discourses and practices with a non-liberal impetus without either identifying them as deviating from or gradually adjusting to the liberal norm. In this light, the question [framed by Moghissi and other socialist or modernist Muslim feminists] of whether feminism and Islam are reconcilable turns out to be a 'false' question, or at least one that

potentially prevents us from addressing other crucial questions. (Amir-Moazami et al. 2011, 3)

Mahmood (2001) insists that docility should not be read as an abandonment of agency but more as "malleability" (208). Ironically, when liberal feminists argue that it is such compliance that benefits totalising institutes such as *madrasas* (religious seminaries) and that it sustains jihadist organisations, they are accused of overstating the political undertones of the quietude of pietist agency. Some have argued that within Mahmood's theory there is an implicit invitation to read agency as even substitutive for women's rights in Muslim contexts (Abbas 2013). In any case, much post-9/11 anthropology has elevated the notion of Muslim women's piety to a sort of epistemological status and encourages Mahmood's study to be read as a kind of meta-theory of piety (Bautista 2008). In much of this literature, concepts such as embodied agency, desires and ethics of Muslim women have been explored, yet the actual political consequences of piety have remained under-examined or deliberately side-lined. A case is made for the appeal of subjugation over autonomy and self-fulfillment over progressive politics as equally normative desires amongst and for Muslim women. This is done through a simultaneous critique of a universalism that is premised on liberal democratic aspirations with emancipation as its end. Moreover, Mahmood and her immediate adherents have challenged liberal and secular feminisms as imperialist impositions on those who may wish to embrace docility, submission, conservatism, patriarchy and even, Islamism (Mufti 2013).

Several commentators have noted the intellectual lineage that informs Mahmood's work – from Talal Asad's call for a concept of agency that is suitable for specific institutions, to Foucault's and Butler's poststructuralist emphasis on subjectivity, and even Bourdieu's linking of agency with habitus. All these are considered to be influential to Mahmood's focus on the body as a repository, an instrument and agent of conscious self-fashioning. Bautista (2008) acknowledges that

> Mahmood's work, then, is remarkable for its refashioning a universalised notion of agency prevalent in the social sciences . . . The argument she makes is that no concept, whether in the academic or public sphere, has a causal, deterministic relationship to the reality it claims to denote. In saying this, Mahmood is not championing a blind form of cultural relativism . . . Rather, the significance of her work is in acknowledging the specific fields of power in which our subjects circulate and form. (80)

Mahmood's central thesis of agency argues for a re-evaluation of Muslim women's capacities through references other than the normative instrumentalist or functionalist perspectives. This enables her to contextualise the docility of the pietist women of the mosque movement in Egypt and review it as a form of submission towards acquiring a higher end (like an apprentice would to achieve mastery of a skill). Mahmood (2005) then offers a reading of her subjects' sacrifices, struggles and desires in a certain cultural milieu as agency (a form of capacity for action), which may result in their becoming "virtuosos" of piety. (The term "virtuous" itself, is used approximately 40 times in the book while "virtue/s" appears nearly 70 times. Interestingly, the connection between piety and righteousness is not discussed).

Inspired by such Deleuzian concepts of non-linear agency, a growing body of ethnographic work is now flooding the world of anthropology, referencing Muslim woman's docility as agentive (Ladbury and Khan 2008). Clearly, there's considerable evidence of female docility that is available for re-definition in Muslim contexts. It is accurate to state that not all these studies (nor Mahmood's) necessarily make the case for crude exceptionalism or religious relativism while exploring Muslim women's docile agency. Instead, these studies argue that pietist and even political Islamist women are desirous of modernising the nation – not through the prism of liberalism but instead by and through an Islamic pietist discourse. This is by no means, a novel or recent observation regarding Muslim women's *desires*. In fact, the notion of re-visiting the hierarchy of Quranic values, as they were first applied in the formative period of Islam was explored by Esposito, as early as 1982. Esposito (1982) differentiated between the socioeconomic and the ethical-religious categories in Quranic legislation and his work has been an instrumental reference for the first wave of academic scholarship on women and Islam. Based on an acceptance of this divide, many Islamist and pietist women in Muslim contexts concede that while women's status is inferior to men in socio-economic concerns, they are full equals as ethical subjects, and despite the specific spiritual and moral obligations imposed upon them, they will be compensated in the Hereafter.

However, Mahmood's definition of agency extends beyond or outside of emancipatory ends in arguing that pietist women are not just challenging the binaries of religion and secularism but in fact, their model of agency is repackaged as "speak[ing] back to normative liberal assumptions about freedom and agency" (Mahmood 2001, 203). Such a proposal necessitates an active critique of the limitations of agency as defined and adopted by liberal, secular movements, campaigns, activists and scholars in Muslim contexts. According to

Abu-Lughod (2002) and other like-minded critics of liberal-feminism, the latter has become a site of complicity with imperialism and Western hegemonic designs against Muslims, their practices and politics. The academic support for such observations requires a critique of the Enlightenment, colonialism, universalism, secularism and feminism, not simply as parochial or provincial but also, inherently orientalist and hegemonic.

Mahmood's (2001) effort is to de-centre liberal/secular feminist assumptions of agency as a synonym for resistance to relations of dominance, and to explore agency instead as a capacity for action through the "performance of gendered Islamic virtues" (203). Mahmood's study on pietist women of Cairo also challenges earlier scholarship produced by modernist feminists who performed the "worthy task of restoring the absent voice of women . . . of Middle Eastern societies showing [them] as active agents who live an existence far more complex and richer than past narratives had suggested" (205). However, Mahmood considers such scholarship to be a presumptive barrier in its ultimate association of agency with resistance and liberal freedoms. Instead, she seeks to "uncouple the notion of self-realisation from that of the autonomous will, as well as agency from the progressive goal of emancipatory politics" (208).

At this point, it just seems self-defeating to call it agency, particularly if the term is so loaded with liberal emancipatory historical political baggage. One wonders why she doesn't just call it anti/non-emancipatory desires or the capacity to act towards patriarchal/conservative or illiberal ends or even transcendentalism? Indeed, one is not quite clear why this kind of agency is even a gendered interest, since it could apply equally to Muslim male pietist movements such as the *tableghi* or *daw'a* (proselytisation) movements. But Mahmood does not allow for a reading of the mosque movement as either resistance or subordination but more so, as a place of happy purgatory or what I call a political nunnery (A.S. Zia 2009a).

Despite acknowledging feminism's contribution to the idea of a "politics which must be pursued at the level of the architecture of the self," (2001, 217) she argues feminism has been too parochially dependent on left-liberalism. Mahmood argues for moving beyond the "teleology of emancipation" (201) – to what, is unclear – while conceding that she does not offer an answer as to how one should imagine "the politics of gender equality when situated within particular life worlds, rather than . . . from a position of knowledge" (224). Such a theoretical limitation can then make a case for how "agentive capacity is entailed not only in those acts that consult in (progressive) change but also those that aim towards continuity, stasis, and stability" (invoked through the virtue of *sabr* or patience) (Mahmood 2001, 212). Such a framing means that analysis does not have to extend to nor confirm how such agency also has the capability to facilitate political action, or that it is very capable of informing, converting and sustaining subversion and insurgency. The implication through such omission is that Muslim pietist agency is always bound to (apolitical) conservative (non)change.

Mahmood (2001) argues that criticism of any "situated analysis" of Islamist movements, which reads them as other than theocratic, militant and patriarchal, is a result of secularist readings (224). She also objects to the demand and expectations of a simultaneous *political* critique of such docile movements (even though, she does the same by critiquing liberalism or secular-humanist projects while exploring traditions such as the mosque movement as alternative forms of "valuable human flourishings" (225)). Moreover, what is ignored is how patriarchy is also a very valuable anti-emancipatory tool that enables many men to "flourish" but to suggest that political critique of this should be suspended while analysing its cultural and religious situatedness is hardly a definition of the critical engagement and unsettling that Mahmood herself demands of secularists and feminists.

The Foucauldian conceptualisation of power encourages anthropological works that borrow from his theory to re-visit the poststructural, the less tangible, discursive fields that focus on performance, relations, concepts, imaginaries, subjectivities, agency, affectation, morality and injury with reference to the Muslim subject. Hence, the inordinate focus on the veil and piety (ethical conduct) rather than polygamy and child-custody (familial, juridical and state institutions), and an emphasis on discursive rather than material (non)emancipation is a feature of such post-9/11 anthropology. Mahmood's defenders argue that it is not her intent to resuscitate liberatory possibilities for Muslim women but simply to explore their subjectivities with a bias towards alterity, rather than transformation. The implication is that while liberal-secular feminism is orientalist and prescriptive, such anthropological epistemology is in contrast, a disinterested, corrective project.

Pakistani Postsecular Scholarship

A body of postsecular scholarship on Pakistani women that evolved in the post-9/11 era has been invested in the reinvention of Islamists, with a focus on their performativity rather than their politics. This has been well-received in the Western market, hungry for such voyeuristic peep-shows into the world of Islamists. Such scholarship follows on the heels of postcolonial studies in Western academia, and has resulted in a postsecularist drive to rescue Islamists and Muslims from secularism and Western liberalism, feminism and the human rights discourses. "The Muslim" has been framed and reframed, packed and unpacked, feminised, de-radicalised, and anthropologised. A case has been made for Muslims to be recognised as a 'cohesive' entity rather than expected to be part of Western multi-culturalism. Islamists' subjectivities have been recovered, their *madrasas* depoliticised, patriarchal politics rationalised and violent ideologies suspended, in the search for accommodating Islamist religiosities in both Muslim and non-Muslim contexts. Muslim identity has served as an academic cash cow, leading to a proliferation of all sorts of Islamic studies departments, seminars, projects, research, publications, Ph.D.s and of course, scholars.

The new postsecularist[2] scholarly interest in Islamist politics in Pakistan may be broadly categorised into two schools but both have a common base point; they are dismissive or critical of the contributions of modernist feminists in Muslim contexts, including their campaigns to cleanse Islam of patriarchal interpretation and locate rights within a broader, universalist and liberal framework of women's rights. Similarly, socialist and/or secular feminists, who had been involved in the struggle to restructure and challenge a theocratic state and who call for women's rights to be located outside of the Islamic framework or discourse,[3] have been targeted for maximum criticism and their activism vilified.

The first school of critics falls within what I term the retro-Islamist body of scholarship which includes, along a broader revivalist imaginary, the proposal to seam together secularisation *with/as* Islamist politics and which suggests that Islamists are the harbingers of a Pakistani secularism (Iqtidar 2011). This aligns with a host of post-9/11 academic works by other scholars (see Introduction) who build a case for contemporary Pakistan (like other Muslim majority countries) as both postfeminist and postsecular.

The second source of critical scholarship is observed by a group of Pakistani scholars and students who call themselves "scholar-activists" and are mostly located in North America where they teach or study. Given that their own lifestyles and choices are secular, liberal and sometimes, purportedly left-oriented, they do not advocate for Islamist alternatives but target feminist and human rights activists in Pakistan for their perceived Islamophobic and liberal-secular politics. The consciousness, politics and activism of this set of postsecularists tends to be polemical and is almost exclusively web-based and their politics are almost entirely shaped and informed by and take their cue from post-9/11 debates (discussed in Chapter 6).

Both sets of scholars reveal a new ethnographic interest in Islamist men's politics and Muslim women's "subjectivities" and the works of Talal Asad and Pakistani émigré, Saba Mahmood, have been influential on their scholarship. In the post-9/11 period,[4] the very relevance of any Enlightenment-based ideals (liberalism[5] and secularism, in particular) and indeed, any form of feminism – both of which used to be the primary target of conservatives and Islamists – have since been challenged as commissioners of anti-Muslim orientalism (Mufti 2004). Feminism in particular has become a suspect handmaiden in the post-9/11 era that is dominated by the analytical framing of all Muslim related matters through the lens of Islamophobia, and especially when it challenges Islamic laws, patriarchy or male norms in Muslim contexts.

Many of the postsecular scholars in the post-9/11 period, especially diasporic ones, are reluctant to disparage their predecessors in the social sciences who have been contributors of, or at least strongly influenced by, left intellectualism. So, these new-age researchers circumvent a straightforward rejection or even nuanced critique of Marxist ideologies (which some members of the Subaltern Collective did in India and others elsewhere, continue to do so) and instead, attempt to reinvent contemporary Islamists as successors of some Leninist legacy. This allows them to mention and then bury, the historical materialism in the relations between Islamist parties, the military and jihadist[6] activism. Instead, they reify the Islamists' personal and political identities as if these exist in some theoretical, anthropological vacuum.[7] Retro-Islamist scholarship on Pakistan[8] then attempts to make a case for recovering subjectivities (which were never really "covered" in the first place) by claiming to resuscitate the Islamist Woman from obfuscation in Pakistani feminist literature and politics. Some Pakistani scholars cite the purpose of such endeavour as simply an effort to show-case – through the pious subjectivities of Islamist women – that there can be 'another way of being'.

However, this is not a neutral and disinterested project in itself. The fact that such efforts popped up post-9/11 and as a timely (and in the negative) response to Lila Abu-Lughod's question, "Do Muslim Women Really Need Saving?" (2002), is not a coincidence. In fact, Abu-Lughod's question is sometimes interpreted as required post-9/11 rethinking or a pre-requisite for research on Muslim women and activism in Muslim contexts (Amir-Moazmi et al. 2011). Several of the academics mentioned and referenced have received recognition and been embraced by Western governments and academia as the authoritative scholarly voices on Islamic studies. What is often ignored is that many others have been precluded from academic sites and publications for harbouring critical political views on the politicisation of mainstream Islamists' subjectivities. Further, within this scholarly effort there is also disagreement, cross-purpose and often, selective application of principle. Some Muslim scholars are considered apologists, whose purposes seemingly serve US imperialist agendas as designed by US think tanks. Others, who may also be advising European and US governments or are tenured academics in Western universities, are celebrated as successful examples and authoritative voices on inter-faith, multicultural initiatives and trail blazers of a new anthropology on this topic.

As a historical and academic exploration, the works of a new generation of postsecularist scholars may lend interesting insights, particularly for Western readership. However, this scholarship remains deliberately aloof from or suspends the articulation of Islamist political activism (particularly, those of Islamist women) in the context of Pakistan and therefore remains an untested and theoretical fantasy. Historically, traditionalist and modernist feminists in Pakistan have been differently concerned with empowerment of their gender within a "rethought Islam," reinterpreting and re-examining a masculinist reading of the Quran and Sharia (challenging Sharia as a male epistemology). They have not supported the call for a theocratic state. Postsecularist scholars, however, while quick to point out the importance of Islamic law as resonant with Muslim citizens, tend to be non-committal on the nature of the state.

Admittedly, there is a value to any scholarship or policy studies that attempt to debunk myths and revisit orientalist interpretations of any historical literature or indeed, that challenge traditional masculinist readings in any discipline. These are not to be undermined at all. However, in their wake, many of the post-9/11 endeavours have thrown up new challenges, particularly for pragmatic political activism in Muslim contexts. Such projects suggest that the only tool for analysing people and in my interest, women in Muslim contexts, is with reference to faith-based politics. In other words, our foremost identities that need to be analysed have to do with our relationship with religion and how we choose to, or are forced to articulate or resist this relationship politically. This narrow focus becomes singular in its lens – the acceptance or resistance to religion and its expressions.

This interest has also lent itself to divisiveness in that women have become symbols for Western audiences – demonstrating or representing either the progressive, modern potential of the nation in question or as veiled, traditionalist, threatening reminders of what the wrong kind of faith-based politics can potentially lead to. Muslim identity was not merely being framed but the title of a series of conferences held in British universities suggest that there is a need to first "frame" and then "reframe Muslims."[9] The spaces for Muslims to be anything other than a religious category has become increasingly narrow over the last decade and it is not only governments or the neo-conservatives who are doing this. Academics around the world are increasingly complicit in encouraging a kind of Muslim exceptionalism which is blunted through the lens of anthropology and justified through a concentrated critique and rejection of universalism, secularism and Enlightenment-based rights.

Recovering Postsecular Rights

In this backdrop, some Pakistani postsecularist scholars have revisited the debate over Islamic laws and made the argument that religious laws may be more culturally relevant than Pakistan's lay or common (colonial) laws (e.g., Aziz 2005; Cheema and Abdul-Rehman 2008–2009). The proposal is that Islamic law can serve as a more appropriate buffer to the cruelties of the discriminatory customary laws, which many feminists also recognise as oppressive. Modernist feminists in Pakistan have held cultural patriarchy as the culprit/cause of gender discrimination and advocated that it is the formal lay law that can serve as an effective sanctuary of equal rights and not Islamic laws. But it should be noted that these feminists have been historically split on the matter of the effectiveness of legal interventions, in general. Most secular feminists in Pakistan are very clear that national laws should comply with universal human rights and continue to adhere to the principle that all women's rights fall within this category.[10] They maintain that cultural specificity or religion is no excuse for denying these rights. Prominent human rights activist, Asma Jahangir (1998), while discussing the double jeopardy that Pakistani women face under the dual legal systems, states categorically that

> women's groups should not accept laws based on religion – whether they be family laws or Islamic criminal laws. It is now a foregone conclusion that a true liberal interpretation of Islam will never be widely accepted. On the other hand, the half hearted liberalization of Islam will be more detrimental for women. Laws which violate the rights of women must be repealed. Those which give women no rights must be reformed. (103)

On another rung are those activists who would also categorise themselves as secular but subscribe conditionally or cautiously to universal human rights. They ascribe the weight of gender inequalities to culture and customs rather than religion. Farida Shaheed (1998) points out that the emphasis of human rights discourses and activism on universality underestimate and disassociate the interface of culture with law and the social moorings in which women's lives are bound between culture and the formation, interpretation and implementation of law. Shaheed (1998) and those within the collective of the Women Living Under Muslim Laws network have argued for a more ambivalent position that seeks a flexible "shifting back and forth from the legal arena to the realm of customary practices" (76).

One step further on this spectrum of debate are the retro-Islamists, who valorise the "implantation of Islamic legality . . . [as] a greater bulwark against such practices [such as child marriage] . . . subject to reinterpretations . . . " (Aziz 2005, 67). The appropriateness of Islamic law as a defence against cultural atavism is premised on the advice to be "cognizant of the originary importance of Islamic forms of legality" and which critique the "forced diagnostic-prognostic couplings" of "equality-espousing human rights norms" (Aziz 2005, 58). The retro-Islamists either reject or recommend a rethinking of the corrective possibilities of lay colonial laws or modern/Western human rights laws. They make the argument that it is only Islamic law that may serve as the appropriate buffer for women's religiously sanctioned protection. The base argument is that Western universal laws have no resonance with native consciousness or traditions. In many ways, the retro-Islamists seem to be answering the question asked by women's rights activists in the 1990s over whether laws for women in Pakistan should be derived from 'divine sanctions' (Jahangir and Jilani 1990). The answer from retro-Islamists seems to be "yes, divinity is the sanctuary for women."

Such analysis that relies on rejecting modernist attempts to reform law avoids referencing historical account and misses the opportunity for more accurate extrapolation. Aziz (2005) and others argue against "forc[ing] equality-espousing human rights norms" but neglect to mention how close such a possible "coupling" came in the earlier part of the twentieth century under colonial rule in India. Mrinalini Sinha (2011) recounts the consensus that developed amongst Indian Hindu and Muslim women across communities (and not via imperialist imposition) and which enabled the Child Marriage Restraint Act of 1929 (or Sarda Act).[11] Sinha argues this was possible because Indian women of both faiths rose above their communal specificities (that reified womanhood) motivated by a collective interest. This makes it possible to read this movement as the construction of an "agonistic liberal universalism" (Sinha 2011, 80). Sinha argues that the 1929 Sarda Act became "the first [. . .] law on marriage in India that was universally applicable across different religious communities each with their own separate laws" (87).[12] Such an alternative reading of historical landmarks in women's struggles challenges the masculinist linear presentation of Islam versus Western liberal universalism as rigidly incompatible and immutable categories.

The idea that Islamic laws will provide sanctuary to women relies on a paternalistic and infantilised notion that prescribes only protective laws for Muslim women. However, this protection as perceived in contemporary Pakistan is not from men per se. Instead, it is from abstractions such as liberal-secular freedoms and local pollutant cultural remnants of Hindu and colonial culture. In this sense, the retro-Islamist perspective overlaps with the critique of patriarchal culture proposed by some modernist feminists (such as Shaheed), particularly with reference to a shared scepticism of the relevance of universalist approaches to the law. In fact, Farida Shaheed, a Pakistani modernist feminist who advocates for a secular state, has criticised other feminists for wanting to counterpose their secular points of references within the broader women's movement. She has argued that for many women, faith is a "living reality" (Shaheed 1999, 161) and a tool towards exercising "self-affirmation" (153). This notion of faith as a channel for self-realisation is very close to Saba Mahmood's theory of pietist agency. In the case of Shaheed, in view of the recent swell of gendered faith-based politics in Pakistan following her pre-9/11 observations, it may be said that she underestimated the political potential of such privatised faith-based agency. Mahmood, however, is un-apologetic about the non-liberal and non-emancipatory motivation for Muslim women's pietist agency and rejects analysis that attempts to grasp the political repercussions of such religious enablement.

Shaheed's problematising of the applicability of universalist human rights juridical tradition in Muslim cultures is close to the project of the retro-Islamists who claim they are not advocating Islamic law, simply pointing out the consonance of religious jurisprudence with Muslim belief systems. On the one hand, the challenge of finding complementarity of human rights and Islamic laws is that while Islamic juridical consideration may be willing to accommodate gender rights, these cannot transgress male religious prerogatives. Are evolving and innovative laws even Islamic then, and why do scholars keep referring to them as humane Islamic laws when, by their own admission, they digress so far from the fundamentals of Islamic jurisprudence and are vulnerable to reversal? On the other hand, hopeful retro-Islamists argue that such efforts to impose Western rights onto a Muslim polity are unworkable and instead, they advocate for a project of redressal through and within the Islamic legal discourse (as more appropriate "bulwarks"). However, what we find is that a series of recent pro-women legislation has been passed by the Pakistani national and provincial legislatures (in many cases, in defiance of religious opposition), directly disproving the caution and advice offered in such hypotheses.[13]

Women's rights and human rights activists have campaigned against the inclusion of the Objectives Resolution[14] into the Constitution and the repeated attempts to Islamise what is seen as a neutral and secular Constitution of 1973 before the amendments made by General Zia ul Haq. Shahla Zia (1998) observes that the Pakistani Constitution is characterised by *more* than its profound commitment to Islamic principles in that it also pledges allegiance to an impressive catalogue of fundamental rights.[15] To suggest that Islamic law is more receptive to and can accommodate and absorb human rights principles seems to be more of a compensatory call that advocates a dependency on the generosity of interpretations and judges, rather than a confirmation of constitutional and permanent legal tenets. Women activists in Pakistan have tended to approach the case for women's/human rights in the reverse order. This is particularly the case in matters of minority rights, where dependence on the flexibility and interpretation of Islamic law is a very tenuous strategic precipice to rely upon. The elasticity of Islamic law as a moral jurisdiction has often served as an extra-constitutional and unpredictable power in the hands of judges, too.

The presumption underlying postsecularist scholarship is that it is itself a disinterested, apolitical and unbiased critique of liberal-secular modernity as it engages in a corrective project to reverse the injustices of Western Enlightenment and secularism with reference to Pakistan. Scholarship on Islamist identities in Pakistan, while critical of the Enlightenment doctrines and grand narratives of liberalism and feminism, does not merely seek to repudiate universal, feminist, liberal, secular rights. This body of work actively looks to recover the Islamist subject's heterogeneity and difference in terms of a redefined politics, freedoms and agency. It is also often committed to rescue the alterity or Otherness that has apparently been denied these subjects. Several postsecularists consider feminists to be antagonistic refuters of non-feminist docility, which is considered a marker of Muslim women's autonomous subjectivity and moral agency (below and Chapter 6).

Recovering Islamist Women's Agency

Post-9/11 interest in women's religious identities dominates the scholarship produced on Pakistan. Amina Jamal (2005, 2009, 2013) argues that secular feminists in Pakistan have Otherised Islamist women by denying them agency and by only seeing them as pawns of male-defined constructed identity. Jamal's work on the political activism of the women of *Jamaat e Islami* (JI) argues that the secular women's movement in Pakistan has refused to recognise the *Jamaat* women's agency and only see them in terms of a passive submission to *Jamaat* men. Jamal warns of the danger of denying the autonomy and emancipatory self-definition of *Jamaat* women. Jamal suggests this denial allows some (secular) feminists to represent the right wing women as victims of false consciousness so that they may construct their own identities as feminists with a modernist agenda, particularly against Islamisation. As a corrective, Jamal's own work attempts to highlight the effectiveness of *Jamaat* women's autonomous attempts to appropriate modernity towards their own ends and their understanding of rights. These modern social and political rights, according to the *Jamaat* women that Jamal interviews, should enhance not repress Islamic values. She quotes from an interview of a woman activist of the *Jamaat e Islami* who explains that while *Jamaat* women are modern, they are not Westernised (Jamal 2009, 19).

Similarly, Humeira Iqtidar's (2011) work on women in the Islamist organisations of *Jamaat e Islami* (JI) and *Jamaat ud Dawa* (JuD), also questions the notion that women are pressurised or coerced to conform to piety movements or join Islamist parties. Her theoretical perspective relies on scholarship that challenges the modernisation framework and looks to include religion as a legitimate category of political analysis. She argues that the religious agency and belief of women activists of right wing political parties in Pakistan is not blind but rather, is historically and culturally grounded and therefore, substantive. Iqtidar goes further than Jamal on two points which argue that women's agency can be mediated by religious belief and does not have to be consciously feminist. Her research finds that resistance to male domination may be incidental rather than purposeful in the activism of these right wing women. This is meant to be evidence of Islamist women's rejection of overt feminist desires. Secondly, her analysis of these religious political parties/movements suggests that by rejecting or failing at secular careers, women who join them find independent avenues which afford these women liberation. Further, Iqtidar contends that by bringing religious belief into the public sphere and recognising it as a motivating factor, this trend is 'secularising' Muslim societies such as in Pakistan.

Iqtidar calls for a conceptual separation of secularism as an (Western, Enlightenment-based) ideology or state policy from (what she considers) the more plausible project of (accidental and Islamist) secularisation. This is based on her reliance on Talal Asad's understanding of secularism, not as a separation of state and religion but the management of the latter by the former. It is precisely because of their intent to dislodge secularism as universal that leads Iqtidar to invest hope in Islamist political parties such as the JI (and more interestingly, the *Jamaat ud Dawa*) as harbingers of secularisation.[16] The fierce competition amongst Islamist groups leads her to conclude that through some kind of social-religious Darwinism, certain Islamist groups can then be contributors of an 'authentic' secularisation for Pakistan.

The academic leap from the *Islamisation* process that Islamist parties have been consciously engaged in for decades, to be now read as secularisation for the Pakistani context is difficult to digest precisely because the political evidence behind such a proposal has not been as oblique as Iqtidar suggests. By excavating exclusively the 'subjectivities' of two Lahore-based Islamist parties, the political records of the *Muttahida Majlis e Amal* (MMA)[17] – of which the JI was a lead member in the North West Frontier Province (NWFP)[18] – have been erased in Iqtidar's analysis. Once in power (2002–2008), the Islamist government (including its women representatives) worked towards actively subverting all Constitutional women's rights, including the right to vote.[19] The MMA also proactively legislated for a vice and virtue police to restrain women's mobility in public spaces. All the while, they were able to represent an authentic politics – one which was *for* (restricting) women *by* women. These anti-Constitutional proposals were formalised under the *Hisba* (Accountability) Bill passed by the NWFP assembly but this was struck down by Presidential veto twice, under Musharraf. Eventually, a watered-down version was passed by the Provincial Assembly but not because of some dialectics and debates within the Islamic discourse, but rather because of secular and constitutional resistance on the part of the state and indigenous provincial politics.

Some of the milder policies applied during the rule of the Islamist government included campaigns against theatre and cultural activities, *basant* (kite-flying festival), films, music, Indian TV/films and family planning messages – all of which are part of the regular activism of the JI women's wing. The vice and virtue police was conceived to limit women's mobility in public and to ensure the observation of strict gender segregation in all institutions. Several women's shelters and NGOs were harassed or shut down under suspicion of complicity with Western designs to subvert Islamic morals through the promotion of women's rights. Many of these are exemplary of where the Islamists' agendas intersect closely with that of the militants. It is this nexus that allowed the militants to devastate the social fabric of the province during the Islamists' rule (2002–2008).

Given that Iqtidar's development of her thesis overlapped almost completely with the five years of the MMA rule, her aversion to using such live examples of the policies and political engagement of Islamists and their "secularisation" of the province is strange. The performances of the Islamists in the provincial and national assemblies between 2002 and 2008 would have provided for rich evidence of the consequences of "Islamist secularisation," particularly when they had replaced what was previously a patriarchal and conservative but non-theocratic secular governance system led by the Pakhthun leadership. Surely, such a living rather than theoretical illustration would have better proven her case over how Islamists fuse the personal and political to engineer the supposed secularisation of society?[20]

What Jamal and Iqtidar do not acknowledge is the purpose of the agency and the conservative ends towards which the Islamist women of these religio-political parties use it. Retro-Islamist scholars use ethnographic accounts to highlight the practices and activism of the right-wing women as indicative of a newly founded liberationist alternative to Western feminism and universal rights. For example, Kalmbach and Bano (eds. 2011a) argue for the importance of studying female Islamic leadership because according to them, it is likely that these women will pose a growing challenge to Western feminism in the future. The warning of these "challenges" by Islamist women to Western feminism have been acknowledged by nearly all scholars on the subject. This is particularly true for those who have historically been on the receiving end of such challenges in the period of General Zia's Islamisation and those who resisted the boost this gave to Islamist parties including their women leaders. Such challenges by Islamists are not limited to "Western feminism" but also target most liberal-minded organisations and individuals in Pakistan who may or may not be feminist or even politically engaged. Theatre activists and media personalities who pursue liberal lifestyles or promote liberal messages are often the target of Islamist female leadership.

Pakistani scholars, Farhat Haq (2007) and Sadaf Ahmad (2009), in their respective work on Islamic women's leadership are sceptical of the depth and/or transformative intent of such "challenges". According to their research studies, Haq and Ahmad respectively and independently find that Islamist and pietist women tend to reinforce nationalist, patriarchal and (as Kalmbach and Bano themselves note), traditionalist, conservative, masculinist religious precepts. Haq and Ahmad conclude that the Islamist and pietist women that they studied reinforce male Islamist politics to their own detriment and against any translation of their agency into tangible rights. On the topic of the spread of female Islamic leadership, leaders of the Pakistan's Women's Commission of the *Jamaat e Islami* have argued passionately not only against those Islamist women who aspire for mosque leadership but also, against any form of secular political ambitions, including representative or (Western-style) democratic politics for women (Brohi 2006). This is ironic because Islamist women have been directly engaged in mainstream politics and served as members of the Pakistani Parliament (in particular, between 2002–2008). Further, it is not the question of the expansion of women's rights that is the point of contest between Islamist women and feminists in Pakistan. Rather, Islamist women openly practise contradictory, fluid opportunistic violations of the same lines and boundaries that they define between women's domestic, and public duties and rights. They are not dupes who may accidentally "secularise" society but well-prepared, politically conscious women who intend to Islamise social and domestic norms and institutions.

Some postsecularist scholars propose to dismantle the presumed homogeneity of Islamist women by showcasing their alterity. But this hypothesis falls apart when applied to their subjects' political aspirations. Kalmbach and Bano (2011b) first make the case for Islamist women's empowerment within a patriarchal religious discourse (one which will challenge Western feminism) then invoke an imagined commonality between faith-based aspirations and the goals of Western feminism. In its haste to legitimise the political possibilities of faith-based aspirations, this scholarship elides over the internecine, competitive and real differences of perspectives within and amongst the Islamists. On the one hand, Kalmbach and Bano argue that female Islamic leadership conforms to the norms and structures established by male scholars and on the other, they make a case that these leaders empower their followers *vis-à-vis* established and confined authority structures. The goals and ends of such 'conformist empowerment' for women are not explained. But more than contradictory claims based on ethnographic studies, these scholarly findings confuse feminist agendas with gender empowerment techniques that have come to dominate the development discourse in developing nations.

Feminism is not limited to vague notions of empowerment, nor is female leadership a singular indicator or a criterion towards achieving goals of gender and class equality and justice. Feminism actively challenges traditional, masculinist, patriarchal and class-based centres of power and authority and does not simply seek to replace male with female leadership. Most strains of feminism are also critical of those women who aspire and adhere to, promote, harbour, or mimic patriarchal ambitions, relations or agendas.

Retro-Islamist scholars repeatedly quote how the MMA religio-political alliance won enough seats for the first time in Pakistan's elections of 2002 in order to form government in the NWFP. However, in not one instance of the scholarship produced by these researchers (see Introduction), including in their Ph.D. theses or indeed, development reports funded by Western governments that they may have authored, have they analysed or even mentioned the nature of governance that followed in a province that was previously and traditionally patriarchal and conservative but ruled by a politically secular governance. The role or specific contribution of female Islamic leadership of that period is neither referenced nor formally documented and this silence extends to the manner in which this power was acquired. While eulogising leadership, such scholarship avoids any discussion of the exercise of this "leadership" in the period that the Islamists ruled the province. The manner in which female Islamist leadership took up the challenge of governance in what is now, Khyber Paktunkhwa province is instructive with regard not just their proposed opposition to 'Western feminism' or liberalism but indeed, to any interpretation of basic liberties and freedoms. There is no evidence of the "empowerment" of these women leaders in the political process in subsequent years either.

The simple fact of participating in mainstream electoral processes and holding intra-party elections is evidence enough for postsecularist scholars to uphold the agentive and participatory credentials of Islamist parties. The hierarchies of most mainstream religious parties are severe and women cannot head them nor integrate into their mainstream decision-making process. The gendered principles that inform many of these parties dissuade Islamist women from fielding as candidates or assuming leadership roles, unless they are forced by secular compulsions such as a reservation system for women and minorities, which compels them to participate towards the realisation of overall political gain for Islamist male leadership/parties. However, Islamist women's intellectual/pietist agency or odd acts of dissonance are unlikely to translate into any tangible influence on party policy or lead towards public leadership roles for women. The only way for this to happen is if Islamists subscribe to the lay rules of political participation, such as quotas to ensure women's equity or minimum participation in representative politics – a policy they reject on religious principle but which historically, they have adhered to out of compulsion. Islamist women owe a debt to the liberal, secular principles that seek to ensure women's participation at all tiers of national level politics. This has been the only opportunity available for Islamist women to actively author and debate Islamic policies and to resist liberal legislation on a range of issues during their stint in national and provincial government in Pakistan.

The Islamist groups' *political support* to General Zia and *political governance* under General Musharraf also needs more serious attention if postsecularists insist on alternately merging any distinction between Islamists' pietist and political agendas. The same caution applies if scholars completely suspend the relevance of Islamists' specific politics in order to suggest that they are contributors to some broader democratic imaginary. One is content with any examination of Islamist politics but interested scholars need to come to terms with a framework where either the Islamists' credentials are up for discussion in their entirety or not.

Muslim Exceptionalism

Pakistani postsecularist scholarship seeks to expose the bias of secularism in Muslim contexts but, unlike earlier feminist scholarship, does not examine the source of demands for Islamic particularism/exceptionalism in the form of veil practice, sharia laws, dispute resolution mechanisms, polygamy, the authority of all-male *ulema*, as well as the effects of these on Muslim communities. It presumes through selective ethnographic accounts rather then broader or deeper social scientific inquiry that these are truly reflective of the entire community and their effects would be uniform and beneficial. There is little to suggest whether such exceptionalism has been beneficial for Muslim women.

The implicit proposal in postsecular critiques is that women's movements should redirect themselves or adjust their local struggles based exclusively on the apparently, game-changing events and aftermath of 9/11. This is an interesting invitation – one that insists that the nature and consequences, indeed, the continuity of patriarchal norms that underscore local, religiously determined politics, have magically been erased. It implies that even the actors, sympathisers and collaborators of Islamist politics have been replaced or their actions suspended and interrupted because of 9/11. The objection to the "Muslim fundamentalism" is accompanied by the suggestion spectrum of Islamist politics not be maligned but be reconsidered as the more benign, "Muslim political activities" (Akbar and Oza 2013, 164). This kind of scholarship advises that feminist activism[21] must reconsider its critical commentary and campaigns against fundamentalist groups or Islamist politics. A generic reference to Islamists or fundamentalist groups now qualifies them as victims of the backlash of the "imperial violence" that followed 9/11 and thus all local resistance against such male groups must now reconfigure its aims and reassess its strategies, vocabularies and priorities, on the basis of the terrorist attack on the World Trade Centre towers in New York and the ensuing so-called, WoT.

By interrupting the feminist challenges to local patriarchal politics, Muslim men – including Islamists, who may be involved in very local violations and abuse of human/women's rights – stand absolved of their actions and politics. It is helpful that a case against women's human rights has already been made through Saba Mahmood's and Lila Abu-Lughod's appeal for a redefinition of such rights and a delinking of these from universal basic rights – one which is also to be found in the narrative of local religio-nationalists. The implication is that resistance activism should desist from campaigning against the discriminatory practices observed by Muslim men or that this should be postponed for fear of painting them (with the imperialist brush) as "bad Muslims". The definition of the dehumanising projects of human rights discourses in such polemics (see collection in Satterthwaithe and Huckerby 2013) relies on targeting individual activists, rather than assessing the sites of abuses and violations.

Erroneously, Pakistani scholars overstretch their theses by borrowing and applying the Iranian or Arab cases in their effort to discredit the case for secularism in the country.[22] If, as is sometimes argued, Egypt was a secularising state in character but not in practice (Hafez 2011), then Pakistan's constitution, several laws and policies, and courts have in many cases, been secular in their practice(s) but that

te has been a secular one.[23] Unlike in Egypt,
not consider Islamisation (of the streets) to
spite its nuisance value. In avowed secular
hetoric by conservatives and/or faith-based
rks successfully (for example, India and the
or Islamic republics, even after the "Arab
ertly for political advancement is viewed
tani state and the electorate. Religio-polit-
modulated in the public campaigns of
endent on whether they are in opposition
vith the government.

In the wake of 9/11, the already contested notions of emancipation and freedoms, women's rights and autonomy have been revisited across the old/new turf and invoked, once again, the ideological contest of Western liberal-secular versus Islamic authenticity politics. The idea of the imperial rescue of the brown woman, well-explored by postcolonial scholars (Spivak 1988), became graphic in the symbol of the Muslim woman. Post-9/11 global reactions have ranged from concern over Muslim women's perceived submissiveness, suppression of their sexualities and hostilities to their embrace of the veil. On the one hand, it has been a period of policy bans on the veil in some European countries and on the other, its reclaim by believing women considered as representative of their "agency". This is not to undermine or ignore the physical manifestations of the ensuing "War on Terror" – the fallout of which, arguably, Pakistan has suffered perhaps as much as Iraq and Afghanistan. Nor is it the intention here to underplay the torture, incarceration and terror suffered through insurgencies and counter-insurgency operations (including in and by, the US) sustained for over a decade now. It has simply been my argument that in fact, the anthropological excavation of the discursive characteristics of Muslim women's faith and the academic effort of reclaiming a redefined and alternative Muslim women's agency, has rendered women as the biggest losers of this "WoT".

Over the last decade, during the period that Pakistan was coerced into becoming an ally on the "War on Terror", there have been systematic and targetted murders and torture of those resistant to Islamist militancy. While such violence has almost always been attributed to extremists or the Taliban, there have been many cases where mainstream Islamist parties or actors have been the perpetrators. The victims include liberal politicians – high-profile, as well as less known politicians. While social activists, policemen/ women, local tribesmen, minority sects and professionals from prostitutes to musicians and barbers, have been the targets of Islamic militants, particularly in the conflict zone of Khyber Pakhtunkhwa, mainstream Islamists have not voluntarily condemned nor campaigned against such pogroms. Islamists too, have been killing each other in bloody sectarian competition even prior to 2001, but these crimes have peaked and become bold in recent years. Even "moderate" Islamists such as Javed Ghamdi[24] were unable to survive in this environment of competitive Islamism. Pakistan has been anything but a haven for liberal/secularists, or indeed, moderates, in the last decade. The implications of all these developments have shown that political progress for women's legal and material rights necessarily require secular modes of resistance and organisation, rather than faith-based hopes and governmentality.

Summary

Saba Mahmood's influential study on Muslim women's pietist agency has been scrutinised not simply because it challenges liberal/secular readings of Muslim women's piety. Rather, it has been the post-9/11 timing and (US-based) location of Mahmood's scholarship that has given fillip to a previous methodological approach of empowering women from within the framework of Islam. Mahmood's proposal goes one step beyond the 'working-from-within' project. By subverting the notion that women should be empowered or motivated to struggle for rights *at all*, Mahmood has made a case for pietist women's "docile agency" and argued that this should not be assessed according to liberal norms or expectations of women's rights or empowerment. This has encouraged the emergence of a post-9/11 generation of referential postsecularist scholars who are critical of Western modernity, feminism and liberalism.

In the case of Pakistan, two streams of schools challenge secular feminist activism. The first group comprising of retro-Islamist scholars are not so much apologists and not consciously cultural essentialists but those who are invested in political possibilities (especially for women) that may be found within Islamic history and a non-Western discourse and where subjects do not necessarily seek political confrontation with either men, money, *mullahs* or the military state. The other set who identify themselves as scholar-activists includes those who do not void secular politics as a strategy but accuse Pakistani liberal and secular activists of behaving as "native inform-ants" and of being complicit with Islamophobia as their activism feeds into imperialist designs (details in Chapter 6). This has led to a more organised questioning of the motives behind human rights campaigns in Muslim contexts and even the accusation that 'native' feminist activists (but oddly, not male left or liberal activists) are invested in the scheme of Otherising The Muslim Man.[25]

I have contested postsecularist scholarship for circumventing the effects of Islamist women's leadership that is celebrated in their works. And argued that this agency and activism may defy the allegations of Muslim female passivity but at the same time, in practice, these are deployed to actively subvert women's progressive rights. Islamist agency and activism promotes patriarchal policies and putative morality-based politics. A series of recently passed legislation in Pakistan contravenes the hypothesis that universal human rights laws are ineffectual and inapplicable for Muslim contexts where Islamic provisions and juridical traditions would be more appropriate. In any case, the strategic positionality of the secular women's movement cannot base its approach on hiatus, where its members neither support nor protest the normative legal or societal process of Islamic laws or modes of societal relations. On issues relating to women, including marriage, divorce, violence, mobility, their sexualities or autonomy, neither the state nor activists can be expected to respond with silence or passivity.

3

Beyond Faith and Agency: Working Women and Secular Autonomy

The problematic of religious agency in theory and application to Muslim women's development and politics has now been discussed in some detail. In particular, Saba Mahmood's (2005) influential theory on Muslim women's pietist agency was unpacked since it relies on an academic subversion of the concept of feminist agency. Mahmood's (2001) avowed intention is to "uncouple the notion of self-realization from that of the autonomous will, as well as agency from the progressive goal of emancipatory politics" (208). The specifics of such 'uncoupling' are now explored in light of the experiences of working women and their encounter with religion in Pakistan.

It will be seen that in consonance with Mahmood's theory, autonomy is not always willingly or consciously embraced by Muslim women through engagement with emancipatory politics. But, neither is self-realisation necessarily defined in the narrow light of discursive pietist strategies and outcomes in which Mahmood locates Muslim women's agency. More directly, according to various studies, 'autonomy' for working women in Pakistan has been comprised of a defined combination of self-sufficiency, independence, physical mobility and economic and personal decision-making (Jejeebhoy and Sathar 2001; Khan 2008; Saigol 2011). This is not to suggest that these are always mutually exclusive of religious sentiment or pietism but the experiences of working women in Muslim-majority Pakistan draw attention to the search and struggle for autonomy in ways which often require them to defy, contest and challenge cultural and religious norms, actors, codes and the limits that these impose on women's choices, freedoms and mobility.

The interrelatedness of gender, work and religion in Pakistan, with a focus on the notions of empowerment and autonomy that researchers have consistently emphasised in their studies on working women, will be reviewed below. The example of the government's Lady Health Workers Programme is detailed here as their historic and most recent experiences exemplify the direct encounter between aspirations for secular autonomy against the limits of religious agency.

Women, Work and Religion

It is beyond the scope of this chapter to recount the various theories on empowerment and autonomy. However, since this publication juxtaposes these values against the concept of religious or pietist agency, the broad feminist perspectives on these terms is briefly summarised here.[1] Following the case made by scholars working on Gender and Development (GAD) against male-centred development paradigms, "empowerment" became a tool for feminist scholars to refer to grassroots movements and women's struggles within these. Perhaps the most commonly used definition of empowerment in gender studies is the one suggested by Kabeer (1994; 2012). She argues that empowerment should be viewed as a process of change that enables one to make choices and that it is through choice that real power is exercised.

While much feminist scholarly attention has been given to studying the link between women's control over resources and their empowerment, there has been no consensus over the specific determinants of empowerment. Some studies argue that access to microcredit programmes enhance women autonomy overall (Hashemi et al. 1996; Schuler 1997) and that financial control leads to greater participation in the household, but others conclude that microcredit loans have instead deepened "the gendered processes of accumulation and, in the case of loans that use land for collateral, the loss of secured land" (Keating et al. 2010, cited in Collins 2016). The importance of decision-making in the household has been similarly contested. Studies in the South Asian context tend to agree that paid employment and education for women increase decision-making in financial matters, but they argue that this has less impact on decisions relating to social and organisational matters or, for that matter, over choices regarding reproductive health (Malhotra and Mather 1997; Sathar and Kazi 2000). Geography, education levels and socio-cultural impediments have variably affected women's empowerment and these factors have been emphasised in scholarly attempts to measure it.

While there has not been any consensus on a set of common determinants of empowerment, feminist scholars and activists have come to view empowerment as a process of self-expression and self-under-standing. Feminists have further clarified that while legal reforms and access to resources may help in this process, they are not in and of themselves empowerment, which is a process rather than a quantifi-able goal or end. The key concern for feminists has been the promise of empowerment towards transformative ends, which is only possible through challenges to social hierarchies and patriarchal exclusion and politics (Cornwall and Rivas 2015). Kabeer (2012) looks deeper into comparative sites of empowerment across geographies and points out the intended and unintended consequences of development and economic policies. She argues against the notion that any community of (Muslim) women is homogenous or sealed off from the wider world. She cautions against discarding the importance of the universalist values of individual rights by suggesting that "if liberal arguments for justice are premised on false universalism, the cultural relativist case rests on an equally false essentialism" (Kabeer 2012, 230).

The critique of women's "empowerment" as a buzzword and magic bullet solution as used in contemporary times has been two-fold; that of its oversimplification by scholars and policy makers (Collins 2016) and, its cooptation for market-oriented business models (Cornwall and Rivas 2015). This has been linked to the narrowing down of the definitions of empowerment and the instrumentalisation of gender content in development policies. Collins notes the shift from empow-erment as a means to challenge hierarchies, to one that includes women in markets as business actors, loan recipients and labourers. She argues that this reflects a return to the Women in Development (WID) development planning literatures of the 1970s. Her argument is that "instead of pushing an agenda that empowers women to self-actualize and challenge existing hierarchies according to their own needs, 'women's empowerment' has become synonymous with lowering gendered barriers to the marketplace" (3). Further, Cornwall and Rivas argue that this has managed to successfully empty empow-erment of most of its progressive content. As Batliwala suggests, "empowerment" has transformed "from a noun signifying shifts in social power to a verb signalling individual power, achievement, status" (Batliwala 2007, 563).

The relevant point here is that the concept of empowerment for women's progress has become sandwiched between two separate but complementary narratives. The first is the stated claim of scholars such as Mahmood, who argue for a dissociation of self-realisation and empowerment from progressive ideals, and recommend that feminist theory needs to move beyond the binary of resistance and subordina-tion to understand the complex ways in which women express their agency without the endpoint being emancipation. The other challenge, using a similar rationale, comes from neo-liberal institutions and policies, which have appropriated the concept of empowerment "to connote economic participation rather than the disruption of social relations" (Collins 2017, 13). Both approaches are disinterested in the unsettling of the patriarchal status quo or social relations in an unequal society.

I use the term "autonomy" in the way it has been referenced in some of the literature on working women by Pakistani researchers. Ironically, Mahmood's project to delink "self-realization from autonomous will" has always been applicable to many working women's experiences in South Asia. As will be seen below, the bulk of studies on the subject find that South Asian working women do not *realise* autonomy by consciously willing to do so, neither do they venture for sovereignty through their work experiences and nor is their intent to be involved in any project of emancipatory politics. Instead, overwhelmingly, women in South Asia are often compelled to work out of necessity, and inevitably and inadvertently, acquire some form of independence and self-worth in the process. However, this does not guarantee an enhancement of their status within the domestic realm, nor does it necessarily enhance their decision-making in reproductive choices although in many cases, their financial choices and authority do improve.

The unquantifiable results of personal empowerment have been under-researched in Pakistan, but experiential evidence has been confirmed by women activists who work in organising women's labour and political representation and which points to how working women's confidence and personal choices expand and are exercised more freely. Very often, this is done with a risk that sometimes costs them their lives[2] (for a list of Pakistani government and Non-Government Organisations working on "women's empowerment", see Saigol 2011). In most documented cases and observations, the viability and prevalence of struggles and gainful strategies for personal or professional progress by Pakistani women are seen to be consciously temporal. Moreover, prevailing religious factors and cultural norms are something that these women have to negotiate against or directly confront. This is particularly difficult since these influences are closely and intrinsically linked and beneficially cemented together by the bonds of patriarchy. Women's visible struggles and aspirations contrast with the kind of faith-based potential and activism that has been offered in recent scholarship and development paradigms for Muslim women. The theory of religious agency has encouraged a kind of religious exceptionalism of Muslim women's divine needs and linked these to their material, developmental needs and aspirations too.

This investment in a hopeful, faith-appropriate alternative form of empowerment weighs in stark contrast to some of the tangible and political realities and expressions of working women in the country. The chapter will outline the causes and efforts of these women in light of their class background and strategies for autonomy, which I argue, are secular in method and aspirations and distinct from those that are limited to faith-based consciousness, ends, means or methods. These contributions have been rendered invisible or unworthy of documentation or commentary precisely because they are secular and do not fit into the now popular meta-theory that associates Muslim women's religious agency as a permanent fixture that defines and directs them, and as if they are immune to any secular characteristics – whether these are personal, professional or political.

Working Women in Pakistan

According to the Pakistan Labour Force Survey of 2014–15, the overall national labour force participation rate remains one of the lowest in the world, at 45.2 percent. Of this total, the male participation rate stands at 67.8 percent and women's hovers at an abysmally low 22 percent. Agriculture remains the main occupation for women (comprising 72 percent out of a total of 43.5 percent employed in this sector) and they are the lowest paid (earning less than half of the minimum wage in Pakistan). Several studies note the increase in the female labour force in agriculture and ascribe it to rising poverty, which leads to increased male migration from rural to urban areas and abroad for better opportunities (Jejeebhoy and Sathar 2001; Khattak et al. 2008). Further, the PLFS (2014–15) and various human rights reports also note that an increase in smaller land holdings has led to an increased engagement of female family members in cultivating land and fulfilling labour requirements. New technological trends have created an informal pattern of men using the machines and women being involved in more labour-intensive jobs (Khattak et al. 2008; PLFS 2014–15). This is further exacerbated by the most basic issue of the delays in payment of wages and government agencies are the main violators of this offence.

The informal sector accounts for 72.6 percent of non-agricultural employment. The informal sector as a whole is fairly horizontally gendered overall but comparatively, women's employment is higher in the urban formal sector (31.5 percent) and rural informal sector (78 percent), as compared to men's (inverse) employment rates at 24.3 percent in the rural formal and 69.3 percent in the urban informal sector. Within this informal sector, vertical segregation is such that manufacturing accounts for the majority of female employment at 63.9 percent and men at 18.1 percent and wholesale and retail account for 6.7 percent females compared to 37.5 percent males. In community and social services, women comprise over 28 percent compared to the male work force of 13 percent (table 17 of the PLFS 2014–15).

Khattak et al. (2008) make an important critical observation about global human development indices when they argue that while both the GDI (Gender Development Index) and GEM (Gender Empowerment Measure) are "useful tools of analysis, there are nevertheless several problems with these indices" (10). They note that the GDI, as the simple difference of the averaging of life expectancy, education and GDP (Gross Domestic Product) indices for men and women, fails to capture complexities such as the cross relation and interdependence of these three variables. More importantly, the authors point out that aspects such as political empowerment of women and legal rights are not taken into account and give the example of women in Saudi Arabia, "who might score well on the index, in terms of education, and life expectancy, but the fact that they cannot drive, which in turn restricts their freedom of mobility, is not reflected" (10). The authors note that the three components used in the HDI (Human Development Index) and the GDI are given arbitrary weights. For instance, literacy is given the same weight as life expectancy but for a majority of women, they argue that, "literacy, defined in the narrow sense of the term, might not be as important as freedom from disease, reproductive health, and life expectancy" (2008, 10).

Another caveat to point out is that unlike research on women in the Middle East and North Africa (MENA) region (Moghadam 2005), there is no recognised or definitive, comprehensive academic work on women, work and social class in Pakistan. Most short papers and NGO studies have attempted to explain the low female labour force participation by noting the social and cultural impediments to women's access and absorption into paid employment. The overarching commonality in all these studies is the acknowledgement that while poverty and gender are closely inter-related, the nature of women's employment and income are not reliable indicators of social class (Mumtaz and Shaheed 1987; Kazi 1999; Sathar and Kazi 2000).

Given this issue of contested reliability, lack of a recognised official or academic base analysis of women and class, and the very scant research on women's labour force in Pakistan, it is difficult to categorise women into official "classes". One recent potential source for developing a partial analysis of women and class is the Benazir Income Support Programme (BISP), initiated in 2008 as an unconditional cash supplement provided to women of the poorest households with the assistance of the World Bank. This has now become the largest social safety net programme in the country. Criticism of the programme in its initial phase included the fact that women beneficiaries used to be identified by parliamentarians, making the programme susceptible to the politics of patronage rather than merit. In 2010–11, a new government introduced a major transition and the beneficiaries were identified through a Poverty Scorecard Survey (PSC) based on household demographics, assets, and other measurable characteristics.[3]

Based on a Proxy Means Test (PMT), the PSC data now includes a poverty profile of each household but also provides data on 12 key indicators that include household size, type of housing and toilet facilities, education, child status, household assets, agricultural landholding, and livestock ownership. There have been several independent evaluations of the BISP, the most recent of which reported that the programme has continued to have an impact on reducing poverty for the target group and that it is reducing long-term impact of malnutrition amongst girls (Cheema et al. 2015, v; 68). Most significantly, this qualitative research also aimed to measure women's empowerment by looking at "women's agency (or the endowments of assets that underpin her ability to make strategic choices and actions) and women's relation to structure (as constituted by formal and informal institutions that prevail)" (v).

The report observes a marked change in the status of women in beneficiary households and notes that almost all the women interviewed reported that they were now being given more importance in their households as a direct result of the BISP. The report concludes that the programme "appears to have facilitated an improvement in the intra-household relations within beneficiary households as the BISP cash reduced economic pressures, as well as facilitating women's involvement in household decision making" (vi). Since the BISP has made a Computerised National Identity Card (CNIC) a mandatory requirement to receive the cash transfer, this has enfranchised millions of women who never possessed an official identity and could not open bank accounts nor even, vote in elections. The evaluation report of the BISP notes that the programme "continues to be associated with increased proportions of women in beneficiary households voting" (Cheema et al. 2015, vi). Potentially, this data, once collected and collated, could lend itself to an economic and sociological differential analysis of the poorest and/or, working-class women in Pakistan.[4] It seems that these initial findings may even challenge the conventional notion that delinked any direct correlation between (supplemental) income and women's empowerment in the domestic realm.

It is due to current limitations of authoritative studies that I term the women's movements discussed below and in the final Chapter 7 as simply "working women's movements" even though these predominantly comprise of women from what is conventionally considered to be the "working classes". Certainly, there is a reckonable class difference between the health workers discussed below and the peasant women mentioned in a later chapter but the example of the women councillors demonstrates how mobility, geography and autonomy become more compelling features than income or assets and interrupt the boundaries of class imaginaries in Pakistan. Some recent legislation (Sindh Industrial Relations Act 2013)[5] has proposed to absorb peasant classes or agricultural workers into the definition of "workers" but this has not led to any registration of peasants with the labour department. Also, not all Lady Health Workers (LHW) across the country belong to the same social class even though the basic criteria of educational levels in order to be selected is the same and they may have experienced upward social mobility over the duration of their services (Khan 2008). Even in the more prosperous province of Punjab, a study by Mumtaz et al. (2013) finds that "working as an LHW was a poverty-pushed option. Only poor women were willing to ignore the strictures of honor as they could not afford to adhere to the requirements of seclusion (purdah) in the way that better-off women could" (54). Despite the status and respect that has developed over the years for Lady Health Workers across the country, Mumtaz et al. find that the poor status and caste of the Attock district health workers invited ignominy, harassment and insults if they ventured outside the "social geography" related to their own *biradari* (endogamous clan).

Noting the absence of any overarching analytical frameworks in Pakistan, it has been difficult to develop conclusive empirical evidence or theses that relate the experiences of working women to class identities or economics (Khan 2007).[6] However, there are several studies that have considered the social transformative characteristic of women's work in the informal sector and amongst lower income groups. The bulk of these locate their research within the broader ambit of "women's empowerment" rather than class identities. Although there is general agreement on the importance of autonomy and mobility in association with women's professional, personal, physical and emotional lives and well-being, these studies also acknowledge the critical role of physical, tangible, quantifiable autonomy, empowerment, choice and freedoms for women. They point out the specific challenges faced by way of patriarchal cultural practices and codes, and gender-blind or discriminatory state policies that obstruct women's holistic autonomy.

Autonomy, Empowerment and the Threat to the Islamic Gendered Order

For Jejeebhoy and Sathar (2001), there is a distinction between autonomy and economic empowerment. Their comparative study on women in India and Pakistan attempts to assess female autonomy by drawing up indexes along the following four components; (1) economic decision-making; (2) mobility; (3) freedom from threat from husband; and (4) access to and control over economic resources. They observe that in India and Pakistan, "wage work for women is often unacceptable and poverty-induced, [and] not necessarily an indicator of autonomy" (695). A common finding regarding working women in South Asia is that not only are wage-earning women not likely to have made the decision to work on their own, they do not always have control over their earnings. Instead, the authors argue that "traditional factors conferring authority on women – age, marital duration, number of surviving sons, nuclear family residence, and dowry – have a more powerful effect on women's autonomy" (2001, 705). The authors found these factors particularly compelling in settings with wider gender disparities.

Additionally, education (even a primary education) plays a prominent role in enhancing almost every dimension of autonomy. The authors above note that the purpose of their study was to prove that regional considerations rather than religious ones obstruct women's autonomy. However, there are several methodological and academic limitations to this study. The two contrasting regions of Hindu-majority India are studied against one region of Muslim-majority Pakistan and the survey discusses intra-religious communities in the former but only majority Muslim women in the latter. Further, the study avoids any broader political or legal contextualisation. However, it makes the more important and broader rights-based argument that "education and employment do not necessarily [radically] enhance women's autonomy and [. . .] traditional factors conferring status on women remain strong" (709). The authors recommend that

> strategies to enhance women's autonomy need to expand beyond
> education, employment, and delayed marriage. More comprehensive,

direct, and context-specific strategies to increase women's autonomy must simultaneously be sought. These include raising women's gender consciousness, enabling women to mobilize and access community resources and public services, providing support for challenging traditional norms that underlie gender inequities, facilitating the acquisition of usable vocational and life skills, enhancing women's access to and control over economic resources, and enabling women to establish and realize their rights . . . particularly . . . for the northern cultures of the subcontinent – whether Pakistani or north Indian, whether Hindu or Muslim. (709)

So, for Jejeebhoy and Sathar, the journey to autonomy is intertwined with the task of not just empowering women by way of intellect, choice and potential or even economic empowerment but also, specific material access, rewards and opportunities. However, these authors do not include political empowerment as a stepping-stone towards enhancing women's autonomy. Further, the authors do not identify the sources or sustainability of restrictive "traditional norms", nor do they analyse where these customs acquire legitimacy or their connectivity to the lever of religion.

Grünenfelder (2013a) argues that Pakistani women's non-domestic work has been conceptualised in three major ways: as a contribution to national development, as a danger to the nation, and as non-existent. She traces the contestations in the development of the subjectivities of the 'ideal' woman – for example, during the Islamisation years of General Zia ul Haq (1977–1988) – and documents how the notion of the Pakistani women was replaced by that of an "Islamic woman" within a state discourse that constantly painted women as a danger to the nation (72). She cites historical documentation of how religious parties have always seen working women as liabilities to Islam (72). However, she also references existing literature on how religious parties permit the notion of working women in the disciplines of teaching and health work, if only to facilitate a gender segregated Pakistani society at large.

Several Pakistani scholars have observed that the social implications of the state's religious discourse are more compelling than juridical ones (Jahangir 1998; Shah 2016). This has encouraged various groups and collectives to "act as enforcers of religious mores" (Grünenfelder 2013a, 75). Further, as will be demonstrated in the examples cited below, this shift of moral responsibility to the public at large has meant that working women and those serving in public office or public figures have become the most primary and vulnerable targets of vigilantism. Increasingly, in Pakistan, sex crimes and murder have come to serve as methods of punitive lesson and control over women's mobility. The majority of such acts are often what would be categorised as honour-based crimes and fall under the loose sociological explanation of cultural atavism. Traditionally, these are either settled through tribal or community based male-exclusive justice systems (to the advantage of men). If the case should make it to the state legal system, the male perpetrator is often exonerated under the Islamic law of *Qisas and Diyat*,[7] which permits forgiveness of the crime by the natural heirs of the female victim (parents, siblings). The overlap and imbrication of culture and religious motivation continues to extend moral impunity to Muslim men. Khattak et al. (2008) point out that where religious laws contradict a civil statute, the latter is meant to prevail. However, they stress that this is "only in theory because in practice this does not occur" and that there are "many contradictions in the two sources of laws, especially with regard to personal law- marriage, divorce, custody of children and inheritance" (55).

Khan (2007) maintains that "the relationship between women's work and the political environment, and women's work and the sexual politics of Pakistani society is also very close" (21). She considers a deliberate ideological purpose behind state policy which promotes gender segregation by deferring to "culture and traditions regarding *purdah* as an explanation for women's inability to take greater part in employment outside the home and access social sector services or have greater political participation" (22). Khan suggests that the threat of sexual violence has helped to keep women obedient and that the double burden of *purdah* and household work have become "an invisible triple burden of *purdah*, household work and paid work" (29). Additionally, the role of counter-intuitive programmes, such as the one conducted by USAID for home-based workers ('Behind the Veil', USAID 2008), only reinforces and limits women's empowerment to one within the framework of religious/cultural agency, rather than challenging social barriers against the 'burdens' mentioned above by Khan which adversely affect women's autonomy overall.

Considerable deconstruction of the purdah has already been studied in South Asia with regard to its role in the institutionalisation of strict gender segregation (Papanek 1973; Syed 2010). Despite the existing gender segregation in many spheres of life in Pakistan, female employment has never been condemned in principle (Papanek 1982; Syed 2010) and increasingly, women have been able and willing to take up employment outside the home despite restrictive gender norms (Khan 2008). This is particularly so where the gender-segregated societal structure has required women professionals (Papanek 1971). The distinction between the physical veil and discursive *purdah* segregation is more complex than simply a religious adherence. However, the issue of autonomy is still relevant in this regard, with reference to mobility, gender segregation of public spaces and decision-making on issues that challenge or go against prescribed patriarchal cultural or religious norms. It becomes more critical in relation to women's active roles in and access to any public office, employment or services or for that matter, independent choice in matters of marriage, sexuality and reproductive decisions.

Khan observes there is a positive impact on prior social norms when the state employs women in professions even in remote areas, as in the case of the Lady Health Workers. A Village-Based Family Planning Workers scheme was launched at a national level as part of Pakistan's Eighth Five-Year Plan (1993–98). This grew into the current Lady Health Workers Programme. It is considered a successful government programme in large part because it has promoted widespread reversible, modern contraceptive use in rural and otherwise inaccessible areas of Pakistan. Khan (2008) lists the requirements to qualify as a LHW (at least eight years of education) and the responsibilities that entail working from her home (with a designated "Health House") from where she sees community members, holds meetings, maintains her household register, and stores contraceptives, medicines and communication material. The work involves registration of all the population in her catchment area in order to identify their need for health and family planning services and distributing information on basic health, hygiene, nutrition, and even providing essential drugs for the treatment of minor ailments. Additionally, the administration of polio drops to children during regular government-sponsored polio drives and participating in emergency relief activities in the event of natural disasters has become part of the duties appended to the LHW programme.

For Khan (2008), the most interesting aspect of the LHW programme is that the health-worker has proven to be an instrument of positive change in her community. She notes that although LHWs are privileged compared to other women in their communities by virtue of their education, "this does not necessarily indicate that they are financially more secure, or that they will marry into families with relatively better income earning strategies" (14). Her 2008 study confirms the difficulty of categorising working women into classes since all LHWs have to have attained high school education to qualify, yet the families she interviewed state clearly that if not for their earnings, these workers "may well have died and [their] marriage[s] may not have survived either under the pressures of poverty" (14). Even some husbands' families reported being grateful for the LHWs' financial contribution and regretted not putting them to work earlier.

Several scholars testify to the historical change in understanding empowerment and autonomy with regard to women's work in Pakistan. Earlier studies relied on broadly defined empowerment indicators. For example, a study on women piece-rate workers in the city of Lahore stated that they were experiencing "more say in family matters, more respect and consideration in the household, and relaxation in the home due to their status as earning members of the family" (cited in Khan 2008, 2). Later research on working women in Karachi found that "there had to be a two-fold change along with paid work: the work had to be both valued by society and give women an improved self-perception for it to have a strong positive impact on the women's lives. Women working in formal sector occupations had the greater advantage here" (Khan 2008, 3).

Khan's (2008) own analysis goes on to include those characteristics that define autonomy by way of choice and decision-making, rather than just the expansion of economic, social or political opportunities. She points out that other positive benefits of work, even in the informal sector, "included a decrease in urban Pakistan in gender discrimination against sending girls to school [and that] . . . the most important rural study . . . showed that paid work outside the home potentially increased women's autonomy" (3). She notes that autonomy was defined "in terms of indicators such as domestic decision-making, financial decision-making, access to household resources, type of mobility, and even communication with husband" (3). Khan considers more direct linkages between women's paid employment and the social change that accompanies this in cases of women in social services such as the government-appointed community-based women health workers. In other words, for Khan, autonomy is linked to being charged with social responsibility.

This is an important point of distinction. Social responsibility is closely associated with religious duty, particularly in the imaginary and discourse of religious politics in Muslim contexts. Practically all religious organisations in Pakistan (including the banned ones – the most prominent being, *Lashkar e Tayyaba* with its active charitable front, *Jamaat ud Dawa*) have fully functioning charitable wings and their fund-raising work is a prolific industry that is commonly considered nefarious for jihadist causes. These charitable fronts are very active in times of humanitarian crises in particular, but they also run community schools, medical aid and welfare centres. There is little known about any assistance offered by way of any formal legal aid but this is likely because they often tend to settle small disputes within their own privatised justice systems. Women volunteers are very active within these organisations but not necessarily as paid professionals.

Paid social work and women working in this field, therefore, offer interesting insights into the intersections of gender, work and social change in such a context. There have been several studies that have drawn attention to the political and ideological constructs of the role and place of women, work and religion in Pakistan. Grünenfelder observes in one rural setting of Pakistan that Muslim professional women negotiate gender relations by developing strategies in order to be able to participate in formal labour markets. Her study recognises social organisation (also called community mobilisation) as a formal occupation that emerged in Pakistan in the 1980s. Grünenfelder 2013b explains that

> the rationale behind this new form of activism was at least twofold (Rasmussen et al., 2007). On the one hand parts of society were eager to bring change to Pakistan and above all to improve the situation of marginalized individuals (for example, women) and rural communities (Idrees et al., 2008; Jan and Jan, 2000). Women were needed to reach the female clientele, as this is hardly possible for men in the highly gender-segregated rural areas. On the other hand, previous state-led rural development had so far focused merely on technical interventions and was not likely to succeed in future without social change on the ground, that is, in villages or communities. (Shah 2009, 604)

One of the difficulties regarding social mobility is related to Grünenfelder's (2013b) finding that "social access to villagers, including village women, can be gained only via key men in the village. And since – according to prevailing gender norms – a female social organizer cannot approach a man, she is always dependent on her male colleagues to obtain access to a village and its inhabitants" (606). The other challenge is with regard to the perception of social organisers as agents and "represent[atives of] imperialistic gender discourses [who] endanger local gender values" (606). Grünenfelder observes how "development is widely perceived as a Western instrument to destabilize the traditional gender order [and this] has important consequences for women development workers in the Hazara region" (600). The importance of hostels for women, cell phones and male companions play a critical role in working women's mobility. (As an aside, it is important to point out that in other parts of Pakistan, including in rural areas and small towns, the role of local "NGO women" and their (often) controversial activism against Islamist politics is neither characterised as 'elitist', nor does it conform to any pietist expectations. These women who take risks in their open challenge to male Islamist preachings are acknowledged, respected and sought by community members for assistance in several matters (Marsden 2008)).

More formally, since its inception in the 1990s, the Lady Health Workers Programme had always inverted the traditional gender equation, since this programme relies on the reverse logic and on women's easy access into the homes of communities where men would never be permitted due to codes of privacy. This programme has destabilised the traditional gender order in an unconventional way and differently from what Grunenfelder describes above. As seen below, this has had far-reaching consequences in the story of women's empowerment in Pakistan in general, as well as in terms of being at the receiving end of the backlash of religious politics more specifically.

Lady Health Workers: The Neutral Interface

The experiences of the LHWs, who are the primary original army of social organisers across Pakistan's rural and low-income areas, bear witness to a departure from normative social perceptions of working women. The most obvious difference in terms of the roles and representation of LHWs from other social mobilisers or organisers as studied by Grünenfelder is that the latter are seen as "embodiment of NGOs" and in some cases, suspected as perpetuating a foreign agenda and one that seeks to subvert the traditional and patriarchal order. However, the Lady Health Workers Programme (LHWP) is a government-run project that employs over 110,000 trained female community workers involved in delivering basic health services at doorsteps in communities. Benazir Bhutto's government in 1994 initiated the programme. The LHWP directly addresses women's reproductive health needs by providing information, basic services and access to further care if necessary, directly into women's homes and communities. It has been termed a successful government programme in large part because it has succeeded in increasing reversible and modern contraceptive use, particularly in many inaccessible rural areas. What interests most researchers is that the LHWP has proven to be an instrument of social change in the communities to which they belong. Not only have these women successfully broken the private-public dichotomy quite literally, they also provide an essential service to women in their child-bearing years which would otherwise be absolutely denied to them.

Ayesha Khan's (2008) research on the LHWP argues that

if empowerment is to be understood through changes wrought in the areas of body, voice and paid work, this project in effect touches all these themes. The nature of the [Lady Health Workers Programme] is directly meant to increase women's control and decision-making with regard to their health, well-being, and reproductive decision-making; it is a community-based project that strives to empower men and women to make their needs heard through health committees and increased interaction. (3)

Khan observed that "all LHWs interviewed [had] negotiated some expanded version of the traditional gendered space" and that mobility was expanded sometimes through a reconceptualisation of *purdah* requirements or honour codes (21). These were not openly defiant nor through any explicit confrontation with structures of male control and domination, even though such structural changes may be taking place in an implicit manner. Pakistan was witness to such a change on a large scale in 2010.

One LHW serves a population of 1000–1500 persons, which is approximately 100 households, and she regularly visits them to maintain her health records. Her monthly stipend, until recently, was equivalent to approximately US $25. For a negligible stipend, the LHWs are also routinely recruited for administering polio vaccinations because they are such an expansive and effective labour force. In 2010, intermittent protests over unfair termination, salary increase or harassment that had been brewing for the past decade, grew into a countrywide boycott of the polio vaccination drive scheduled for February of that year. The LHWs in Sindh province were especially active and there was even a deeply symbolic protest demonstration at the mausoleum of the assassinated Prime Minister and founder of the LHWP, Benazir Bhutto. This may be read as a political and alternative rendering of a "performance of gendered *secular* virtues," when compared to Mahmood's (2001) readings of pietist women's "performance of gendered Islamic virtues" (203). The daily *Dawn* reported that at this protest the LHWs demanded that the promise to regularise their work, made by the late Prime Minister, Benazir Bhutto, should be fulfilled ("Anti-polio Campaign Faces Threats of Boycott," *Dawn*, Feb 9, 2010).

In September 2010, after protracted nationwide strikes and protests and a legal battle, the Chief Justice of the Supreme Court of Pakistan ordered that the LHWs should be paid the minimum wage of a skilled (full-time) worker (at the time, Rs.7,000 or roughly US $70, per month). The President of the All Pakistan Lady Health Workers Employees Association, and leader of these protests, Bushra Arain, told the press that "whatever success Pakistan has achieved towards bringing down infant and maternal mortality rates, or in meeting the targets for the Millennium Development Goals four and five [8] would not have been possible had the LHWs not been going door to door" (Ebrahim 2011).

In early 2011, the Sindh provincial government was forced to delay the launch of its three-day polio campaign because the LHWs now staged further city-based protests against the government's non-implementation of the Supreme Court's legal orders. This was followed by nationwide protests, which included direct action by the LHWs in blocking major highways, courting arrests and following up their legal case at the Supreme Court. When the Supreme Court passed a judgment in favour of the LHWs' demand for a minimum wage, the Chief Justice (CJ) based it on an interesting observation. Reportedly, the deputy attorney general representing the government pleaded that the LHWs were always meant to be contractual workers hired by the government and were not entitled to receive the rights they were demanding. In response, the CJ is said to have asked the representative what the name of the programme was. When told that this was the Lady Health *Workers* Programme, the CJ is reported to have asked for a definition of 'Worker' according to the ILO convention. In a meeting with members of Women's Action Forum, one of the more experienced Lady Health Workers involved in this struggle, reported that based upon the clarification of the definition of "worker", the CJ passed the judgment that since they are officially, legally and universally recognised as "workers" according to the international agreement, the LHWs must be awarded the minimum wage.[9] So, apart from framing their own rights in a liberal, universalist light, the Supreme Court of Pakistan chose to interpret the case of the LHWs in this frame rather than any Islamic provision or indeed, cultural specific code or ethos. The matter did not end for the LHWs, who had registered another case demanding regularisation of their jobs, which was adjudicated in their favour (2012–2013).

Silencing Secular Resistance

Against the backdrop of these developments, the proceeding wave of attacks on health and aid workers in Pakistan that same year signified the tense and entangled relationship between women and religion. Of the 15 aid workers targeted by militants across the country in 2012, nine of the victims were health workers associated with the national polio campaign. At the time, Pakistan was one of three countries where polio still persisted. Some 57 cases were registered in 2012 and the World Health Organisation warned of travel/visa restrictions and sanctions to be imposed if polio continued to spread. The majority of cases are found in the tribal areas, which are less populated but where militants have actively resisted the vaccination programme terming it an un-Islamic practice and believing it to be a conspiracy against Muslims.

The Lady Health Workers are also contracted to administer polio drops in recognition of their successful access to communities and involvement with post-natal services. In so far as they represent modernist ideas and transgress the patriarchal division between private and public roles for women, as well as the fact that they are officials of the Pakistani state, the LHWs in recent years have been specifically targeted by the militants in the Taliban controlled areas (which reach beyond the tribal areas and in several metropolitan centres). Between 2006 and 2009, the Taliban's invasion of Swat in the Himalayan region of Pakistan was followed by their systematic and violent pogrom to enforce its version of Sharia on the already Islamic, Republic of Pakistan. The Taliban destroyed Swat's famed tourist industry through a series of public beheadings and hangings (of prostitutes, barbers and entertainers) in town squares. Once they controlled Swat, over their three-year siege, the Taliban prohibited polio vaccination campaigns, destroyed 122 girls' schools, 22 barber shops, and banned all music, cinema and most NGOs in the area. According to regular news reports, the Taliban also killed those health workers who attempted to save people wounded in suicide blasts.

A British Medical Journal (BMJ) study entitled, "How the Taliban Undermined Community Healthcare in Swat, Pakistan," (Ud din, Mumtaz, and Ataullahjan 2012) conducted in-depth interviews with Swat-residing, Pashtun LHWs, to gauge the effects of the Taliban's threats and violence against them. According to the study, not only did the overall infrastructure of community health suffer drastically, but maternal mortality increased and individual LHWs were socially ostracised through a vilification campaign, while many left or stopped working due to direct threats to their lives. Some of the strategies adopted by the Taliban are quoted in the BMJ study, based on the direct experiences of the affected LHWs (although the authors make the proviso that the worst affected could not be interviewed due to the high risk this entailed for those women's lives). The most effective strategy employed by the Taliban was to name-and-shame the LHWs on FM radio and the issuing of three *fatwas* (religious edicts) against them. The LHWs interviewed in the BMJ study cite specific examples of beheadings, as well as public beatings and firing on their houses and murders of their colleagues' family members. The study notes that the LHW programme to provide family planning services made it "an ideological target" (2). This is very similar to the campaigns and political positions taken by some mainstream Islamists who argue that family planning, contraception and sex education promote "vulgarity", "obscenity" and encourage extramarital sex. The BMJ study cites allegations by the leader of the Taliban, Maulana Fazlullah that "LHWs want to promote prostitution and sin in our society" (2).

According to the BMJ study, about 15 percent of the LHWs of Swat resigned, others simply stopped working while several left the city. The Taliban's persecution of the health workers resulted in an increase in maternal mortality, at least seven forced marriages (according to the sample interviewed), and abortions have been on the rise. The most effective strategy employed by the Taliban was to name-and-shame the female health workers on FM radio and to issue three *fatwas* (religious edicts) against them. The BMJ study notes that these religious pronouncements had a more serious impact than even the threats of kidnapping, execution of forced marriages and in some cases, death. The reason is that these *fatwas* were not directed at health services *per se* but against the very notion of women in public spaces, which was declared a form of public indecency. The *fatwa* (as cited in the BMJ study) also declared that "it was a Muslim man's duty to kidnap the women health workers when they paid home visits, to marry them forcibly (even if they were already married women), or to use them as sexual slaves" (1). Specifically, Maulana Fazlullah, the Taliban chief of Swat even went so far as to declare the LHWs as *wajibul qatl* (fit for murder).

The second *fatwa* declared that it was illegal for Muslim women to work for wages and the third that Lady Health Workers were subverting the gendered social order and in fact, "were men because they travelled unaccompanied in the streets like men. Like all non-family men, they should not be allowed to enter homes" (2). The BMJ study notes that these "divine" rulings were instrumental in discrediting the primary care work because the health workers were now cast as "prostitutes" and "servants of America" (2). The Taliban's (now famed) use of FM radio for religious propaganda rationalised that since these women health workers carry condoms, it was obvious that they were house-calling prostitutes.

In varying degrees, the substance or rationalisation of all three *fatwas* overlap, and can be found in the rhetoric employed by several hardline and mainstream Islamists. When the Taliban occupied Swat, the Islamist alliance of the MMA was ruling Khyber Pakhtunkhwa (2002–2008). The socio-political environment created by the MMA policies had instituted a form of gender apartheid in the province, which made it conducive for the militants to further their radical agenda there. The suggestion that violence perpetrated in the name of Islam can no longer be viewed as a crime – committed by individuals, aided and sanctioned by local Islamist clerics and groups – is dangerous. Such a defensive stance defuses the criminal act as an imperative of a "broader discourse" (Manchanda 2012, online) and depicts feminists and human rights activists as alarmists who focus exclusively on faith-based violence.

The targeted killings of the polio workers that spread across the country in 2012 may or may not have always been the work of the Taliban, but their narrative of anti-polio campaigns is consistent with that of religious fundamentalists in Pakistan. The main religious polit-ical parties support polio vaccination (since they proclaim to be anti-fundamentalist) but never condemn the Taliban for their atroci-ties in this regard. However, postsecularists are reluctant to identify all those crimes perpetrated against women that are directly connected to religious fundamentalism. The implicit suggestion is that violence cannot be inspired by religious fundamentalism and should only be seen as motivated by and reactive to imperialism or the "context" created by external causes. The argument is that while religion may afford political agency, religious actors void themselves of the patri-archal reservoir available in Islam when they exercise such agency.

On the other hand, if, as it is explicitly argued, such violent crimes must be viewed as stemming exclusively from "a broader discourse . . . of heteronormativity . . . and neo-liberal development" (Man-chanda 2012, online) then these critics should be making the case that polio vaccination and girls' education/political empowerment are in fact very much part of the neo-liberal development agenda. Would it be logical then to review anti-polio, anti-education drives as part of a rational rejection by those who oppose health and education pro-grammes particularly for and by women, because these are part of the trope of liberal universalism? This form of rationalisation allows any person who claims to act in the defence or promotion of Islam to be absolved of "criminal intent" or, from being called 'violent' and to be viewed as Manchanda suggests, permanent victims of external (his-torical) conditions and a "global political climate."

The attacks on the polio vaccinators did succeed in convincing many for the need to retreat and abandon the programme because of the risky "political climate". Development advocates protested such a call for silencing as a policy of defeat and argued that there needed to be a coordinated, public response by Pakistani and foreign NGOs to the attacks. The government and other groups argued it was safer to simply stop public education campaigns altogether and just allow aid workers to operate quietly. A report in the Christian Science Monitor quoted the Lady Health Worker President of the time as saying, "the less attention we get, the less vulnerable we will be as targets for the terrorists," Ms. Arain says, "we are involved with anti-polio drive, infant health awareness programs, family planning, etc. and if the government does not pull its act together, many deadly diseases can spread rapidly in Pakistan . . . . The situation can get out of hand" (Siddiqui 2013, "5 Female Teachers Killed: Pakistan Aid Work Imperiled," *Christian Science Monitor*, 2 January).

During their protests, the LHWs also made some important political statements regarding the instrumentalisation of religion. Historically, mainstream Islamist political parties and groups have been actively inducted into national health related campaigns and programmes, including for the promotion of the use of contraception and polio vaccinations. In this regard, both UNICEF and WHO in Pakistan have sponsored the inclusion of clergy in national campaigns, in order to demonstrate the compatibility of modern health methods/procedures with Islam. Most "non-fundamentalist" Islamic groups (and here, the term is an important signifier of the differences amongst Islamists) support polio vaccination and use of contraceptive devices (albeit, in the case of contraception use, with less active involvement but more so, by passive non-resistance). Given the backlash against polio vaccines, particularly after the militants' take-over of Swat and the Taliban's ban of the vaccination, many of these Islamist groups were encouraged to reactivate the drive for polio vaccines. In this regard, UNICEF had sponsored a programme called "Polio Eradication Campaign and Endorsement by Islamic Scholars" and provided supportive material for the polio workers who conducted the vaccination campaign in Pakistan. Some of these folders were found blood-drenched, next to the bodies of those polio workers who were assassinated in the largest city of Karachi, Pakistan's largest city, in 2012. It read as a tragically ironic comment on the futility of the attempt to synthesise religious scholarship with modern developmental progress.

There were several subsequent local meetings and international conferences for Islamic scholars to meet and strategise on devising methods to counter the resistance in those Muslim contexts where the polio epidemic has become endemic. The language of these scholars reveals a deeper concern. A newsletter of the Global Polio Eradication Initiative dated 7th March 2013, carried the views of these scholars who repeatedly referred to the importance of polio eradication as an obligation on the part of "Muslim parents" and who claimed to have reached "a consensus that the Muslim Ummah faces a serious problem of persistent polio that threatens all Muslim children." Further, the newsletter reported that at the Islamic Scholars' Consultation held in Cairo in 2013, the Grand Imam of Al-Azhar, Dr. Ahmad Al Tayyeb warned that "crippled children lead to a crippled Muslim Ummah."

This anxiety for the Muslim child and protecting the "Ummah's children" is matched by an equal anxiety regarding a "re-profiled" Muslim-appropriate methodology to make polio eradication successful. The Regional Director of WHO (Eastern Mediterranean Region) said the following, as he addressed the Islamic scholars in Cairo in 2013:

> We need your wisdom to guide us through these challenging times and your advice on the way forward. We want to hear your views on whether you feel there is a need to re-profile the programme. *Would it help if the programme is distanced from the West?* Would it be preferable if it is seen and perceived as being owned and supported by the entire ummah? Will *a neutral interface delivering the services* in the highest risk areas of these countries help? How can we work together? [emphasis added][10]

The Lady Health Workers of Pakistan have a different view regarding this proposal for some external "neutral interface" for delivering such health services. At their protest demonstrations against the killings of their colleagues in the assassination spree of polio workers in 2012, the LHWs were seen burning and defacing some of the official posters that carried images of and endorsements by, Islamic male scholars and prominent 'born-again' male cricketers and celebrities. These (male) personalities are engaged by the government and donor agencies to popularise the vaccines. Such advertisements and posters are ostensibly meant to promote the subliminal message that polio vaccines are sanctioned by the clergy and are therefore, suitable (*halal* or legitimate) for Muslims.

In this vein, several multinational health corporations have introduced what are advertised as "Halal Vaccines", suggesting (falsely) that the polio drops have been prepared differently or by some 'kosher' method to legitimise their use in Muslim contexts. Peddling Islamic products has become a false alternative and lucrative for their proprietors, and the defenders of such reinventions justify such market strategies as creative adaptations. However, as the LHWs clearly realise, such circumambulations simply diminish the worth of their own worldly contributions and deflect attention from how these women are in fact, the primary and practical "neutral interface" for such services.

The Politics of Secular Autonomy

The secular methodologies of the LHWs for delivering essential basic health services for women may be prosaic and understated but are effective, successful and dependent only on state support, rather than on competing *fatwas*, distortions, deception or performativity – as a method of delivering basic services to all members of a community, regardless of religious affiliation. Autonomy has become synonymous with these women in terms of mobility (physical and class) and an empowerment that is not limited to or dependent on income only. Status and a pragmatic and purposeful social calling defines this programme in contrast to those who may be involved in charity or social welfare work that is motivated by divinity or piety. Clearly, the religious militants in Swat realised the seriousness of such a secular autonomy that motivated them to murderously prevent these women from transgressing public norms and defying the expectations of women's roles under their Sharia. The passivity of religious agency is not a threat to the patriarchal male order. However, clearly, if states keep abdicating more and more public services and spaces to clerical intervention, then the likelihood of framing a rights-based discourse in anything other than a faith-based proposal is going to be fully implausible and its success, equally contestable.

While vocal against the murders of the polio workers and supportive of the continuation of the polio vaccination campaigns, members of the *Pakistan Ulema Council* (comprised of various clergy) and religious political parties have not extended any interest or support to the pragmatic class-based concerns of the LHWs (including those workers who also work on polio vaccination teams). The only collective political support extended to the LHWs, other than women's rights activists and individual women Parliamentarians, has come from the left leaning, rural-based, secular nationalist party, the *Awami Tehreek Sindh*.

Historically, the base and cadre of this secular party falls in the same province as where the LHW protest began (Sindh) and is associated with and steeped in Marxist tradition. The leadership and cadre of the *Awami Tehreek Sindh* focus primarily on their sub-nationalist agenda. But, in relation to their province, their ideology pivots around class-based issues, including re-distribution of wealth and around the management of natural resources. The party has always identified itself as secular and socialist. It was not surprising that it was the only political party that raised the issue of the LHWs' right to minimum wage at an event that marked the International Women's Day in 2011. Moreover, the event was not organised at any urban centre under the aegis of some UN platform, but rather held at a district council hall (the lowest tier of the political structure in Pakistan).

The male President of this nationalist party, Ayaz Latif Palejo, linked all the issues that would usually fall under the secular feminist agenda. These included criticism of the discriminatory Islamic law of *Qisas and Diyat*, which Palejo described as "exposed" after the Raymond Davis case.[11] Palejo argued openly at this forum against the selectivity of invoking Islamic laws in a discriminatory way for women as opposed to men, even for non-Muslim foreign men such as Davis. He also confirmed the risks that women experienced if they chose to contract free-will marriages and identified the flaws in the marriage contract (*nikahnama*) that institutionalised the control of women's sexualities. At the event, the cause of the LHWs was collectively supported as a basic human right ("Women's Rights Amendments to Nikahnama Proposed," *Dawn*, March 31, 2011).

Soon after the spree of killings of the polio vaccinators across Pakistan, UNICEF (Pakistan) shifted the strategy of commissioning religious endorsement from its peripheral position to a central one. In March 2013, UNICEF hastily published a booklet of multiple *fatwas* or religious decrees that endorsed polio vaccination and clarified that this was not against the Sharia (Bhatti, 2013). The *fatwas* were sourced from a wide range of international scholars, mosques, Islamic centres, collectives, and councils and even spanned the different multiple schools of Islamic jurisprudence, religious sects and thought within the country. An attempt was made to include the endorsement from every possible citadel of theocratic influence and the idea was to equip polio workers in the field with this religious cover, since the door-to-door visits had been severely curtailed after the killings. Despite the fact that this strategy failed to prevent the systematic murders of polio workers and that there is no quantifiable way to measure the success of such a strategy, international agencies continue with this religio-cultural methodology of delivering basic services.

This is often at the cost of other pragmatic responses that are indifferent to and even defiant of a dependence on religious endorsements and references are clearly visible and can be documented. One example of the latter is of those women who belonged to the same polio vaccination team as their assassinated colleagues. Just a few weeks after the killings, undeterred by the continuing threats, the women of the attacked team resumed their work and participated in the next round of vaccinations. This resilience and determination could be seen in the 15-year old sister of one of the victims who took her place on the vaccination team for the next round (McNeil Jr. 2013). Other tangible strategies include those employed by the deputy commissioner of

Karachi (Malir district), Dr. Jan Muhammad Qazi. He combined the strategy of "carrots and sticks" which included, having the police impound entire apartment compounds where Pashtun residents were shooting at the vaccinators, until all the children were given the vaccine. He would even resort to bribing children at playgrounds to receive vaccines and block traffic in busy town centres so teams could administer the drops to children in cars and on cycles, on the spot. The *New York Times* reported that as a result of the use of such unconventional methods, Qazi's district was one of the few that tested negative for the polio virus (McNeil Jr. 2013, "Pakistan Battles Polio, and Its People's Mistrust," *New York Times*, July 21).

It is not simply a matter of contrasting the effectiveness of pragmatic strategies against appeals to mystical persuasion. The emphasis given to the latter by a failing governance structure, ineffective and opportunist donors and, anthropological inquiry that places extraordinary stress on the "effectiveness" of Islamist welfare work and their grass-roots linkages, deflects our attention from the possibilities, successes and value of non-religious, even impious approaches and methods.

Summary

The key argument regarding the entanglement of faith and feminism in Pakistan was advanced. It counters the notion that Pakistani women's rights may be more appropriately appraised if framed through the lens of religious agency and demonstrates that in fact, working women's struggles are predominantly invested in and advance secular autonomy. It is a testament to the attention given to religious identities that there are multiple theses on women and Islam in Pakistan but a gaping absence of academic or social scientific work on women and class identities. Key studies were sourced that point to Pakistani women's empowerment by highlighting the contradictions and contrasts between secular, material-based autonomy and abstract religious agency, with reference to the work and activism of the Lady Health Workers of Pakistan. It contrasts the charitable work and proselytisation as the ends of women who exercise religious agency against the sense of autonomy, decision-making and status that are the side-products of paid social work taken up by working women. These need not be always mutually exclusive but more often than not, the image and experiences of working women or those who transgress into the public sphere have been viewed with suspicion and cast as liabilities to Islam. The extension of this patriarchal vision that played itself out through the systematic targeted murders of Lady Health Workers by religious militants for their work as state representatives in carrying out polio vaccination campaigns across the country was documented.

4

The Limits of Religious Agency in Pakistan

This chapter discusses the (re)construction of the "agentive Islamist woman" across the sites of religious nationalisms, Islamic extremism and popular culture in Pakistan. It reviews the manner in which women are cast in various forms in order to canvas male religious political schemas. The three cases studied demonstrate how women have been valorised as bearers of Islam and national culture. Through each case, we see how masculinised Islamic politics seeks the political deliverables of Islam, depending on whether its utility supports corresponding ideological agendas and material ends.

What's In It For Women?

As 2010 drew to an end, Pakistan's first (veiled) female suicide bomber reportedly blew herself up at a World Food Programme queue in the north-western tribal district of Bajaur (bordering Afghanistan), killing some 47 people including security personnel ("Woman Suicide Bomber Strikes at WFP Centre; 45 Killed," *Dawn*, Dec. 25, 2010). Despite a strict social code that relegates all public spaces as exclusively masculine, a female transgressor performing a militant act against the polity was half-expected. This is especially true since suicide attacks in Pakistan had escalated drastically in the years between 2005 and 2010.[1]

Unlike the Arab or even other South Asian experiences, Pakistan's history carries no anecdotal ethnography, nor archival evidence of women militia. Even the activism of women of the right wing Islamist groups has not been radically violent in its mode or political expression.[2] Instead, the more relevant debate in Pakistan has pivoted around the notion of pietist Islam and the political articulations of the agency attributed to women from such movements (A.S. Zia 2009b). As potent symbols of Islamic resurgent movements globally, Muslim women's agency and its co-option by masculinised religious nation-alisms have been well documented in postcolonial feminist critiques (Lewis and Mills (eds.) 2003). Recent academic attempts to recover the agency of pietist/Islamist women challenge feminist theories that assume that agency must be substantive and informed by a feminist consciousness. In Chapter 2, it was noted how Saba Mahmood (2005) has argued that in fact, piety movements prove that agency can be attributed even to passive, docile non-action and preservation of the status quo and that feminist politics is not a natural desire. Humeira Iqtidar (2011) concludes through her dialogue with a woman member of *Jamaat ud Dawa* that Islamist parties can be oppressive for some but liberating sanctuaries for others. Masooda Bano (2012) argues the case for recognising the rationality of thousands of young Pakistani women who graduate from *madrasas* and demand the national adop-tion of traditional Sharia law, despite its highly restrictive limits on female agency.

The political experience in the Pakistani context has shown, however, that faith-based agency of women is not just innocuously adopted for non-liberal, non-feminist ends nor as a willing embrace-ment and celebration of gender inequality only but increasingly, to actively support a patriarchal Islamic agenda (Haq 2007; Ahmad 2009). Moreover, in the context of Pakistan there is a simultaneous (pro-masculinist) counter-narrative that now celebrates the agentive possibilities of Islamist women.[3] In such literature, Muslim women's virtuosity is not simply defined with reference to nationalist Islamic identities and the colonial encounter and not even simply as cultural resistance to Western modernity and its discontents. Rather, Islamist women's agentive possibilities are now the site for communal, sectarian, internecine contests *within* the Muslim-majority society of Pakistan. This is particularly true, when the *normative* nationalist reli-gious discourse contests with the *radical* or extremist Islamist challenge[4] and competes for more legitimacy and credentials as an authentic form of Islam, in comparison to the aims and acts of reli-gious militants.

Multiple Views of Agency

The romanticisation of Muslim women's faith-based agency has largely allowed Islam to become a tool in a schema under which "women symbolize the varied ways Islam can be deployed to loosen or control the body politic" (Ong 2003, 405). This translation has been quicker than anticipated in the Pakistani context. The regulation of women's agency is patent in the overtly controlling prescriptions found in the narrative of anti-state, Islamic extremists in Pakistan. Extremist ideologies seem to be appropriating women's militant agency as an exclusive recourse for their specific militant ends. Comparatively, the mainstream religio-political groups and fundamentalists – depending on their location on the ideological spectrum – tend to be more selective in their engagement with the potential agency of the modern Islamist woman. They are interested in a cultivated 'unveiling' or nuanced showcasing of the agency of Islamist women. This demonstrative or performative agency should be read as a dual concept. It is simultaneously exploited to: i) demarcate and limit pre-defined feminised spheres, in order to particularise (im)mobility; and yet, ii) is also usurped and reclaimed as an identity marker of free will, in order to counter the (Western) stereotype of the traditionally oppressed, veiled Muslim female subject.

Meanwhile, liberal elites in Pakistan attempt to develop some form of a vague secular strategy to counter the resurgent wave of religiosity. One such attempt has been the initiative by (liberal) cultural doyens and artists-cum-activists to deploy fashion as a form of resistance to religious militancy. A host of fashion designers, musicians, performers and painters have embarked on a national project that presumes to reclaim and appropriate nationalist and religious symbolism to resist religious extremism. The politics of these "lifestyle liberals" hinges around campaigns that aim to (re)frame cultural production as a liberal, postmodernist, performative, artsy resistance and alternative to religious forces (Chapter 6).

The (lack of) politics defining these latter projects do not measure up to the serious challenge posed by resurgent Islamist politics that is radical in nature. Neither can it compare to the organised, robust and patriarchal campaigns aggressively launched by mainstream religious conservatives. Moreover, such campaigns have tended to offer a spectacular combination of religious and nationalist symbolism and rhetoric. The only consistency in the various expressions of power politics is that they have been premised and played out, increasingly literally, across the bodies of women. This tussle directly influences gendered identities and redefines cultural and national identities exclusively along the lines of religion. It leaves Pakistani women's imagined and real spaces squashed between old and competing new male orthodoxies. With just weak and benign liberal resistance to such campaigns, there is the possibility of rescuing some social but not necessarily much, political autonomy for women today.

Extreme Agency

In March 2009, the video image of a young woman being publicly 'flogged' or whipped by tribesmen (allegedly, the Taliban) in the Swat valley of Pakistan, as a form of prescribed Islamic punishment, made international headlines.[5] The video was recorded on a cell phone, anonymously released to the media and was played repeatedly, first on national TV channels and then all around the world.[6] The woman, identified as Chand Bibi by the media, was variously reported as having been punished for committing *zina* (adultery) and/or entering the public sphere with a *na-meheram* (ineligible male escort – a kith/kin whom a Muslim woman can legitimately marry). The reaction of Western observers to what would be perceived as an inhumane, atavistic Islamic practice was predictable. However, the dynamics of responses within Pakistan make for more interesting reading. Across the board, from the most right wing, fundamentalist, religio-political parties to the liberal, left-leaning organisations and progressive women's movement, there followed unanimous condemnation of the act. Such interpretation and imposition of Islamic law, as well as the entire social-justice system of the (banned) *Tehreeq e Taliban Pakistan* (TTP) in the north-western tribal belt of the country, was denounced as "un-Islamic" by practically all groups across the political spectrum, including fundamentalist ones ("Religious Scholars Denounce Whipping of Girl by Taliban," *Daily Times,* April 4, 2009; "Flogging of Girl in Swat Widely Condemned," *Dawn,* April 5, 2009; Baabar 2009, "Swat the System," *Outlook India,* April 20).

In a state increasingly theocratised as part of an Islamisation campaign initiated by the military dictator, General Zia ul Haq (1977–1988), this was certainly not the first case of public punishment of women – either state sanctioned or driven by patriarchal customs and traditions. Why did this particular case elicit such sympathy, especially when the woman was not killed, as is often the norm in cases of gender violence, but in fact, survived the brutality? The proposal is that the Muslim woman's body as a spectacle has taken on a new political meaning, across which post-9/11 international and local politics are played out. Whether it is the veil, crimes of honour or occupation of public spaces or mobility, the Muslim woman's body has transformed beyond being just an international signifier or a marker of the Islam-versus-the-West debate. It has become a signpost over which local religious narratives compete, in order to manipulate its symbolic power and in order to construct their version of Islam as the normative one. Since the flogging was video-taped and played repeatedly on media channels, it became a particularly graphic exemplar of the disposition of Islamic militant insurgency as it swept control over northern Pakistan. However, other than feeding the media cycle, the spectacle of violence against women is also a useful propaganda tool for militants to demonstrate their opposition to Western values, especially those associated with freedom – sexual or spatial – for women. Such 'performance' also serves the interests of mainstream, modernist and fundamentalist religio-political groups alike, as a means to essentialise and reject the bearded, unkempt, 'barbaric' Taliban as the inconvenient Muslim. In comparison, conservative religious groups are able to present themselves as the more moderate face of Islam.

Distancing themselves from the more brute tribal militant form of Islamist politics, fundamentalists and mainstream religious nationalists wedge in their worldview of an Islamic *millat* (imagined Muslim universe) as the ideal commune for women's protection. Their Islamic continuum is promoted as a viable alternative to tribal brutality and/or lay or customary cruelty. It is also offered as an appropriate substitute to Western/universal, rights-based, juridical and (immoral) feminist agendas. Before discussing the political appropriation of the newly-founded Muslim woman's "agency" in a cross-section of Islamist narratives, the case of Islam Bibi is discussed below to help connect and trace the role of how women's agency has evolved in the context of the War on Terror and the resultant insurgency in north Pakistan, peaking between 2004 and 2014.

Helen of Waziristan

One of the iconic female symbols that make a coterminous link between tribal resistance, nationalism and religion in Indo-Pakistan's history is that offered by Islam Bibi (Hauner 1981). This Hindu woman in the 1930s had contracted a free-will marriage and converted to Islam. While she was being forcibly returned to her natal family by the colonial British Resident administration, a young Pathan tribesman, Mirza Ali Khan, or 'Faqir Ipi' rescued her and is still revered and remembered in Pakhtun folklore. He was the Pakhtun warrior from Waziristan (a tribal agency in current day Pakistan), who mounted one of the most challenging insurgencies against the British colonial administration of India. The pretext of rescuing the converted Muslim woman became his call for an all-out jihad against British rule.

Faqir Ipi captures the imagination of resistance literature and embodies cultural honour amongst Pashtuns in particular (Haroon 2007). More recently, in the context of the NATO occupation of Afghanistan and military attacks on Pakistan's tribal areas, Faqir Ipi's role has been simultaneously evoked as the historically "notorious jihadi" or, the heroic precursor of the Taliban, depending on who is recounting his character (Tharoor 2007, "The Original Insurgent," *Time*, April 19).[7] However, often what is omitted in historical recollection is that the cause of the armed resistance was sparked by Faqir's rescue of the woman renamed, pertinently, *Islam* Bibi. Feminist memorialisation of events such as these reclaim the historic and traditional agency of women's right to choice of marriage.[8] These readings recognise that colonial encounters with tribal history were designed to sustain colonial domination by re-writing tribal myth and traditions as innately patriarchal and militant. In the same vein, contemporary state nationalism brands tribal identity as "anti-Islamic" due to resistance and refusal of the tribal areas to be part of the state of Pakistan after Independence in 1947.[9] Similarly, current Islamic militancy seeks to purge Pashtun tradition of its indigenous religious idiom and replace this with its own modern militant version.[10] Against the construct of "tribal tradition," a whole new narrative of nationalist and religious modernity competes and in the process, submerges the tribal woman's historical relevance.

Interestingly, contemporary commentary refers to the elusive Faqir Ipi as the "Scarlet Pimpernel" for the British Raj, in order to underscore an important lesson for modern political warfare (Hauner 1981; Haroon 2007; Tharoor 2007). By transporting the tribal reference of Ipi as a symbol of Pakistan's tribal intractability, the comment serves to highlight the futility of penetrating present-day tribal resistance with reference to the "War on Terror". At the same time, the analogy served as a warning to the NATO Allied Forces over the impossibility of success in their pursuit to capture Osama Bin Laden. As a corollary, the attempt to tame the tribalised 'heart of darkness' is deemed to be a historically doomed task for some Western commentators. Equally, for Pakistani nationalists, this is evidence of tribal resilience and national 'honour'.

While broader nationalist narratives elide Islam Bibi's role, she is alive in Pakhtun cultural recollection. Equally interesting is the reference to this, 'Helen of Waziristan' in Pakhtun blogs.[11] She is immortalised as a romantic repository of the cultural bravery of Pakhtun masculinity and as a mythological mute convert rather than the original rebel who exercised her personal agency for autonomy. Ironically, both these references – the indigenous, anti-Western resistance of Faqir Ipi and feminised religion that is Islam Bibi – are compared to and read through a cultural evocation of the pre-modern, Western personae of Scarlett Pimpernel and Helen of Troy!

One of the most insightful and influential discussions on the theme of radical alterity dates to the much-cited investigative question posed by Gayatri Spivak (1998) asking, "Can the Subaltern Speak?" Related to this has been her sentence "White men are saving brown women from brown men" with reference to the relationship between the imperialist subject and the subject of imperialism, which Spivak says is "at least ambiguous" (Spivak 2010, 269). Spivak revisits the original discussion of *sati* or widow immolation/sacrifice which the early British colonisers abolished in India and which is generally cited as the metaphorical exemplar of the white rescue of brown women. Spivak reminds us that posited against this is the "Indian nativist statement, a parody of the nostalgia for lost origins: 'The women actually wanted to die . . . '" (Spivak 2010, 50). Significantly, Spivak confirms how both these statements, representing imperialism as social mission and *sati* as reward, respectively, "go a long way to legitimize each other" (50). By way of a counter-narrative of *sati*, Spivak makes the observation that "between patriarchy and imperialism, subject-constitution and object-formation, the figure of the woman disappears, not into a pristine nothingness, but into a violent shuttling which is the displaced figuration of the "third-world woman" caught between tradition and modernization" (61).

As an example of corrective resistance to both (patriarchal, nationalist) narratives, Spivak offers the example of a young woman's suicide in Calcutta in 1926 with reference to the question of free-will and agency.[12] The suicide was later linked to the woman's failure to carry out a political assassination that she had been entrusted with, as member of a group for the armed struggle for Indian independence. However, at the time, to circumvent the expected suspicion that the motivation for her suicide would be believed to be the result of an illicit pregnancy, Bhuvaneswari Bhaduri waited for the onset of menstruation before taking her own life, mindful that otherwise "her death would be diagnosed as the outcome of illegitimate passion" (63). This was a kind of a pre-emptive strike! Spivak considers this to be a rewriting of the "social text of *sati*-suicide in an interventionist way" (63). Bhaduri deliberately displaced the notion that this was a *sati* suicide, since the prescription for *satis* is to be postmenstrual and 'cleansed' prior to the act of suicide. Spivak observes that in her reading, "Bhaduri's suicide is an unemphatic, ad hoc, subaltern rewriting of the social text of *sati*-suicide" (63).

However, as in the case of Islam Bibi, the subaltern as female cannot be heard or read, squeezed as she is between patriarchal, nationalist and religious narratives. Spivak (1998) ends her original essay with the insistence that there is no virtue in global laundry lists with "women" as a pious item. Representation has not withered away. The female intellectual as intellectual has a circumscribed task which she must not disown with a flourish. (308)

Perhaps those interested in the discussion of brown women, impe-rialist rescue and subaltern resistance need to go beyond titles and excerpts such as, "Can the Subaltern Speak?" and "white men saving brown women . . . " and engage more deeply with the text that follows these titles, in order to justify their arguments for docile agency, or before making a convincing case for the brown/Muslim woman's pietist agency.

Given the various stakes that hinge around women, the nation and Islamic identity, at the national level, the response to the 2009 Swat whipping of Chand Bibi is easier to understand, since it presented an opportunity for the Taliban militant to construct a new body politic, quite literally, across a woman's body. It allowed the most conserva-tive Islamists to distance themselves from the tribal Taliban such that the latter are labelled as "extremists" who appropriate religion for inhumane purposes. According to this constant, all other Islamists can then project themselves as the more acceptable, moderate, benevolent alternative. The competing appropriation of the female body by both extremist and fundamentalist/nationalist articulations suggests that women's bodies continue to act as repositories of religious and nation-alist identity in the context of Pakistan, as well as in the global attention on Islamic militancy.

However, the female suicide bombing on Christmas Day, 2010, in Bajaur, reads as a disruption of the linear narrative outlined above.[13] In this case, contemporary extremist strategy seemed to be deviating, as it turns from simply victimising women to immortalising them in temporal terms. This was through the recognition and instrumental-ising of the Islamist woman's agentive potential in militant terms. The Taliban claimed responsibility for the Bajaur attack and issued a warning that the organisation had "a large number of women suicide bombers" who would "carry out more attacks in the near future" ("Woman Suicide Bomber Strikes at WFP Centre; 45 Killed," *Dawn*, Dec. 25, 2010). The female suicide attack prompted anxiety amongst Pakistani male politicians and media commentators over the potential of the veil as a tool for future breaches in security. Newspaper colum-nist, Yusufzai, suggested that the all-engulfing veil makes for "perfect . . . concealment of explosive devices and even suicide jackets" (Yusufzai 2010, "And Now, Women Suicide Bombers," *The News*, Dec. 29). The columnist goes on to warn that "there should be no doubt that militants would use females to launch suicide attacks, particularly in places difficult to penetrate."

This anxiety reflects some of the themes explored in a host of post-colonial feminist critiques, which highlight how the study, rescue and eroticisation of colonised women served the project of colonial powers. For example, Woodhull writes on how, in the cultural and political imaginings of the French colony, Algerian women were perceived in their dual capacity as, "'emancipatory seed' and the gateway to penetration" at the same time (Woodhull 2003, 573). In Pakistan too, a similar attitude towards the tribal woman has led to a concern to study, document, educate, liberate and celebrate her. She serves as the point of reference for tribal resistance against cultural intrusion and military aggression but presents a quandary for funda-mentalist and liberals alike. The predicament is over her potential for reverse 'penetration'. Fundamentalist and liberal men may both be agreeable on the need to rescue her from the extremist narrative and tribal traditions. However, there is fresh fear and therefore, tacit agree-ment on the need to regulate her agency as it now potentially poses a security threat. However, they do not want to be complicit in unveiling her to this end either. A new challenge inverts the resistance motif due to the impenetrable security threat presented by the tribal Pakistani woman.

The concern at the time was deflected as newspaper coverage of the Bajaur suicide bombing fell into a brief debate over the gender of the veiled bomber and then dropped the issue. While claiming they had many female recruits who would be used in future, the TTP did not confirm if the veiled attacker in this case had been a woman at all (*Dawn*, Dec. 25, 2010). Interestingly, an earlier suicide attack in 2007 in Peshawar city, where the suspect was thought to be a woman, is discounted as the first "official" female suicide bombing. Although, the female bomber was transporting explosives on her body, the deto-nation itself had been conducted by a remote control device – presumably by male Taliban commanders (Yusufzai 2010, *The News*, Dec. 29).[14]Agency remains a nebulous claim for women even in its more radical expressions and at the cost of extreme sacrifice.

Lesser Militants, More Agency

A research study on the mothers of martyrs recruited by the militant outfit, *Lashkar e Tayyabia*[15] (LT – Army of the Righteous) in Pakistan, observes that women members "serve more as props or a supporting chorus for the . . . mission rather than as active participants" (Haq 2007, 1033). Women leaders are not given military training but taken to camps to witness men's training. However, the study suggests that the "LT leaves open the possibility that women may take part in active fighting and suicide missions if that becomes necessary for the survival of the *ummah* [global Muslim imaginary/community]" (1031). With reference to the mothers of martyrs, the LT is seen to appeal and use their grief in order to garner support for its jihadi[16] agenda. LT literature claims a successful mobilisation of willing mothers who offer their sons for jihadist missions and hence, martyrdom. However, Haq's research findings from a lower-middle-class neighbourhood in Lahore suggests that "the majority of the mothers of martyrs are victims of a negligent Pakistani state, not Spartan mothers ready to sacrifice their sons for the mission of the *ummah*" (1022).

By speaking the language of the global *ummah*, the narratives of these mothers of martyrs transcend nation-making such that their biographies become "social texts . . . produc[ing] inspirational narrative for the jihadi community" (Haq 2007, 1035). They are mothers of all young Muslim men but with reference to their agency, the study is more sceptical when it surmises that there is "no adequate means to adjudicate the question of agency for [the] mothers" (1043). Rather, the agentive potential of the mothers is sapped by the "LT leadership [which] becomes the agent that mines the mothers' private grief to enact a public jihadi community" (1043).

Another example of recent radical activism by Islamist women was witnessed in the uprising of the *Jamia Hafsa* (JH) women students in Islamabad in 2007 – the only serious political confrontation to General Musharraf's dictatorial regime of nine years by any group of women activists. These students belonged to a religious school or *madrasa*, attached to the *Lal Masjid* (Red Mosque) in an upscale location in the capital city of Islamabad. The women clerics who ran the girls' *madrasa* were related to the male *imams* (clerics) of the main mosque, who in turn were suspected for their affiliation with radical religious militants in the north of the country, in the wake of the "War on Terror". In 2007, the young women of the *Hafsa madrasa*, after a series of vigilante activities in the city, illegally occupied the premises adjoining the mosque land. This was in protest against the government's threat to demolish and reclaim this property (and other illegally constructed mosques in the city) because it was suspected to have become a hotbed for terrorist indoctrination. The JH women wore complete black veils and carried bamboo sticks and kidnapped a woman from the neighbourhood whom they accused of running a prostitution enterprise. They only let her free once she 'repented.'

An all-out military operation followed (Operation Silence), leading to the death of several male clergy in the *Lal Masjid*, as well as state law enforcement officers (Farhan Bokhari and Jo Johnson 2007, "Pakistani Forces Kill Red Mosque Cleric," *Financial Times*, July 10). The JH women claim several of their female students were killed although the state denies this and there has been no evidence or legal testimony confirming this assertion. In the process of documenting this event, however, the very autonomy that feminist organisations seek for their own activism and the way they have historically deployed direct (often, illegal) action was denied to these right wing radicals in their criticism. Instead, many liberals condemned the activism of these Islamist women as a "misguided" moral crusade and condemned such action as demonstrative of extremism (Afzal-Khan 2008), as if the JH women were new arrivals on the scene or exclusive products of a *madrasa* politics and not a wider, insidious conservatism that has steadily dominated the social fabric. From another perspective, scholar Faisal Devji described the activism of the *Lal Majid* as not characteristic of a militant group but that of a "civil society organiza-tion" (Devji 2008, 21) resisting the state's attempts to exclude women radicals from such activism.

This very tangible and live consequence of women's religious agency and empowerment, as motivated by faith was not problema-tised nor analysed by either Islamic feminists or postsecularist scholars. They were silent on the issue or deflected discussion on the radical agenda of the JH women. Those commentators who are sympathetic to the agency and leadership potential of Islamist women are silent when this agency is translated (inconveniently) into activism – as expressive or desires derived of that very same agency. All forms of agency have the potential to convert into political activism and for either the liberals or postsecularists to deny these radical women that progression and recourse is a classic example of doublespeak.

Using religion as a source for mobilising spiritually empowering practices amongst Muslim women has not been strictly limited to Islamists. The strategic use of Islam has been co-opted and developed into empowerment projects by some non-governmental organisations and sponsored by foreign funds. Farida Shaheed's (1999) work cites the empowering strategies of *darses* (pietist or Quranic study circles) and *khatams* (literally, "the end" prayers usually held at funerals followed by a sermon) as reclamations of religious modes that strengthen women's personal and social relationships. The argument offered by Shaheed and others who were convinced by faith-based empowerment possibilities was that such piety projects would chal-lenge politicised religion. Instead, religion got both privatised and yet politicised. The resurgence of the *hijab* (veil), home based women preachers and the growth of female religio-political leaders is the result of many years of faith-based empowerment, which turned the focus of such women away from the political, public agenda and inwards instead, towards a private, theological enterprise. Incubating in the private realm, such movements gained momentum, shielded from the gaze of the State. Whenever the environment is conducive, such faith-based empowerment is revealed and tends to resurge in and through public expression but very much towards religious, conservative causes and not apolitical or neutral ones.

It may be argued that such in-admissibility of Islamist woman's agency on the part of men, or its qualification by liberal feminists elsewhere,[17] has pushed her into the subaltern of national religious (and feminist) discourse. Diasporic scholarship emerging from Western academia seeks to revive the subalternised Islamist woman and celebrate her agency in religious terms (Mahmood 2005; Iqtidar 2011). This falls into the same category as the presumptive rescue of indigenous Muslim women by the colonisers and which postcolonial feminist critiques originally targeted. Mahmood and Iqtidar[18] presume to rescue Muslim women from Western, liberal, secular feminist agendas by resuscitating the interiorised subjectivity of non-feminist but nonetheless, consciously pietist Muslim or Islamist women. That such religious agency can spill over into political action is a continuum that remains ignored and uncommented upon. This dilemma is recounted in Woodhull's essay on Algeria, which discusses how French colonisers had "positioned Algerian women as living symbols of both the colony's resistance and its vulnerability to penetration" (Woodhull 2003, 574). Woodhull's essay also criticises Fanon's omission of the positive effects of the colonial relation for Algerian women and points out how masculinised nationalism continues to prop women as living symbols of threatening social divisions within Muslim nations.

In the case of contemporary Pakistan, postfeminist writings challenge the viability of universal feminist advancement and its potential for equal rights. Instead, such writings advocate for a replacement of universal liberalism with and through the communitarian logic of religion as an indigenous alternative. In most cases, this project merely ends up strengthening male nationalist agendas. This pulls women activists into the trap of making feminised spaces within masculinised nationalist and religious discourse, rather than pursuing transformative agendas. The spaces for women's political and social expressions narrow down, as do expectations, resulting in the tightening of what Woodhull (2003) calls the "double knot" that fatally ties "culture and politics between definitions of femininity, and religion and nationality" (576).

Right-wing Agency

The case of Dr. Aafia Siddiqui,[19] the US-based Pakistani female scientist incarcerated and sentenced for suspected terrorism in 2010, allowed for a re-visitation of the symbiotic relationship between femininity, nationalism, religion and now, global Islamic politics. A persistent theme within the ambit of religious nationalism has been to warn against the dangers of the cultural corruption and libidinal possibilities offered by Western social values, if they should penetrate Islamic consciousness. The right wing Islamist groups constantly compare the degradation of Western women against the honour of Muslim women, as if the former's "symbolic prostitution is the only alternative to seclusion and veiling" (Woodhull 2003, 579).

The case of Aafia Siddiqui however, raised these stakes further in Pakistan. She became the personification of vulnerable Muslimhood, US injustices and global Islamophobia in a post-9/11 world and after the occupation of Afghanistan by Allied Forces. Siddiqui's survival of alleged incarceration in Afghanistan as Prisoner 650 and title as the 'Gray Ghost Lady of Baghram' was redefined after her indictment and life-sentencing by a US court (Suzanne Goldenberg and Saeed Shah 2008, "Mystery of 'Ghost of Bagram' – Victim of Torture or Captured in a Shootout?" *The Guardian*, Aug. 6). Through national campaigns in Pakistan, her individual status was symbolically transformed to that of a global Islamist resistance against US injustice and earned her titular ranking as the, *Qaum ke beti* (Daughter of the Nation) or *Dukthar e Millat* (Daughter of the global Muslim Community).

The (predominantly) male nationalist response to the Aafia Siddiqui case signifies how the normative femininity of the Islamist woman is continuously re-constructed through nationalist and religious representation. The trans-historic and trans-geographical references used in the campaign to 'Free Aafia' depict her simultaneously as an archetypal victim (of an American, anti Islamic agenda) and free agent (representing national sovereignty).[20] Such debates took place in the vagueness of unverified information regarding Dr. Aafia's US citizenship/green-card status. Ania Loomba (2003), with reference to the colonial reception to *sati* (widow immolation) in India, speaks of "the fascination, the horror mingled with admiration, the voyeurism, the oscillation between regarding the widow as victim or sovereign agent" (243). So too, Aafia Siddiqui has invoked a similar response and been pivotal in the political consciousness, imagery, rhetoric, positioning and campaigns of national political parties in Pakistan. This includes primarily the religious party of the *Jamaat e Islami* (JI), the conservative *Tehreek e Insaaf* and even the sub-nationalist, urban based, non-religious, *Muttahida Qaumi Movement* (MQM).

The ideal, patriotic figure of Aafia Siddiqui is based on the construct of both traditional, as well as modern nationalism. The most important point of departure that enabled Aafia Siddiqui to qualify as an icon was that despite her mobility, social class, divorced status and Western residency, she retained the veil and pursued Islamist politics. All such transgressions from traditionalist ideals of the domestic Muslim woman is acceptable, since Islamist nationalism does not rely on the passive Islamist woman – rather, it looks to engage her potential Islamist agency. The agitprop posters pasted across Pakistani cities glorify Aafia Siddiqui as the archetype tortured Muslim subject but more so, as a symbol of national sovereignty subjugated by the United States. This metaphor is best exemplified by the images used in the campaign to 'Free Aafia' where the silhouette of a veiled woman stands in relief against the map of Pakistan. There is no palpable symbol of political agency in the popular visuals of a pious Aafia Siddiqui that are carried at rallies and in the media. Instead, there are many photos of her in a black graduation gown in the US (denoting achievement), counter-posed with another picture of her in desolate condition and in a black *chador* after her capture.

Despite her personal achievements and ascribed political status as Daughter of the Nation, her agentive role is in fact, static, proscribed and ex post facto. She was never part of the nation's political consciousness when she was posted on the wanted list of the U.S. Federal Bureau of Investigation in 2003, nor up until the time when she was reportedly captured by Pakistani intelligence agencies and extradited to the US in 2008. Instead, Aafia Siddiqui's status as Daughter (and not Mother) of the Muslim Nation is a deliberate ascription, since she cannot be used as a live concept to evoke future sacrifice, as is the case of the appeals for future jihadists made to the mothers of the *Lashkar e Tayyabia*. Rather, Aafia Siddiqui is mourned as the martyred but innocent daughter and as one who is not guilty (but therefore, also not an agent) of anything other than being a veiled Muslim woman.

Within male Islamist vocabulary, there are no fixed rules of application of these fluid terms of the traditional and modern. So it was not surprising to see revisionist tableaux enacted on the streets to memorialise Aafia Siddiqui over the last few years. *Pasban* (formerly the *Jamaat e Islami's* youth wing but now an independent group) takes out regular street rallies and renditions to keep her memory alive in the public conscience. One such rally borrowed its references from both indigenous and exogenous models of Muslim identity ("Unique

Rally to Demand Dr. Aafia's Release," *The News*, Aug. 21, 2010). This rally on the streets of Karachi used camels and Arab head-dresses and swords as props to invoke the historical bravery of Muhammed Bin Qasim, the original Muslim conqueror of Sindh (now a province of Pakistan) in the 8th century. The newspaper item reports that in this rally, the right wing youth leaders recalled Qasim's invasion of Sindh under the Hindu ruler, Raja Dahir[21] with reference to its partial motivation to rescue Muslim women. The purpose of the spectacle of camels and Arabised costumes was to evoke the historic chivalry of Islamist leaders rescuing Muslim women. The political comment was targeted against the failure of the Pakistani government, shaming it for its comparative impotency in the negotiations for the release of Aafia Siddiqui from US incarceration. In May 2013, this iconography was reinforced by the *Jamaat e Islami* when it ran its campaigns for the national elections under the slogan, 'Vote for Aafia.'

Amina Jamal (2013) has argued a case for the agency and agenda of modernisation of the Islamist women of the *Jamaat e Islami* in Pakistan. The counter-argument to Jamal's line of argument is that it does not scrutinise the political record of these Islamist women and their performance in Parliament and provincial assemblies. Precisely because Jamal appeals for the activism of Islamists women to be understood "on their own terms", such proposals by-pass a discussion of how the agency of these women converts into an activism that contradicts and restricts other women's empowerment if it does not conform with the religiously prescribed mould (A.S. Zia 2009b, 242).

Even the Pakistani state today, despite its vacillations and historical conservatism, does not impose some uniformed citizenry on Pakistani women. It does not propagate a dress code nor overtly prescribes an appropriate role, identity nor specific symbols that make for a prototype Muslim woman. This does not mean it is any less discriminatory or patriarchal in its legal construct. However, in recent years, other than in the narrative of religio-political groups, it is in piety movements that such attempts at closure over the constructions of the authentic Muslim woman can be found. In seeking to do so, the women of the right wing and pietist movements collude with patriarchal definitions of their place in society (Kandiyoti 2003). While acknowledging the agency of these women, it is not enough to suggest that this may be innocuously non-feminist – it is equally important to identify how actively patriarchal they are.

In *Resisting the Sacred and Secular* (Basu and Jeffery (eds.) 1999), Patricia Jeffery warns that "the question is not whether women are victims or agents but, rather, what sorts of agents women can be despite their subordination" (223). The chapter on Pakistan by

Farida Shaheed in the same volume suggests that while the women's movement resisted state Islamisation in the 1980s, religion carries importance for women due to its participatory aspect and its contribution towards social collectivity. Shaheed recognises that "religious beliefs and tenets are bound to play an important role in justifying existing patriarchal structures and informing attitudes toward gender and, specifically, women" (Shaheed 1999, 154). However, she makes the counter claim that according to her research, "women did not express such a linkage [with political religious discourse] when they could have" (154) and that the possibilities of religion cannot be reduced to its use "as a mobilizing force in the political arena" (145). Shaheed goes on to argue how most women, particularly in rural Pakistan, escaped the effects of the political discourse of religion and managed to maintain a personal relationship with the strategic resistance it offered them in their daily lives. Shaheed's study concludes that in fact, reclaiming religious practices and rituals provide women the liberatory, or at least resistance potential against their "everyday experiences of patriarchy and religion" (160). She suggests that "the vast numbers of women whose faith is a living reality" should be recognised and respected as their "right to [exercise] self-definition" (161). The argument warns "self-professed feminists" against imposing their secular points of references in the broader women's movement (162).

Enter, the *Al-Huda* pietist movement, which followed the above script of empowerment through reclamation of religious practices almost like a blueprint to Farida Shaheed's thesis. Except the aim was not to bolster women's "self-affirmation . . . of personal psychology and . . . social collectivity" (Shaheed 1999, 153) and not even as a tool of indigenous feminist resistance, but rather their aim is to actively reject all such notions. It is tempting to concede that at the time, Shaheed's defence of women's idyllic piety was a prescient testament to the failure of the progressive women's movement to tap into the huge reservoir of potential faith-based resistance and that as a result, this potential was usurped by another (conservative) force instead. However, the dynamics and direction of this and other pietist movements completely negate Shaheed's misplaced faith in some subaltern feminist resistance theocracy simmering permanently under the surface.

Pietist Agency

The *Al-Huda* social movement has defied much of the contemporary feminist analyses cited above and proven to be neither a resistance nor an alternative political organisation.[22] Rather, the purpose of this institution is to allow its fast multiplying graduates who are looking for an ideological engagement with Islam to transform themselves into pious subjects. Sadaf Ahmad's (2009) research identifies the conscious aim of *Al-Huda*, which is to bridge the gap between religio-political discourse and daily lives and which Shaheed had insisted was irrelevant to pious women. Instead, it is exactly in this informal, non-institutional space where the pietist *Al-Huda* woman resides. By drawing upon the indigenous culture, idiom, language, symbols and identities, such movements tend to resonate with their constituents. However, rather than through *dars* (piety lessons) and *khatams* (literally, the end, sermons offered at funeral), the cultural references for this pietist movement, according to Ahmad's research, are nationalist Islamic history as taught in textbooks and the mass media, including the Two Nation Theory.[23]

A succinct feminist analysis of the Two Nation Theory is offered by Veena Das (1996) where she observes that during the partition of the Indian subcontinent (1947), women's bodies "became a sign through which men communicated with each other. The lives of women were framed by the notion that they were to bear permanent witness to the violence of the Indian Partition. Thus, the political programme of creating the two nations of India and Pakistan was inscribed upon the bodies of the women" (56). Similarly, Haq (2007) observes that

> in contemporary jihadi discourse women's bodies are the sites of communication with the other in two ways. The veiled body of the Muslim woman is a signal to the rest of the world of the purity of the revitalized Muslim *ummah*. The violated body of the raped Muslim woman turns into a call to action for young Muslim men. (1040)

Faiza Mushtaq's (2010) analysis of the *Al-Huda* phenomena is more ambivalent. Mushtaq suggests that some feel this movement represents a "radical rupture of the status quo" and others believe it is "doing nothing to challenge women's subordination" (Mushtaq 2010). Mushtaq is more hopeful of the possibilities offered by *Al-Huda* when she observes that

> whether they end up supporting liberal, feminist visions of women's liberation or undermining them, the changes wrought by this movement are already disrupting existing power relations and institutional arrangements in Pakistan. (para 48)

Ahmad (2009), on the other hand, challenges this notion of the disruptive power or indeed, feminist possibilities offered by the *Al-Huda* movement. She finds that the founder of the *Al-Huda* movement, Farhat Hashmi, emphasises on a dialectical relationship between faith and rationality but she and the other teachers at *Al-Huda* aim to attain a hegemonic status for their ideology where a "monolithic form of Islam is propagated as truth" (75). Ahmad argues that "Al-Huda reinforces a patriarchal system, highlights the idea that men and women have different natures and therefore variant gender roles, and claims that a man is the natural manager of a woman and that a woman must obey her husband unless he asks her to do something un-Islamic" (89). The author acknowledges the "interpretive agency of subjects" in hegemonic contexts with potential for dissonance but according to Ahmad's study, "the instances of discourse transformation and disruption . . . among Al-Huda graduates . . . are not as common as one might expect" (90–91).

Similarly, there are other challenges to the Shaheed thesis that religion provides only apolitical succour and acts as a routine resistance tool for women. The documentation of the *Al-Huda* women's stories "clearly show their commitment towards ridding their lives of behaviors that they no longer consider acceptable" (Ahmad 2009, 146). In condemning "foreign" influences, these women construct their own identities. Ahmad writes that, "Farhat Hashmi's denouncement of various cultural practices and disapproval of Westerners and Indians helps women redefine their own identity as Muslims" (146). This reconstruction of a pure and authentic Muslim identity is a deliberate aim which enables these women to become a distinct Other within mainstream urban society. Ahmad suggests that, "[Al-Huda's] ideology is not very different from the hegemonic religious ideology that is propagated by many *maulvis* – Al-Huda, too, is reinforcing a patriarchal system with gender roles as natural and the man as head of the household" (73). The Islamist women of mainstream religio-political parties in Pakistan, such as the JI, testify to the boost that such pietist groups provide to Islamist politics. The reinvention of agency, whether it is by nationalist masculinist discourse or by pietist women's movements, converges almost as testimony to Jeffery's (1999) warning that

> while we can celebrate women's everyday resistance and demonstrate that women are not wholly subdued by their situations, we must beware of overoptimism about the efficacy of such resistance and of conflating women's resistance with their agency. (222)

Summary

Some of the contextual symbolic and political conditions and challenges under which Islamist women's agency is currently being articulated in Pakistan, and its limitations for feminist progress, has been outlined. Discussing three specific case studies (Chand Bibi, Islam Bibi and Aafia Siddiqui), it identifies the stringent requirements that insist that all expression of such agency must be compliant with the larger male-dominant ideologies of Islamic politics. This, in turn, makes the feminisation of Islamic politics a far less attractive proposition than imagined at first glance and marks the limits of religious agency for Muslim women in Pakistan.

The attempt to substitute or replace universal minimal human rights with abstract conceptions of Islamic nationalism and culture, simply serve to reinforce patriarchal traditions. They end up confirming that male-dominated, postcolonial historical values are viable sources of authenticity. For the survival of their identity, Islamist men depend on the cultural capital provided by the entity that is the Muslim Woman. By placing emphasis on women as vehicles of Islamist authenticity, it provides leverage to male politics and accordingly, any threat to disengage from the overall male agenda stands to disrupt the entire Islamic order. This justifies violent prevention of any perceived threat or rupture to the order, as illustrated in the case studies presented above.

The Limits of Capital: Commodifying Muslim Feminity

The notion of an Islamist imaginary as one that is modernising, accommodating market forces or secularising the political landscape of Pakistan towards its own unique version and flavour, depends on a recovery of Islamist women's alternative agency. The use of the form and potential of the Islamist woman and her scope for performance and spectacle is based on the need for Islamists to take charge of their identity. This applies to those who wish to showcase Islamist women's agency as a modern interpretation of gendered identities within the global Muslim *ummah*. The agentive Islamist woman also serves as a visible representative of the Islamic nature of the Islamic Republic of Pakistan. The tension between traditional Islam and the necessity of reinventing mobilising practices in the current context is important for politically engaged Muslims. The most authentic, visible and consistent code for this struggle is the Islamist woman. However, for her, there is no evident return from such a project in terms of individual autonomy or independent rights. The notion that piety movements will offer new modes of partnerships and agency is not just unlikely but also a risky proposal, considering the vertical and deeply hierarchical collaboration of patriarchal religious politics that is defined by Muslim men and practised within Muslim-majority countries such as Pakistan.

Capitalism as an Equal Opportunity Offender

The anthropological postsecularist scholarship referenced seeks to resist orientalist stereotypes of observing Muslim women by reclaiming their independent subjectivities, as represented through pietist practices, the *hijab* and other Islamic signifiers. The motivation for a project that seeks to distance and emphasise the *essential* independence of the Muslim subject is well explained by Kwame Appiah (1991) in his acclaimed essay that compares the 'posts' in postcolonial and postmodernism (with reference to postcolonial Africa). Appiah refers to the need for "clearing a space" in the postcolonial narrative in order to reinvent and market (or in his term, commodify) a cultural product. This need for distinctions in the market is a feature of postmodernism, which Appiah defines as "the project of transcending some species of modernism, which is to say some relatively self-conscious, self-privileging project of a privileged modernity" (343)· This distancing is important, particularly for the commodification of culture, as discussed by Appiah, but has now come to apply to the issue of religion too. Appiah makes the argument that "the triumph of reason, secularization and 'end of religion' is not just a marginal achievement and conversely it is religion instead, that has been commodified and thrives in and by expanding the market" (346). He also tempers the "Weberian talk of the triumph of instrumental reason" as a "mistake" (344) by arguing that

> the disenchantment of the world, that is, the penetration of a scientific vision of things, describes at most the tiny – and in the United States quite marginal – world of the higher academy and a few islands of its influence. What we have seen in recent times in the United States is not secularization – the end of religions – but their commodification; and with that commodification religions have reached further and grown – their markets have expanded – rather than died. (344)

With reference to Muslim women's religious identities, the market forces of capitalist consumerism necessarily compete against any limiting, purist notions of *inner*, spiritual, non-material desires. Instead, the market seeks to tap into and reify, re-inscribe and reinforce (therefore, profit from) Muslim women's *outward* identities, external lifestyles and public belonging, in relation to their beliefs. Retro-Islamist scholarship attempts to reconcile and rationalise the increasing trends of Islamic consumerism as reflective of a shift in Islamism and the designs of Islamists in Pakistan (see contributors in Iqtidar 2011b). This scholarship argues that Islamists are engaging with (the temporal) global market forces, rather than their a priori exclusive fixation on state forces. This is meant to be evidence of the potential of the market rather than the state as a (Weberian) mobiliser and game-changing competition for and influence over Islamists' interests or "Islamist imagination" (Iqtidar 2011b). The conclusion is that

Islamists' interests have substantially moved "beyond the state" and turned instead to "secular interests" such as the market, as a possible "engine for the formation and transformation of the moral community" (Iqtidar 2011b, 536).

A body of work on the intersection of consumerism, capitalism, women and the Islamic culture industry demonstrates that Muslim women believers navigate and consciously engage in Islamic practices through various modalities of capitalism. In the diverse examples cited in such global research, there is no evidence that these Islamist women resist becoming commodities themselves. In fact, it is argued that the centrality of gender in Islamic forms of consumer culture serves as a "territory on which capitalism stakes its claims (once again)" (Gökariksel and McLarney 2010, 3).

It is tempting for Pakistani postsecularist scholars to read this willing merger of the pietist expressions of Islamist women with the temporal forces of the secular market as a testament of their pragmatic (non-pious?) desires. However, such celebrations rely on the role of pietist women only as consumers or as agents in the marketing of commodities. Postsecularist scholarship dismisses the very framework of liberal or Marxist feminist politics that necessitates campaigning against and resisting such commodification. Postfeminist readings are able to celebrate pietist self-fashioning as expressed through the consumption and exhibition of fashionable hijabs and other Islamic accessories, such as the 'hijab shampoo' launched by Unilever in Pakistan. Marketing for Islamic finance however, does not target women believers, presumably out of the pragmatic realisation that the majority of Pakistani women do not have access or control over finances or decision-making in this regard. Neither does such post-secular scholarship begin to grapple with the cosy relationship between Islamist interests and consumer capitalism. So, it does not comment on the resultant combination, which indicates a simultaneous emergence of not just an Islamist but also, a bourgeois imaginary. Such scholarship is too busy celebrating the fact that the Islamist imaginary has moved "beyond the state" (Bano 2012b, Iqtidar 2011b), so it does not trace how the shift of Islamist consumer interest has extended to a place where its leading members now qualify as the new Islamic Bourgeoisie.

The 'post' position is admittedly liberating. Scholarship on the Islamists now reinvents Pakistani Islamists in a post-Maududi[1] frame, delinking the *Jamaat e Islami* (JI) from its founder. However, the derivations of contemporary Islamists actually continue uninterrupted from the original source – simply reframed in a number of new combinations. This is particularly true of gender roles and relations. So, postsecularist scholarship on Islamists makes references to how the JI in Pakistan has dislodged the original Maududi formula of Islamic economics but does not point out that this has been not through a rejection of the capitalist system but only by redefining and reframing it as '*sharia*-compliant' capitalism. Their political opposition to Western lifestyles and values does not prevent Islamists from sponsoring global or Western economics or capitalism. The key method of legitimising this engagement is by converting the temporal identity of the market (into something called "market Islam") through the operative term, "compliance". This enables "market Islam" activity to be read as evidence of Islamists' willingness to adapt or survive in a redefined modernity and which qualifies them as actors seeking an "international political imaginary" (Iqtidar 2011b, 562–563).

In many ways, this emphasis on a post-Islamist reformulation is an attempt to distinguish modernist Islamists from the earlier postcolonial (fundamentalist) characteristics that informed religio-politics in Pakistan. Such reinvention is a part of the project of retro-Islamist Pakistani scholarship. Appiah (1991) is accurate in suggesting that in this sense, the 'post' in postcolonialism is the same as the 'post' in postmodernism but he paints this as an optimistic exposure of those elites who seek to sentimentalise the past in order to authorise their present power. Thirty years later though, the 'post' argument in Pakistan seems now to have become just a masquerade for the refutation of secular thought, modernity, science and Western philosophies of the Enlightenment and rights-based ideals of universalism. The adoption of liberal values (by liberals, but not by Islamists or conservatives) in non-Western contexts are described as neo-colonial, neo-imperial, rationalist enterprises and adventures. The projects of Western wars, education, media, culture and ideas are read by conservatives in Pakistan, as well as the postsecularists cited herein, as secular assaults on the faith-based, post-9/11 Third World – not as rational, capitalist (even Weberian) exploitations (often with the complicity of the Muslim clergy) by globalised nation-states. According to these worldviews, there are only two options for the native Muslim subject; s/he can either be a liberal/secular citizen, complicit with Western philosophy, committed as s/he is to the notion of equal rights for women and minorities or, a good Muslim/docile (capitalist) theologian.

The trouble with academically assisting such reinventions is that it offers practically *all* Islamist expression as indigenous alternatives when, in fact, with reference to capitalist consumerism, it simply mimics secular activity. Islamists and secularists may consume and produce different products but this does not challenge or change *the means of production*. Mimicking does not mean that the act of consumer transaction or the motivation of the consumer has any socio-political impact on the management of capital or its structures in a given society. In other words, Islamic products and consumerism neither Islamise nor secularise economic or social relations nor the means of production – despite any lofty claims by postsecularists.

Further, capitalism is an equal opportunity offender in the commodification of women regardless of their pietist motivations. In the case of the Islamic industry, the opportunity to promote Islamist conservatism is much wider. It also opens up the "marketization processes [which] tend to produce universal essentialist tendencies to create a "Muslimwoman" in the singular who stands for global Muslim society" (Gokariksel and Mclarney 2010, 5). Muslim women's *difference* becomes a "marketable product, a logic of profitability" (6). It also privileges some representation (for Muslim women) and renders others undesirable. Such products range in representative form and include Muslim women's memoirs, autobiographies and images of veiled women in a plethora of Western publications that invite their readership to be a part of a fashionable self-Orientalisation.

The Veil as Commodity

Arguably, the most over-discussed piece of clothing – the veil – continues to be circulated in academic discussion and popular culture. However, unlike "Islamic money," which is mostly just currency, the veil is anything but an empty signifier (Moellem 1999; Gourgouris 2008b). Apart from serving as (simultaneously) a marker of belief, identity, duty and unfreedoms; a pragmatic method of portable mobility or conduit in the journey of spiritual self-discovery; a defence mechanism, instrument of postcolonial nationalist resistance, metaphor of visibility/invisibility of the female body politic; an icon of liberation, exoticism, culture, class; a symbol of gender apartheid, a prop of performativity and even, a means of disguise usurped by militant Islamist men or Western journalists, above all, the veil sustains itself as a commodity (substitute) of Muslim femininity.

This form of commodifying gendered identity fits neatly within and contributes unreservedly to the logic of neo-liberal capitalism. This is not unlike the way Islamist women's politics avails of the opportunities afforded by liberal political democracy such as special quotas or reserved seats for women in electoral procedures. Pakistani Islamist women who participate in electoral democracy do not liberalise the process on entry but instead, use the site and tools of liberal democracy (via reserved seats/quotas for women in Parliament) in order to subvert and then, Islamise previously secular spaces and relations. Similarly, the neo-liberal market is an equally conducive site for displaying, marketing, consuming and peddling religious goods, values and ideas that may promote and endorse Islamists' illiberal religious politics, conservative values and the censorship of ideas. While Islamist economics may proffer re-wrapped religious products, neo-liberal economics offers itself as a politically neutral territory (market) determined only by profit and loss and so poses no secular resistance to it.

Arguing the case for the postsecularists, who reclaim the relevance of Islamic identity markers (but against their conclusion that Islamists in Pakistan are lurching into some post-Islamist or commercial secularisation phase), the male head of the JI, Lahore chapter, Amir ul Azeem on World Hijab Day in 2012, protested that "the West is now trying to separate Hijab from Muslim identity" ("No Female Speakers at Jamaat e Islami's Hijab Day Rally," *ET*, Sept. 4, 2012). Voiding the symbol of its religious significance and emptying it of its potential renders it useless to political Islamists. Deploying it for a cause other than Islam is considered a (Western) conspiracy that they will resist at all cost. At the same event, Azeem drives this point home by praising the Turkish female parliamentarian who sacrificed her political position by resigning rather than surrendering her hijab. To suggest that the Islamists are inadvertently going against the grain of their own political consciousness and that this activates a process of accidental "secularisation" is to accuse them of being dupes of a different false consciousness. The scholars who argue along this line undermine their own defence by imputing Islamists of a consciousness that is not based on ethnicity, class or gender but simply, a culpability emerging out of a crisis of realisation. While many Marxist and modernist feminists in Pakistan would agree to the idea of religion as a weapon of numbing mass obedience, postsecularists have objected to such a view as a deliberate oversight of the complex aspirations of the conscious, agentive Islamists. Postsecularists have spent much academic energy trying to overturn such misreadings. By rehearsing the idea that under some circumstances, Islamists are *not aware* that they are agents (of an Islamist secularisation), such scholars encode on them the same Orientalist themes they seek to resist.

Overlapping with modernist feminist critiques against the objectification of women, Azeem of JI also, "criticis[ed] advertising agencies and multi-national companies for using women in commercials for various products [and] mocked the presence of female models in advertisments [sic] for shaving razors" (*ET*, Sept. 4, 2012).[2] Of course, this opposition is not emerging from any feminist consciousness but rather the objection is that in the Islamist imaginary, women's visibility must remain opaque and that their full autonomy is unacceptable – for commercial, political, sexual or social purposes. Commodifying women for the purpose of marketing or selling Islamic goods would be acceptable, provided women are discreet marketers and asexual commodities, committed exclusively to promoting religious purposes. This process is reminiscent of capital formation as outlined by Marx and Engels (1848):

> These labourers, who must sell themselves piecemeal, are a commodity, like every other article of commerce, and are consequently exposed to all the vicissitudes of competition, to all the fluctuations of the market. (Chapter 1)

The notion that the lure of the market ("market Islam") is pulling away Islamists' interests, "beyond the state" or beyond Islam and that this process is therefore, accidentally secularising Pakistani society, is wishful apologia even if it pretends not to be. Such analysis attempts to dilute too many of the conscious expressions and articulations of Islamist politics that inform their consumerism too. Just one example of a conscious, political, *anti-consumer* stance of Islamists would be their resistance to any access or consumption of Western/Indian forms of popular culture, objecting to it as a form of cultural imperialism. Similarly, they are strongly opposed to having trade relations with any infidel 'enemy' nations (such as the US, Israel, India and any European country that tolerates blasphemous expression under the pretext of freedoms).

The suggestion that sociological outcomes and consequences of Islamists' engagements with the public realm, including the market, are simply an "accidental" product of their genuine move towards democracy and (economic) liberalism (Iqtidar 2011b, Jamal 2013), depends on the idea that all this is indicative of a post-Islamism with a twist, that is, a condition that is not secular. The notion that Islamists may be involuntarily rendering a sociology and politics which is quite incidental to their original imaginary (which is just imagined, after all) contradicts the appeal by the same proponents who argue that Islamists' agency and conscious engagement with modernity and markets should be acknowledged. Given the unlikelihood of any rejection of the demand for capitalist and/or, religious products, a more likely result of such critical combinations of Islam, capitalism and consumerism in Pakistan is that at best, an Islamist Bourgeoisie and Muslim Proletariat may emerge and influence rather than "clear the space" or subvert the nature of the market, or the political economy or indeed, the social imaginary of gendered or societal relations.

Observed since 2004, World Hijab Day[3] used to be a fairly lacklustre annual event in Pakistan, until recently. Organised across the country by the *Jamaat e Islami's Halq-e Khwateen* (women's wing), the event only gained increased visual coverage in the media when it stepped up its rhetoric after 2008 (A.S. Zia 2009c). Subsequently, the aims of the hijab movement have clearly moved beyond a simple demonstration of solidarity with European Muslim women who observe the hijab. Instead, increasingly, the JI has been positioning the hijab as an active symbol of resistance against the imagined threat (of anti-Islamic forces) to Pakistan's very sovereignty.

The hijab has never been prohibited nor enforced in Pakistan. The attempt to institute an Islamic dress code on women under the Islamisation period of General Zia ul Haq was strongly and successfully resisted by the liberal feminist movement (Mumtaz and Shaheed 1987). No government has ever attempted to resist the preaching or coercive practices observed in some communities for the cause of the hijab. Nor has the state upheld the right of women who have been harassed for not observing the veil. If anything, conservative governments explored the possibilities to institute its practice in schools in 1997. Yet, the JI leadership has worked hard to maintain the notion of a constant perceived threat to Islam as symbolised by the unveiling of Muslim women. Such themes have been well rehearsed by religio-nationalists in the Muslim context and are equally well documented by feminist scholarship on postcolonial nationalisms (Jayawardena 1986; Lateef 1990; Kandiyoti 1991).

The theme for 'Hijab Numaish [Exhibition)] 2012,' borrowed its slogans and spirit from gay pride parades held in Western countries. This is ironic, since Islamists in Pakistan condemn homosexuality as un-Islamic and unnatural and it is a criminal offence in the Islamic Republic. Countrywide banners advertised the preparation for the Hijab Parade and on the day, hundreds of veiled women held up signs announcing that "Hijab is My Right and Pride". In 2012, the event also stepped up its political rhetoric by more than just a few notches. Using the occasion, *Jamaat* women (Multan chapter) for the first time, called for making the hijab a constitutional obligation for Pakistani women (Jafri 2012, "Pakistan Constitution Should Make Hijab Compulsory: JI," *ET*, Sept. 2). This is not the first ideological shift from a reformist agenda towards more orthodox interpretations of the Quran and/or hardline, right-wing politics that the *Jamaat* women are incrementally endorsing. Earlier, the discriminatory Islamic law of *Zina*[4] was tabled for reform under the Musharraf government. The JI women (several of whom were members in the National Assembly) for the first time took a clear departure from their historic prevarications over the *Zina* Ordinance.[5] Some 25 years later, these Islamist women shifted their strategic position on the law and followed the conservative male dictate, which insisted that any change in this law would convert Pakistan into a "free sex zone". This can be taken as evidence of the success of the agency of Islamist women, which is not merely non-feminist and non-modernist in this case, but is a very radical step towards ossifying Islamist sexual politics.[6]

The demand to make the hijab a constitutional obligation is contrary to the JI's (Pakistan) stated policy that maintains that the veil must remain a matter of personal choice, although their activism does aim to coerce Muslim women into observing it. So, while the central leadership of the JI officially disclaims any tactless, fringe demand to make the hijab constitutional, by the same token, they also object to other broader aspects of constitutional commitments such as the guarantee of women's right to work. Their ideological base pivots around the concept of complementarity of gender roles and ideally, just as it is undesirable to impose the veil on women, it is equally erroneous to "inflict" on them the right to work. The choice to work should be weighed by virtue of the necessity of a woman's conditions and explicitly, with the permission (and regulation) of her husband.

It is often argued that both the JI and its inspirational archetype, the Muslim Brotherhood, are no longer the genomic progeny of their founders (Abul Ala Maududi and Hassan al-Banna, respectively). However, the essence of gender relations are derived largely from the original exaltation by their leaders which appeals to women and their roles as mothers and wives in their 'noble' mission. Further, the language of protection and refraining from 'unnatural' duties (which often includes voting and fielding as candidates for office) is always derived from an Islamic reference point. Islamist women of the JI cannot head the party and could not be part of the central decision-making committee until very recently (Rehman 2016, "Winds of Change," *The News on Sunday*, March 27). Their women's wing is a semi-autonomous and parallel structure with its own *shura* (deliberative council) and the members can attend joint sessions with male members. However, in 2002, when General Musharraf introduced a quantum leap in reserved seats for women at all tiers of legislative government, the JI did avail of this opportunity and for the first time, the JI women members served in the national and provincial assemblies in a large force. When Islamists embrace such opportunities, much is made of the Islamists' intention to engage with modernity.

Despite their opposition to women's full citizenship, such pragmatic moves by Islamists have only been possible due to the compulsions of liberal-secular ideals and those achievements which are based on the principle of universal citizenship and affirmative action (women's quotas) to ensure gender parlance in the mainstream, at all levels and for all, including Islamists. While it is the right of Islamists to operate an opportunistic politics, it is equally critical that this then be tabled, discussed, and defended in an applied and not just theoretical form, to make their case.

The success of Islamists has been in their ability to not reform but reframe their agendas, particularly on the issue of gender politics (Tadros 2011). The vocabulary of this reframing is no longer prohibitive (such as the one that the women of the JI Multan still seem to subscribe to) but rhetoric is wrapped in a language of a human rights discourse, that is, Muslim women's *right* to protection and to veil. Both may emanate from a wider paternalistic discourse but such patriarchy-boosters are well-disguised when they are drawn from a fashionable discourse of rights, rather than the old-fashioned, oppositional binaries of Islamist versus secular, or human rights versus religious patriarchy. In political terms, it does not mean that the Islamists intend to combine or borrow from adversarial ideologies. They are not committed to gender equality or minority rights or a democratisation at national levels or within their organisations. Nor do they support these at societal levels, either. Regardless of how their *different* democracy, *different* equality or *different* ends may be defined, it is the conditionalities that shape these differences and qualifies their strategic politics as a promotion of the process of Islamisation of society from below. Mainstream Islamists are not averse to influencing a top-down process of Islamisation. In 2012, the World Hijab Day campaign in Pakistan was also marked by a conference held on 15th September, in Lahore. In a sort of gender political coup, the conference succeeded in getting the wife of the Prime Minister of the ruling (liberal) Pakistan People's Party (PPP), to attend as the chief guest. While not observing the hijab herself, the first lady reportedly supported Muslim women's choice of observing the hijab and pointed out the significance of this at a time when Western women were "humiliating" themselves by exposing their skin ("There's No Shame in Wearing a Hijab," *ET*, Sept. 16, 2012).

Scholars from Papanek (1982) onwards have discussed how the veil has served as the ultimate symbol that used to divide the private and public imaginary for Muslim women. Still others have discussed how Islamist women are redefining the hijab as an instrument that now facilitates mobility and enables them to participate more confidently in the public/political service. Most liberal feminists in Pakistan would agree. The post-9/11 period has seen a spilling over of pietist practices – which had been incubating in domestic spheres through *dawas* (missionary preaching), *darses* and *khatums* into the public sphere. Commentators have also noted the contribution of popular female religious preachers such as Farhat Hashmi, towards this deprivatisation (Ahmad 2009). Soon after 9/11, the backlash of hostility towards symbols such as the hijab, has allowed Islamist parties like the JI, to activate a sense of solidarity with hijab-observing Muslim women globally. They have done so through a resistance motif that implies that Pakistani hijab-observing women are also victims of an imagined discrimination. This is smart politics that seeks to deflect the attention away from the radical programmes that Islamist women routinely engage in (as found in the examples of when the Islamists ruled the province of Khyber Pakhtunkhwa (Chapter 2).

Donor-driven Islam

In the 1980s, feminist movements in Muslim contexts were often challenged as a Western imposition and for their secularist intent (understood as anti-religion or *la deen-iyut*). Urban women's groups were critisised for being limited in their cultural resonance with the poor, rural or faith-empowered[7] women of the country. Much of the current postsecularist scholarship that seeks to resuscitate religious empowerment for Pakistani women relies on this same premise but qualifies the traditional argument through two main refinements. The first point of departure from the traditional critique of secular feminist politics and as found in the more recent body of scholarship is that, (supposedly) forced secularisation (premised on the immanent framework of Western secularism) has failed, and that religion has not disappeared from the public sphere as an expected outcome of modernisation. Secondly, such scholarship argues for a review and inclusivity of religion into the mainstream of development research and policy itself. Such calls are expressed in the hope of *Rewriting the Secular Script* (Deneulin and Bano 2009) in development work.

Donor initiatives to re-embed a gendered identity through the lens of Islam, emerges from the recommendations of those who seek to ensconce all women's rights within Islamic-defined rights (see Chapter 2). The interplay of Islam and donor-funded development projects in Pakistan has imposed counter-intuitive effect on the secular women's movement (A.S. Zia 2011a, 2013c). These projects[8] do not involve any discussion of class identities. This reduces all analyses to be viewed through the singular lens of religious identities. These ventures are defeatist, as they employ pragmatic methods that call for negotiating rather than demanding rights. The emphasis is on pragmatic necessities, such as ensuring equal enrolment for girls in *madrasas* as a practical, demand-driven necessity. Or these studies recommend a certain amount of mosque space for women rather than challenging the absence of secular public alternatives. They even suggest that health for women should be delivered through the approval, involvement and mediation of local clergyman or "Rent-a-Maulvi projects" (A.S. Zia 2013c).[9]

Cassandra Balchin (2011) describes some of the overarching effects of the influence of weaving in religion and religious beliefs and practices into the new development paradigm for Muslim contexts. Balchin documents the organisational experiences of Oxfam in Muslim contexts. She notes that the term "Muslim fundamentalism" is deliberately avoided now and testifies to the weighing in of "culture" as a factor in policy decisions. The example she cites is whether a polygamous employee should be considered to be in violation of Oxfam's policy of gender equality or overlooked as a form of respect for religious/ cultural specificity of Muslim contexts.

The ambiguity of secular feminists who subscribed to faith-based developmental methods and practices in Pakistan has been criticised for compromising on secular politics (A.S. Zia 2009a). So, characterisation of liberal-secular feminists as uncompromisingly secular and rigidly antithetical to religion and Islamist women is unfounded and simplistic. If anything, despite the allegations of religio-nationalist groups, it is difficult to identify any wholly Western liberal-secular development project in Pakistan. Many such organisations have observing Muslims working for them and while they may disseminate and conduct training on issues using universal rights documents and through secular (non faith-based) strategies, this does not impede or exclude them from (simultaneously) working on religion, or with religious groups or indeed, employing methodologies such as faith-based empowerment. By and large though, non-governmental development work does seek to empower communities or women through liberal ideals of equality between classes and genders. The consciousness training sessions tend to challenge practices of discrimination, coercive practices or human rights violations inflicted (usually on the poor or minorities) by religious actors, interest groups or communities under the rubric of "honour", or by the state, under the cover of defending sovereignty or Islam. Very few Pakistani secularists in the field of social development would suggest that their ethos is not defined by some kind of cultural Muslimness, even as they remain committed to a secularist resistance to the peddling of religion in politics or as the definer of the state.

Even prior to 9/11, several bilateral and multilateral governmental aid agencies had already begun an exploratory interest in supporting women's groups who worked on women and Islam as a communitarian entry point into communities. These initiatives over most of the 1990s had become well-entrenched project-definers – not only in Muslim-majority countries but even where Muslims reside as minorities. The difference between these earlier religion and development projects and the later, post-9/11 ones is that the former were engaged in a research-based inquiry that looked to distinguish patriarchal culture from pure Islam. These used to be invested in reinterpreting patriarchal readings of holy exegesis and/or, exposing the political misuse of Islam by male authorities. Some of these feminists considered religion to be a private matter but still mined its potential use as a coping mechanism for women and as a method for empowerment in the domestic realm and at community levels.[10]This potential for instrumentalisation has been advanced further to its postsecular logical ends by several developmental agencies.

The influence of postsecular scholarship, such as Saba Mahmood's work (2005), has in some cases directly influenced such donor recommended policies. The authors (Ladbury and Khan 2008) of a British government's development agency study on "Increased Religiosity Among Women in Muslim-Majority Countries," note that

> Saba Mahmood's account of religious study classes in Cairo is our primary reference material for this section. We have chosen her work because of its comprehensive ethnographic analysis [] but also because of her approach. It is not Mahmood's intention either to find a "redeemable element" in what, for many, constitute an illiberal and socially conservative movement, i.e. to look for aspects that would make them more palatable to liberal sensibilities (Mahmood 2005:5). Rather she focuses on what they say about conceptions of the self, moral agency and politics and asks her readers to do the same, thereby discouraging the tendency to assess the movements from a given normative position – liberalist [sic], secularist, feminist etc. (22)

The project to recover the agency of Islamist and pietist women is an interesting one, but the concern is that this carries with it the risk of nostalgic and uncritical reinvention. Neither should this enterprise be considered a disinterested or neutral project. Such scholarly endeavours have encouraged an international perspective that latches onto some confessional mode that then accuses secular political women activists in Muslim majority countries of somehow being detached from their own reality. The authors of the DFID 2008 Issues Paper acknowledge that

> Mahmood was concerned not to use explanatory frameworks derived from normative positions (secularist, Western, developmental, feminist) so she purposively avoids trying to explain the movement in these terms. Nor does she report instances of women saying they felt their knowledge "helped them" in discussions with their families. (24)

Simply the fact that pietist Egyptian women felt they are getting religious knowledge convinces the authors' "own sense" that "these [piety] classes are very important empowerment mechanisms for women, at least in terms of their intra-familial and neighbourhood relations" (24).

Contemporary scholarship on faith and development has questioned the possibility, desirability and even wisdom of relegating religion to just the private sphere (Casanova 1994; Mendieta and Vanantwerpen (eds.) 2011). Deneulin and Bano (2009) consider it an ethical problem to view religion only as a means to promote given ends. They argue instead, that religion is inherently political which includes the expression of authority and power but is equally about how to "live well together" (8). This is indicative of how the new postsecularist scholarship is distinct from the earlier modernist (Muslim) feminist approach where the new scholarship invites the desirability of faith-based development in order to "provide a new analytical grid for studying religion in development" (Deneulin and Bano 2009, 7).

Postsecularist scholarship that aims to "rewrite the secular script" suggests that "development is what adherents to a religion do because of who they are and what they believe in" (Deneulin and Bano 2009, 4). Modernist feminists in Pakistan, such as Shaheed, also recognise that religion operates simultaneously as a potentially spiritually empowering quest on a personal level and as a mobilising force in politics. But Shaheed believes that women's relationship with pietism is not a political enterprise (Shaheed 2002). Both schools invest hope in (tempered) female leadership as an important element of challenge to traditional male interpretations and their monopoly over Islamic teachings/preaching. The reason for using the qualifier "tempered" is that while sympathetic anthropologists view the agentive challenge by women through faith-based strategies as a positive engagement, they simultaneously acknowledge that female leaders will only be acceptable within limits and boundaries.

According to Kalmbach and Bano (and in diametric opposition to earlier research work by Shaheed et al. 1998), those who seek to "confront the gender biases in textual interpretation" or aspire for leadership positions carry little currency amongst Pakistani women and their conservative contexts (Kalmbach and Bano 2011b online). This argues directly against the modernist feminist efforts of organisations such as WLUML and individuals such as Riffat Hassan, and the broader case made by Islamic feminists. Kalmbach and Bano argue against direct textual re-interpretation and instead, for negotiated adherence within traditional Islamic precepts where "Islamic knowledge can provide women living within conservative communities with argumentative tools that increase their assertiveness, their activities within the public sphere, and their awareness of the rights *vis-à-vis* the male members of the family granted to them by even relatively conservative interpretations of Islam" (2011b online). They argue for how this "raises the possibility that women seen publically defending traditional Islamic precepts could be engaged behind the scenes in renegotiating their rights and asserting more autonomy in day-to-day family affairs" (Kalmbach and Bano 2011b online).

If these women subscribe to a traditional, patriarchal and conservative religious ethos, then why would they engage for changing the status quo by negotiating or demanding autonomy or independence? By definition, surely, women who adhere to male-interpreted, traditional or conservative interpretations of Islam and the prescribed forms of social roles and hierarchies of relationships would not aspire towards liberal goals. However, if autonomy refers to daily mobility here, then the practice of bargaining and negotiating within patriarchal limitations is a well-documented feature in Muslim contexts and its operation within familial relationships too have been studied extensively. This is by no means a value addition to the theory on faith and development. Towards what ends are these women jostling and negotiating by using faith as the driver for autonomy, if they are simultaneously adherents of traditional Islamic precepts? What are the emancipatory goals for these said aspirants of leadership if it is not equality, as described by supposedly Western feminism? Moreover, if such leadership is bound to traditional patriarchal precepts, why is this of gendered interest?

The overlapping interest between some sections of the modernist and postsecularist streams that argue for religiously inspired development initiatives is consensual up until a point. Postsecularists argue for 'religion *in* development' rather than 'religion *and* development' citing this as reminiscent of the shift for gender in development studies (Deneulin and Bano 2009). Modernist feminists who support the instrumentalisation of religion in development are consistent and clear about their demand for a secular or non-theocratic Pakistani state. In their demand for the repeal of Islamic laws and separation of religion from state business they look to disabuse religion from polluting effects of patriarchal cultural practices. By this token, they can also continue to simultaneously work on feminising women's relationship with religion within the private or social sector. However, postsecularists challenge this demarcation by illustrating the "everyday realities" of women involved in piety and faith-based movements, and insist that this should be seen as political and a valid instrument of empowerment, mobilisation and expression of women's attempts to cross the private/public divide. While recognising the importance of engagement with religion and its potential to empower them, Sholkamy (2011) is anxious about how such "popularisation of religion" can serve as a "veneer for growing conservatism that is antithetical to change and reflection" (48). In particular, it is the "instrumentalisation of religion and Islam [that is] worrying and problematic" (48).

One large scale donor-funded study acknowledges that "'FBO' [Faith Based Organisation] is a problematic category in the Pakistani context" and finds that "while religion often plays an important role in charitable giving and activities that respond to immediate needs and partially fill social service gaps, it does not play an explicit role in most organizations working on long-term development" (Kirmani 2011, 18).[11] In a reprinted version of the same paper, Kirmani notes that findings from the same project[12] on the welfare work of religio-political party, the *Jamaat e Islami*, needed to be studied more carefully and deeper, rather than taken as conclusive (21). Cassandra Balchin is less convinced of claims regarding the potential of religious political parties in becoming partners in development due to their "extensive networks of voluntary organizations, which have potential to be more cost-effective than regular NGOs, as they rely on managers from within the party rather than paid professionals" (Balchin 2011, citing Bano 2009, on 38 fn 22) and suggests that

> despite the uncertainty of their impact, such religious organizations are judged to be suitable potential development partners purely on account of their reach and financial cost. An identical conclusion is drawn in Kroessin 2009, who argues that the large budgets available to UK-based Muslim development organizations mean they can make 'a significant contribution to development activity' although 'clearly more needs to be known about the work of Muslim NGOS'. (38)

The trend in recent years has revealed how international financial institutions, Western government assistance and Western academia are increasingly mired in reinventing Islamist possibilities so as to qualify them as viable alternatives to indigenous secular options in Muslim majority countries. There is no clarity, nor available guideline as to how the "moderates" are selected. If anything, the Islamist discursive is replete with all kinds of false-positives, by which I mean, *Sunni Tehreeq* in Pakistan is an organised Islamist movement that is considered to be part of one set of an (*Sunni*) innovative school of Islam. They sponsor and support religious visitation to shrines (a practice that fundamentalists and militant Islamists oppose fiercely) and they campaign against the bombings of these shrines. Yet, the *Sunni Tehreeq* also campaigns for the death of accused blasphemers and does not campaign against the bombings of girls' schools in the country. Similarly, the overwhelming interest in supporting Sufi Islam as a peaceful alternative to radical militancy is another misplaced proposal. To fund Sufi teachings is to pervert the fundamental principle of Sufi-ism – which resists the institutionalisation of faith in the first place. None of these strains of Islam have particularly impressive records of being patriarchy-free, either.

Such projects encourage an abandonment of legacies that are secular and rights-based. These approaches are further assisted by the enthusiasm of postsecularist scholarship that looks to cleanse postcolonial histories through blanket critiques of modernity and liberal ideals. The associated methods of faith-based approaches depend on some form of compromise on equal rights for women and minorities. This is reminiscent of postcolonial negotiations over autonomous rights that were often bartered at the altar of national security, nuclear security, or over calls for "saving Islam". Also common has been the practice of denying women's rights by using Muslim cultural particularism as an excuse against the so-called "onslaught" of *Western liberalism* but which simultaneously welcomes and embraces *Western neo-liberal* economic policies. The post-9/11 development paradigm has triangulated the concerns of culture, femininity and now religion, supported by an anthropological benevolence for the Islamist subject.

Modernist feminists such as Shaheed (2010) argue that the operation of gendered power structures cannot be fully understood by focusing on the state or civil society organisations and that

> the interface of religion, politics and gender illustrates the impossibility of separating out the realms of the social from the political, the public from the private, for everyday life is not neatly packaged into

self-contained spaces but flows freely, affecting different dimensions simultaneously. (851)

The question this raises is that if the categories are so dissolved and overlapping, why is there a conclusive need to understand gender dynamics by just focusing on and studying religion? Why are secular, non-faith-inspired/derived expressions not a valid, living and independent subject for research consideration and political organisation?

Women's Roles in Islamic Charities

Some postsecularist commentary argues that women's roles in Islamist charities/religious organisations, such as *Jamaat ud Dawa*, provide them with agency and empowerment (Iqtidar 2011). The authors of *The Charitable Crescent* (Benthall and Bellion-Jourdan 2003) are criticised for purposely confirming the suspicion harboured by the White House that Islamic charities often serve as fronts for promoting Islam and radicalisation (Bano 2005, 385). Suspected duplicity of the authors aside, both the detractors and supporters of Islamic charities in Pakistan have repeatedly refuted some supposed distinction between humanitarian work and coercive proselytisation. In a special report on the Islamic welfare organisation, *Jamaat ud Dawa* (JuD),[13] seasoned journalist, Aoun Sahi, quotes a former JuD activist who argues that *dawa* (missionary work/proselytisation) and jihad (holy struggle) are ideologically impossible to separate and are equally important tasks in the belief-systems of members of this dual identity organisation (Sahi 2012, "Dawa, Jihad, Charity or All?" *The News on Sunday*, April 15). Even though the founders of what was originally a jihadist group maintain that there is a structural or organisational distinction (whereby, *Jamaat ud Dawa* is the charity organisation of the banned jihadist outfit, *Laskhar e Tayyaba*), this does not necessarily translate in the avowed beliefs of the members. Muhammad Amir Rana, a security and political analyst and director of the Pakistan Institute for Peace Studies observes that "all large Islamic militant organisations have huge charity networks. They need to have them in order to legitimize their existence" (cited in Sahi 2012).

In recent years, the JuD has actively widened its charity work to specifically target minority communities in Pakistan. After the terrorist attacks in Mumbai, India, in November 2008, the pressure on the Pakistani government led to a crackdown for hunting suspects believed to be members of the (banned extremist group), *Lashkar e Tayyaba*

(LT), widely suspected of operating under its (legitimate) affiliate and charitable arm, the *Jamaat ud Dawa* (JuD) (Gillani and Sengupta 2009, "Pakistan Court Orders Release of Militant Suspected of Ties to Mumbai Attacks," *New York Times,* June 2). Although, the JuD denies its linkages to the LT publicly, it is interesting that in defence of the *Jamaat ud Dawa*, some two hundred Hindu minority women in Sindh, Pakistan carried out a public protest in support of the mother organisation (LT) which was being investigated by the state for its suspected involvement in terrorist activity – specifically, the Mumbai attacks of 2008 ("Pak Hindus Rally to Support Jamaatud Dawa," *Dawn*, Dec. 17, 2008). These women claimed that JuD supported their poor community and gave them protection and services and should not be proscribed by the state. Importantly, these women crossed gender and religious boundaries to support those who would ordinarily be their religious antagonists.[14] However, the solidarity support from the (non-Muslim) beneficiaries of JuD had nothing to do with its religious credentials. The motivation for the Hindu women's allegiance and defence of the organisation rendered its Islamic identity as completely beside the point. It could have been any secular organisation or the military, or indeed, a local landlord (who often act as patrons or are involved in relief work in times of crisis) that the minority women would have defended in return for such assistance. It was not the importance of Islamic teaching by JuD that served as a source of such empowerment or agency, nor did it motivate the Hindu women's unlikely public demonstration of their support. In this case, charity is a more enabling tool than *dawa*. It would be fair to conclude, therefore, that it is not the imagined pietist empowerment that JuD provides its patrons or members but rather, practical help in the vacuum of a neglectful state or welfare programme.

The contention is then that religious affiliation and empowerment from within the religious discourse may be completely independent of delivering practical needs, or irrelevant for qualifying as a beneficiary for human rights and developmental benefits. This argument would support the view that Islamic charities can be distinct from Islamist political agendas, but would then challenge the proposition that Islamist organisations are unique in their approach or that they have some special religio-cultural resonance with followers and members. They are either apolitical and therefore, neutral Samaritans or, they are faith-driven and consider *dawa*/proselytisation an intrinsic part of their charitable/political duties.

If JuD falls under the former thesis, promoted by scholars like Bano who argue that Islamists are motivated by an apolitical, non-persuasive charitable ethos, then this contradicts Iqtidar's contention that

JuD's pietist agenda is a justifiable *political* effort to deprivatise religion and to Islamise society.[15] On the other hand, if we accept Iqtidar's argument that the charity work of the JuD is motivated by Islamic teachings, then it is impossible to argue (as Bano does) that there is some imagined distinction between charity and promotion of Islam/proselytisation by the JuD. These two views – religious charity/humanitarianism as intrinsically bound to proselytization or as just neutral goodwill – contradict each other even while recovering the multiple layers of complexity that supposedly characterise such religious organisations. In my view, the more important point is that the system of patronage as used by religious organisations extends itself to minority communities (too) while simultaneously making them targets of broader legal and social discrimination as part of their Islamic ethos, which places Muslims in preeminence. Either way, the hegemonistic intent of these faith-based organisations, which are often linked to religious political parties, is clearly political rather than merely charitable. Both ways, such a strategy can work its faith based politics or agency, to liberate and oppress at the same time.[16] This is true for women and minority concerns, alike.

Who Benefits?

Competitive forms of Islamist mobilisation and a wide repertoire of action by nationalist and anti-state actors are gaining ground in Pakistan. Their efficacy depends upon their ability to usurp women's agency, which may then be directed towards producing and reproducing an Islamic religio-cultural order over which Islamist men compete. With reference to the notion of rights, the women's movement in Pakistan has consistently struggled to work out a formula where religious identity finds complementarity with universal and individual rights. The Family Laws of 1961 are a case in point[17] but with nationalist (and academic) challenges that are questioning the authenticity of universal rights for women as culturally or religiously inappropriate, many such progressive legal rights are being reneged upon in the country.[18]

Islamists have accommodated the capital and technology of the West but resist abstract and/or, individual rights for women and minorities. This is based on a tendency to infantilise Muslim women who require protection. The scholarship critiqued below valorises this metaphysical revival and even advocates the literal or legal sanction of Islamic rights. This is particularly true when issues of the age of consent and abortion are debated as a cultural imposition that would be better resisted through Islamic provisions rather than universal laws (Aziz 2005). The reluctance of those scholars who seek to revive the relevance of Islamist politics to identify it as regressive, conservative, anti- or postfeminist is ironically characteristic of the same unwillingness on the part of many liberals in Pakistan who shirk from identifying themselves as categorically secular. Large segments of Pakistani liberals want to (not reject) *reclaim* Islam from the fundamentalists' and militants' narrative and refashion it within their own moderate realm of piety. For example, several Pakistani women activists observe the veil or some form of *purdah* and argue that they do so in recognition of its cultural heritage not as a religious requirement. Their activism however, calls for a commonsensical separation of politics and religion and invokes equal rights for women that is grounded in a cultural collective but not as interpreted by Islamists – men or women.

Between 2008–2013, under the rule of the civilian democratic government of the liberal Pakistan People's Party, the perception that Pakistan's cultural and particularly, its religious identity and very sovereignty was under existential threat, had gained neck-breaking momentum – in the media, political opposition and, even in postsecular scholarship. The sources blamed for such attacks on Pakistan's sovereignty ranged from drone attacks as a counter-terrorism strategy in the tribal areas, to perceived threats against Pakistan's nuclear arsenal. Other foundations for suspicion were aid assistance, such as the Kerry Lugar (Aid) Bill; the Raymond Davis case;[19] the indictment and sentencing by a US court of Aafia Siddiqui for terrorism; and the availability of Indian satellite TV channels in the country. The frenzied response to these events resulted in a flood of overnight Islamist organisations, movements and councils for the defence, protection and recreation of Pakistan, Islam and Muslims, and particularly their women.[20] Such consequences are likely to asphyxiate any space for politicking or conducting social practices that may be deemed anti-Islamic in sympathy or sentiment. Islamic vigilantism has increased multifold in the country and minorities, women and even middle-class liberals are foremost targets.

It is this reluctance and blurring of ethical responsibility that is a feature of both, postsecularist and liberal Pakistani commentary. In the case of the former, scholars are unwilling to openly criticise *or* defend the actions, transgressions and political forays of Islamists, including those by its women members, particularly when it expresses or condones a politics of violence. On the other hand, liberals often subscribe to "lifestyle liberalism" rather than remaining steadfastly committed to a political liberalism and so, increasingly lose ground to religious conservatism in the public sphere. They also tend to be ambivalent in their support for secular agendas, despite confidently espousing the cause of a liberal, tolerant and moderate Islam. This defies the insistence of postsecularist critiques that secularism is purely derived from within the immanent frame of Western liberalism. In Pakistan, one can be comfortably be 'liberal' and 'modern' without advocating secularism.

Summary

Increasing Islamisation of the Pakistani state and society has challenged practically all basic liberties, freedoms or security for women. In this context, there have been some purposeful attempts to reclaim and celebrate the "agency" of the pious Muslim Woman, exclusively in terms of her religiosity. This redemptive project, piloted variously by militant Islamists, religious nationalists and/or, diasporic academics has failed to award any substantive legal or structural autonomy or independence to women in Pakistan. As Islamist women embrace the fold that encourages them to become religio-nationalist symbols and imbibe such masculinist ethos, there is no evidence that this has delivered them any tangible benefit. Muslim femininity has become a consumer category that allows capitalist interests to launch products wrapped in religiosity, or to market gendered developmental programmes that are tailored in an essentialist and limited framing for Muslim contexts. Legal rights – including the much-touted Islamic right to inheritance, remain stubbornly resistant to Muslim women's claims. Unequal status for legal testimony and under the *Qisas and Diyat* laws, high maternal mortality, unequal citizenship laws and restricted mobility (despite the hijab) – all combine to make the country lag abysmally behind the rest of the world in terms of gender equality. It is unclear how women have been "empowered" through their new-founded religious activism or pietist awareness except through ethnographic testimonies limited to affirming 'the (non-material) self'.

At the same time, postsecular interpretations of women's agency within the Islamic framework impede the possibility of developing an independent politics of transformation beyond the male discourse. Their support to the agentive potential of Islamist women means they can only assert a limited bearing and ultimately, hold mainly sacrificial roles for the larger cause of saving the threatened community of the Muslim *ummah*. A culture of recognition, even when it unveils women's agency, can also serve as a sealant of otherwise transformative possibilities for women as individuals or as feminine collectives. To serve as the bearer of culture can turn out to be a "fundamentalist defence of internal power structures – patriarchy, caste, class – rather than a systemic critique of these" (Sarkar 2002, 234).

6

The Limits and Possibilities of Liberal Activism

Having argued against the limits of religious agency for Pakistani women, the compromises and setbacks experienced within liberal and/or secular women's groups in their resistance strategies must of course be acknowledged. This chapter points to the penchant of many liberal activists to celebrate women's empowerment through symbolic achievement, rather than material political progress. However, it also acknowledges that the price paid by even modest liberal resistance by women can put their lives at risk and that rights-based groups are often the only ones supporting other vulnerable collectives against human rights abuses. Meanwhile, considerable postsecularist Pakistani scholarship makes this task a difficult one, since it challenges the very applicability of a liberal feminist framing, standards and tools, and accuses feminist politics as compromised, biased, culturally inappropriate, even imperialist (see the Introduction and below). These intersecting pressures faced by liberal and/or secularist groups, as well as their relevance in the context of Pakistan's religious politics are discussed.

Culture as Resistance Politics

In 1983, at the height of social and political oppression under the Islamic military dictatorship of Zia ul Haq (1977–1988), a group of underground feminist artists in Pakistan came together to draft a secret manifesto. One member of this draft committee was Salima Hashmi, an artist and one of the founder members of the women's resistance movement and pro-democracy struggle of the time. She recalls that all through its anti-women policies, the "Zia era had made women very conscious of the body" (Hashmi 1995, 51). Women artists were painting the oppression but also their "resistance, anger and revolt"

(51) and this response found expression and articulation in their activism, writing, poetry and art. Some of the early works of such feminists, through their art, commented on state policy that attempted to impose the *chador* and *chardewari* (the veil and the four walls/domesticity) as a dress and social code for women. One such work by Hashmi depicted a flying chador that is empty – an expression of the refusal to acquiesce to non-democratic policies and a masculinised, religio-military state's dictates. A young artist, Naiza Khan, recalls these years of resistance in her later work which consisted of imprinted henna hand-printed images of a woman's body on public walls, which would get removed overnight by social vigilante teams and she would repeat these periodically. Several such subversive pieces became the symbols and a force de resistance for the women's movement, particularly in the struggle against laws that sought to punish women's physical transgressions and to control their mobility. This control had extended to all public activity, including the de facto banning of performing arts such as dance and theatre for women, and even participation in sports. The state also encroached into the private realm, laying vigil to suspected illicit relationships or preventing the co-mingling of couples in parks, beaches or colleges by asking for proof of their relationship.

Thirty years later, these cultural campaigns to reclaim public spaces may be read as a resistance that has preserved freedoms of expression and mobility and directly prevented any state-prescribed dress code for women. Today, many women head the performing and fine arts institutions both in government and in the private sector. Sportswomen participate in regional and international arenas and women performers such as the popular singing duo Zeb and Haniya hail from a conservative Pashtun society yet sing and perform with guitars on a popular music TV channel. Women head music studios, perform in public events and produce and star in films, concerts and the arts.[1] There is a national women's cricket team that participates in international competitions. Therefore, cultural resistance has had a direct historical relationship with politics when the repression was state-initiated and perpetrated largely through its institutions.

A Liberal Dictatorship

Conversely, during the self-proclaimed 'Enlightened and Moderate' regime of General Musharraf (1999–2008), something called "culture" became symbolic of the accommodationist politics of a section of the elite class that had welcomed this liberal dictator into power. Many who had fought against the previous ascetic military dictatorship of the 1980s, fell over themselves to support this new age military dictator who liked dogs, dance and drink (Zaidi 2005). A form of "lifestyle liberalism" appealed to those who considered the General to be a bulwark to growing conservatism and many of his liberal supporters were rewarded through appointments as cultural ambassadors and to head projects that were meant to promote a positive image of Pakistan (and legitimise the General's rule).

Under General Musharraf's military rule, Islamic militancy continued to spill over from the "War on Terror" in Afghanistan and coalesced across the Pakistani border. Its violent expressions gathered local momentum in the tribal areas and its repercussions reverberated across all major cities. The militants' pogrom in the North Western Frontier Province was not countered by any secular political resistance by the state. Instead, the militants' violent religious agenda was only sporadically confronted by military action and dogged by repeated violations of peace treaties. Meanwhile, the liberal antipathy towards the systematic and misogynistic decimation of social and cultural expression by the religious militants – which was supported by the conservative Islamists ruling the province – could only elicit a few scattered protests (Brohi 2006). The dead body of "dancing girl" (prostitute), Shabana, killed by the Taliban as symbolic of their protest over un-Islamic Pakistan, swung for days at *Khooni Chowk* (The Bloody Crossing) and was mocked with currency notes strewn across it in Swat in 2009 (Oppel Jr. and Shah 2009, "In Pakistan, Radio Amplifies Terror of Taliban," *New York Times,* Jan. 24; Tohid 2010, "Swat Paradiso in Black and White," *Daily Times*, March 20).

The liberal elite in the major cities, fed now on high cultural symbolism which had once been effective and even subversive against an overtly theocratic state in the 1980s, had no idea, tool nor vision to counter this radical, grass-root, violent form of new age Islamist militancy. The artistic endeavours of the urbanised liberal elite, supported by a liberal dictator's philosophy of 'Enlightened Moderation', were no match for the political challenges offered by the extremists. The blunting of political activism became clearly evident over this period. Towards the end of the Musharraf regime, there was widespread protest over abuse of his dictatorial policies and the liberals began to disband their earlier support. By this time, however, street activism had clearly been replaced by the emergence of a new form of resistance activism. This was primarily through internet blogs, social networking, in random coffee-shop consciousness-raising sessions and, even fashion became interpreted as a political tool. In various degrees of seriousness, a new generation of socially aware youth were arguing, debating and theorising on Pakistan's politics and social issues. This cyber generation carries activist strains that in form, ideology and politics, can only be termed, postmodernist.

The email exchanges on a variety of activist list-servers between many neophyte activists read as Activism 101 sessions for the newly conscientised, looking to be politically active. Many members of this generation are from the upper-middle classes, and often fresh graduates from British and American universities. Their virtual discussions reveal the absence of any reflexivity, and increasingly, cyber activism is not necessarily contextualised in historical knowledge nor is it necessarily connected to street activism in Pakistan. More and more, new-age activists step out of their graduate gowns and plug in their laptops to activism over a cappuccino. Mindful of Islamophobia, they know they are "anti-imperialist" and "post-orientalist" and compassionate moderates but they are unable to locate their own identities with relevance to Pakistan's political context. One lengthy debate amongst these young people over web-server lists (some of whom had participated in the Lawyers' Movement 2007–2009) was on what qualified as civil society – almost as if it were a club to which they were seeking membership. Many of these members opposed critiques of neo-liberal economics and did not wish to engage in discussions regarding the "redistribution of wealth". Instead, their recommended recipe to countering religious militancy was to focus on cultural expressions and media forms as a method of resistance politics. Such resistance remains limited to blogs but has little impact in political reality. It is in this context then, that a sublime new thesis attempted to promote high art, cultural activities and even events such as Pakistan Fashion Week as a counter-terrorist ideology. This revealed just how low the bar of political standards had fallen, qualifying any public activity as political resistance and blunting the edge of meaningful political activism.

Liberal Designs

Towards the end of 2009, Pakistan made international headlines for debuting the Pakistan Fashion Week.[2] Since the 1990s, fashion shows have been regularly held in Pakistan and are the favoured sponsored activity of multinational corporations. These are often touted as a cultural activity with young women modelling (usually) unconventional clothes on a catwalk. However, members from the designers' community, patronised by General Musharraf as the face of a progressive Pakistan, felt they were ready to be promoted as international players in the business of fashion. Partially as a marketing strategy but also due to the market-driven sensationalist response of an international media, a routine event was transformed into an anti-terrorist and anti-Taliban political activity. The fact that many international news agencies dispatched their *war correspondents* rather than fashion editors to cover the event was telling in itself.

Apart from the blatant political opportunism demonstrated above – which attempted to exaggerate the division between the binaries of the modern and archaic, the liberal and the terrorist and, through performativity rather than the politics – the themes of the event in itself proved interesting. Several of the designers participating in Pakistan Fashion Week focused on the theme of the military, the veil and nationalism as inspirations for their fashion lines. They choreographed the showings to *milli* (nationalistic) music, including patriotic songs written for the two wars fought against India and as tributes to the Pakistani soldier. At the time, a military dictator had just been thrown out of power by a people's movement (2008) and a strong critique had built up against the jihadi sympathies festering for years amongst the army ranks. Ironically, the content of the entire week's showings lent it a strongly conservative flavour by evoking nationalist and patriotic fervour, rather than the supposedly liberal modernism that organisers and participants purported in the press coverage around the event. This attempt to reclaim Islamic culture as a resource or prop to consolidate normative social Islam is a completely inadequate corrective under the current deluge of Islamist resurgence in all public expression. It also confirms that the artists' community has been unable to grasp the potential of the spectacle as a site for challenging mainstream nationalist or religious discourse. By merely juxtaposing the head veil over a partially bare body, or parading models in fashionable army fatigues and barbed wired turbans, such social commentary reads as clichéd rather than subversive.

Women's empowerment was a driving symbol of General Musharraf's self-acclaimed rule of 'Enlightened Moderation' and several gender-related laws and policies did emerge during this period (A.S Zia 2009b). However, these are difficult to quantify since so often, the purpose of such policies was more symbolic than transformative. On the one hand, women's visibility in politics and the state machinery was endorsed. At the same time, conservative forces were accommodated politically and the backlash of radical conservatism on women, particularly those outside urban centres was severe and unchecked by this liberal military regime. Such contradictions were mimicked by the political expressions of the liberals such that they channelled their activism through form and lifestyle rather than political content. As identity markers of the liberal potential of a regime, women may have been well canvassed, but in reality, they continued to lose the larger struggle for equal rights.

Underestimating Liberal Political Possibilities

The fine degrees of separation between the agendas and ethos of mainstream and militant Islamists tend to converge on the strategic deployment of the woman question. This is often demonstrated through the selective award of iconoclastic status in the narratives of religio-nationalism and/or Muslim Resistance. From female suicide bombings, to victims of stampedes[3] – the fruits of Muslim women's religious agency has become narrow and limiting, even by its own standards. The trope of nationalism with its mix of religion has been an intrinsic tool of male political rhetoric and it has benefited them the most.

The best exemplars of the effects of challenges to the neo-religio-nationalist politics in Pakistan remain embodied by the female form and liberal/secular activism as its nemesis. The most recent symbol and casualty of this site of contest has been the teenage schoolgirl, Malala Yousufzai, who survived a murderous attack by Taliban militants in Swat, in 2012. The range and multitude of the global response to the attempted assassination of Malala were far-reaching. They spanned from music artist Madonna's puzzling bare-back tribute at a concert just days after the attack ("Madonna Slams Taliban, Dedicates Song to Malala at Concert," *Dawn*, Oct. 11, 2012) to the equally jingoistic decision by the government of Pakistan to name three of its Frontier Corps platoons, 'Malala', 'Shazia' and 'Kainat', as a tribute to all three school girls targeted and injured by the Taliban ("Malik Announces Rs100m Bounty on TTP Spokesman," *The News*, Oct. 17, 2012). While the case received near-universal condemnation, various interest groups in Pakistan ascribed a variety of wide-ranging motives, causes and responsibilities for the attack, excluding religio-political inspiration.

Mainstream Islamists in Pakistan made public condemnations against the assassination attempt on Malala's life but refused to hold the self-acclaimed perpetrators, the Taliban as responsible for this crime. This denial allowed the Islamists to present themselves as pseudo-sympathisers where they acknowledged the criminal *act* but at the same time, defended the perpetrator by blaming externalities and abstractions. By deflecting the direct responsibility of a crime from the individual and placing it on the breadth of society, government, the state, global powers or imperialism, this emptied the perpetrator of criminal motivation and refilled him with a higher, larger-than-life mission. Converting the agent into a victim creates a faith-inspired order of the *noblesse oblige*. This laundering opens a new line of defence. It suggests (as several Islamists, including the JI, did) that under certain circumstances a case of justifiable homicide may be made. However, in the views of the same sympathisers, this flexibility is a limited moral commodity. The defence of a higher moral purpose as the motivation for murder is not a universally available tool for all citizens, regardless of class, creed or gender. It is a selective application, reserved only for those who are deemed Islamic enough and soaked in the cause of promoting/defending Islam as defined by powerful or political clergymen.

Malala was worthy of sympathy due to her status as a minor but did not qualify for justice because of her near-*fitna* (chaotic) activities. In the minds of the Islamists, her would-be assassins were absolved of their crime even before they were caught. This was despite the Taliban's stated motivation, which had not been cited as the drone operations against militants but due to Malala's adversarial intent to "secularise" her society and promote "Western culture" ("Bullet Successfully Removed From Malala," *The News*, Oct. 10, 2012; "If Malala Survives, We Will Target Her Again: Taliban," *ET*, Oct. 9, 2012). In several press releases, the Taliban spokesman refuted all the defences being spun by Islamists and conservatives (such as drone attacks) as the motivation behind the assassination attempt ("The TTP's 'Defence' of the Attack on Malala," *ET*, Oct. 17, 2012). The statements impatiently corrected the rationalisations and confirmed that they attacked Malala specifically for her adversarial intent to "secularise society" by educating girls and according to a non-Islamic curricula. Her aimed defiance to the TTP qualified her as anti-Islamic and the Taliban claimed, "We did not attack her for raising voice for education. We targeted her for opposing mujahideen [those engaged in jihad] and their war" ("Taliban Says Its Attack on Malala Justified," *ET*, Oct. 16). The decision to kill her was the natural culmination of their larger campaign of systematically blowing up girls' schools over the last five years, in northern Pakistan.

In contrast, it was through a process of equivocations – including the call for contextualising the brutality of the Taliban due to their being victims of imperialist violence[4] – that peripheral Islamists begin to utilise such smokescreens, too. This enabled them to make a case for garnering sympathy or to legitimise the acquittal of an "Islamic murder" or justifiable homicide, even prior to a judicial hearing.[5] According to such a world-view, justice must not be blind but dependent on the perceived beliefs or religious weight of the individuals or parties involved. This notion of justice allows the sympathisers of the criminal to act as judge and jury in condemning the act but also, to actively resist any punishment to be awarded to the criminal because they do not recognise the latter as such.[6] In this backdrop, the broader criticism of the military operations against militants and call for "strategic silence" (Pratt 2013a) on the part of (imperialist) feminists (Toor 2012) who actively campaign in support of cases such as Malala's, implied that Muslim women can only either be anti-imperialist passive victims or foreign agents – there is nothing in-between.[7]

Feminists as "Native Informants" and "Imperialist Collaborators"

Some of the criticism of liberal/secular feminisms in Muslim-majority contexts such as Pakistan, imply that feminists are a non-representative minority, ignorant of the dangers and effects of neo-liberal imperialism and therefore, complicit in imperialist wars/violence.[8] Inadvertently, this reads as a form of racialising too – as if, brown women do not have conscious independent agendas but blindly follow the dictates of white feminist agendas. The range of such defensiveness spans from a belittling of the impact of religious politics on women's sexualities, freedoms and mobility and legal rights, to outright accusations that Pakistani feminism is imperialist and its activists operate as native informants.[9] To make a case against their complicity to imperialism, the evidence that is cited aims to indict some select feminists' membership or association with some international or transnational feminist network. But other than the ones indicted by these scholars, there are several other prominent and active liberal, secular feminists who have been engaged for decades in resisting Islamist politics and have organised sustained campaigns against Shariat and Islamic laws and/or, head or work with "neo-liberal" NGOs. They remain unnamed in such critiques, presumably because it would be imprudent to impeach every feminist in Pakistan. As an example, one critique of members of a transnational solidarity network, the Centre for Secular Space, is that its "list of "Advisors and Officers" reads like a who's who of third world feminists" and that this inclusion is "to give the Centre a flavor of authenticity" (Toor 2012, 153). Apparently, third world feminists can only be either unknowing activist dupes of tokenism or cunning collaborators of imperialism.

Specific to Pakistan, such criticism objects (ahistorically) that 'the liberals' in Pakistan harbour a "partiality for authoritarianism" as long as it is of "a secular variety" (Toor 2012, 155) but avoids mentioning that several of those (men) considered to be of the "principled Left" (156) also welcomed the 'liberal dictator' General Musharraf after his military coup of 1999. The same liberals condemned for joining General Musharraf's subsequent cabinet and supporting the Pakistani military included several (one prominent) Leftists and left sympathisers and in fact, many feminists took a public and documented stand against the military rule. With regard to liberal politics, one criticism is that civil society activists generally carry a "deep-rooted fear of illiberal masses" (Toor 2012, 156). This critique objects to the attribution of Islamisation as a method of controlling women's sexualities and suggests that the realities of Muslim men and women in Muslim-majority countries, Muslim communities, and beyond is shaped by more than any one religious ideology or power formation. In the context of Pakistan, for example, Toor (2011) argues that "'Islamization', something called 'Islam' cannot explain the actual ways and means by which women's bodies and sexuality are managed and/or controlled in contemporary Pakistan" (3). One is unsure however, of what the point of this statement is. Yes, Islamisation, which has inspired and institutionalised a series of sexist laws and policies that remain successfully on Pakistan's statute books thirty years later, does not explain *all* the ways women's sexualities are "managed". However, to suggest that the theocratisation policies of General Zia ul Haq "cannot explain the actual ways and means" that women's sexualities have been targeted, reads as an attempt to erase the effects of Islamisation of the State (not just society) which focussed almost exclusively on women's bodies. The contestable claim that "even Zia's regime – which is the closest that Pakistan came to the institutionalization of a theocracy – was not a period in which the shariah trumped secular law" (Toor 2011, 5) is puzzling because to the extent that such a 'trumping' was resisted, it was the liberal human rights and women's rights movements and activism that stemmed such a tide.[10] Such efforts to de-essentialise Islamisation is responsive to and reads as a misplaced defence against Islamophobia in the West. However, this is a limited and counter-intuitive framing for resistance and struggle in Muslim contexts. Further, such a definition of Islamophobia is selective and does not include the intense hate and rejection amongst and between the wide variety of intra-faith sects who deny, campaign, vilify and denigrate each others' Islam and sometimes, rationalise murder of other Muslims in Pakistan irrespective of class divides.

If all analysis is reduced to a crude class analysis which implies that men only deploy sexual oppression as an articulation of class domination then yes, all sexual politics in Muslim contexts may be read as reflective of class warfare and religious laws and ethics may be considered as incidental "tools" rather than motivating factors. The instrumentalisation of Islam by Islamists has not shut down after Zia ul Haq's death in 1988 and women's bodies remain the battlefield of faith-based sexist politics in contemporary Pakistan. This may be seen in Islamists' resistance to legislation against domestic violence and marital rape, the backlash to the Women's Protection Act, their refusal to amend the *Qisas and Diyat* laws, and campaigns to impose an Islamic dress code. It is difficult to understand how these have nothing to do with Islamisation or that they may be unrelated to the control of women's bodies by Islamic fundamentalist politics. Also relevant is how conservative male legislators have regularly colluded with the minority of Islamists in Parliament in order to block reform of discriminatory religious laws and prevent any pro-women ones.[11] The liberal or left-leaning parties do not effectively represent the working classes of Pakistan any more or less than the Islamists and conservatives, yet the sexism that is demonstrated by these liberal/left men also takes equal recourse from religion and tradition. The only tempering of such gender bias comes from those within such parties who do uphold liberal-secular values (however weak) and appeal to universal principles of equality and human rights (however ineffectively).

Conventional Islamic punishment such as stoning to death, which is practised in Iran, Saudi Arabia and Afghanistan, is not carried out in Pakistan. However, informal, parallel legal structures institutionalise extra-judicial practices such as stoning, based on the notion of retributive justice and as culturally and religiously authentic. Such informal justice systems rationalise men's right to control women's sexuality as their Islamically sanctioned right as guardians (*wali*) of Muslim women on whom their honour depends. Further, the *Qisas and Diyat* provisions of the Islamic laws as they stand, sanction retributive justice or payment of blood money, which has routinely allowed men who have murdered their kinswomen to negotiate patriarchal arrangements and legally circumvent punishment for such crimes. This law is not class or culture-specific and is available for the benefit of, and is invoked regularly by the privileged and working classes alike, and violent men in general, and is an institutional legal practice.

If the state continues to embed religious legality so as to reclaim and excavate an imagined 'pure' Islamic culture as distinct from Western ones, then necessarily some historical moments within patriarchal culture and religion will overlap and logically, will condone stoning and retributive justice. Citing relevant examples in Pakistan and emphasising the assimilative relationship between patriarchal culture and Islamic practices, Shaheen Sardar Ali (2006) notes that

> since its initial phenomenal expansion within the first few decades of its existence, Islam has tended to incorporate and assimilate the social customs and institutions of the various regions and communities which converted to Islam. (84)

It was only after 2004, when religious militant groups started their offensives against the state in north-west Pakistan, that the first reported cases of extra-judicial stoning and flogging became part of the narrative of societal violence against women. Prior to this, horrific forms of violence have been perpetrated against women routinely in all parts of the country but stoning has a very specific resonance with prescribed Quranic/Islamic punishments. To suggest that these are not derivative of religion (however much debated) or not related to control of women's sexualities but simply a case of class oppression is to be deliberately myopic.

When a woman minister for social welfare, Zille Huma, was shot and killed at a public event by an "extremist" as the press termed him (although he was not associated with any Islamist organisation), for not adequately veiling herself in 2007 – does that fall under cultural norms or religious sanction? Is veiling to be severed from religion completely, in order to exonerate its motivational influence in this case? Flogging is widely understood as a prescribed religious punishment subject to circumstances, judicial process and interpretation. In cases of adultery, blasphemy, wilful marriages and denying women their property rights by marrying them off to the holy book, cultural sanctions are often derived from or collude with existing religious laws that prescribe unequal inheritance for women or the autonomous right to marry. Further, until the law was amended in 2006, the *Zina* Law became a tool of controlling women's choice or to deny them their free will in matters of marriage, as well as to limit their mobility under the consensual agreement that adultery was a *religious sin*.

Therefore, the "patriarchal opportunism" that Toor (2011) insists men deploy by selecting "elements from an ideological 'toolbox'" (3) in order to regulate women's sexualities would mean that the 'box' would have to store an available reserve of such tools in the first place.[12] To brush aside the Islamic prescriptions on women's sexuality (and especially the concept of adultery) is to deny its patriarchal inclination and availability, regardless of the spirit behind the letter (which is still related to codifying women's sexuality). Even after the contentious amendment of the *Zina* (Adultery) laws in Pakistan, the basic premise of this law centres on the need to regulate women's sexuality as a permanent threat to social order, which emerges as a general patriarchal consensus in many Muslim contexts.

Blasphemy, if proven, is punishable by death but often, enraged Muslims take this law into their hands and use it as a moral justification to attack and even kill (usually) other Muslims with impunity. In most cases (although not all) the issue has nothing to do with blaspheming but is used to settle personal scores in any case. Women's marital choice is de facto subject to permission from her (religiously prescribed) *wali* or guardian. At best, some women legislators have attempted to make the state the *wali* rather than a woman's male relative, which has been resisted by Islamist women representatives in Parliament. Regardless, the concept of a *wali* as a religiously derivative prescription for minors and women remains an infantilising and discriminatory requirement. Even if it is not legally invoked, this rationale seeps into all policies of the state, including the requirement of identities of fathers, brothers or husbands for the formal actualisation of women's citizenry. This is directly relevant to the management of women's sexualities where a single woman does not qualify for a recognisable status without the official reference of a male relative.

An interesting contrast to the approach to reform may be found in the example of the alleged cultural practice of marrying a woman to the holy book (Quran) in one province of Pakistan, in order to deny her due inheritance/property rights. In 2005, the Council of Islamic Ideology (CII) unanimously approved a draft bill aimed at eliminating this custom of *Haq Bakhshwan* by declaring it un-Islamic. Ostensibly, this could be seen as an attempt to uproot and replace discriminatory cultural practices with a progressive Islamic alternative. However, on closer examination, it is found that this reformist bent was motivated not so much from a concern of women's rights but in recognition that the practice was a violation of the holy book. Therefore, the amendment proposed was to the Blasphemy Laws and not to Family Law, as a step to protect the Quran.

The CII recommended life imprisonment for those who 'married' their sisters and daughters to the Holy Quran by amending Section 295-B (Blasphemy Law) of the Pakistan Penal Code (PPC) arguing that the practice amounted to "defiling the Holy Quran" and "desecrating the Islamic institution of marriage" and the secondary concern was the denial of a woman's right to inheritance and her right to choose a life partner (Nasir Iqbal 2005, "CII Okays Draft Bill to Stop Marriage with Quran," *Dawn*, June 17). The proposed amendment by the CII suggested that whosoever wilfully defiles, damages or desecrates a copy of the Holy Quran or an extract therefrom or directly or indirectly allows the Holy Quran to be used for purpose of its marriage with a female or fraudulently or dishonestly induces any person to swear on the Holy Quran never to marry any one in her life time or knowingly *uses it in any derogatory manner* or for any unlawful purpose shall be punishable with imprisonment for life. (Human Rights Commission of Pakistan 2006; Emphasis added)

In this case, the crime was interpreted primarily as an insult to the holy book, not as a contravention of a woman's basic right. The CII only has the authority to recommend or sanction laws in line with the Islamic ideology of Pakistan but not to legislate.[13]So, the law that ultimately did address socio-cultural practices that were discriminatory towards women was the Prevention of Anti-women Practices (Criminal Law Amendment), which was passed by Pakistan's elected Parliamentary body, the National Assembly, in 2011. This law prescribes a range of specific punishments for what it identifies specifically as "anti-women practices" such as forced marriages, marriages to the Quran, denying women their due share of hereditary property, and the barter of women as a practice of conflict resolution in some communities. Similarly, President General Musharraf's (1999–2008) liberal intervention led him to issue a reference against the proposed *Hisba* (Accountability) Bill of the Islamist government in the province of Khyber Pakhtunkhwa and allowed the Supreme Court to strike down the bill (2007) that prescribed (amongst other policies) a vice and virtue police for the province.

Clearly, the references, impetus and priorities afforded in the approach to women's rights are very different in the above examples. The CII seeks to align women's protection with and through a theological rationale only when the religious order is threatened, while women representatives of an elected parliament refer to a commonsensical corrective which is supported by and through a liberal, universal and rights-based discourse. The concern is that often, patriarchal cultural practices are *rationally* beneficial to the patriarchal order and do not contravene the broader Islamic moral and social order, including women's right to *lesser* inheritance or awarding minorities a lesser status as citizens. The notion that since women are guaranteed at least some inheritance rights in Islam and that it would be strategically judicious to argue for *at least* these divine rights and preempt (theoretical) resistance or denial of these rights due to any competing cultural practices, is a defeatist one. If one is to only obtain theoretical rights, then they may as well be equal and prescribed by universal civil code, not religious debate or dependent on interpretations.

Religious sources are not derived from any lay logic that can be translated into acceptable pieces of legislation, particularly if they challenge patriarchal norms. There are occasions when piecemeal logic is applied in some cases and which are then hailed as progressive interpretations of religion and cited as successful implantations of Islamic ethos. These always stop short of being equal for women with the understanding that if such an attempt would be made then these laws would be unsuccessful, since they do not accommodate the expectations of normative religion nor the cultural environment as determined by patriarchy. Moreover, such arguments are more problematic when cultural practice and religious ethos do contravene each other. Then, which will supersede, cultural authenticity or Islam? The argument that there is significant debate within Islamic tradition and *ijtehad* (independent reasoning) and *ijma* (consensus) as the derivative method of legislating a religious law is simply an attempt to justify another way of bringing rationality and commonsense into the religious discourse.

Feminists in Pakistan have been committed to exposing how women's sexuality is the site where both culture and religion collude in a combined effort to demonstrate, regulate and measure society's moral order. Their concerns have been more focused on repealing discriminatory Islamic laws, rather than remaining limited to lobbying for positive interpretations under the recognition that patriarchal culture and/or religion will dominate any translation of the social order. These feminists are not looking for bulwarks but to uproot and transform gender relations to ensure that women's choices are neither divinely legally ordained nor sanctioned by a patriarchal culture.

Sympathising with Men, Silencing Women

With reference to the call for feminists to maintain a "strategic silence" (Pratt 2013a) on women's issues in Muslim contexts that are under siege by the "WoT", it is worth recalling that feminists in the South have historically always been invited to observe such silence but usually by religious/conservative and even, liberals, nationalists and those men who warn feminists to not wash their 'dirty laundry in front of Western eyes' (A.S. Zia 2013b).[14] Such appeals urge concealment of (private) cases of domestic violence, rapes and other violations in times of war and insurgencies and plead against the exposure of 'collateral damage' to women in times of national crisis or conflict. The advice seems to be to maintain this moratorium (over rapes and murders and misogyny) at the very least, until *after* the conflict, *after* modernisation, *after* gender consciousness, *after* neo-liberalism, or *after* a true Islamicate has been established.

One collective of US-based scholarship (Satterthwaite and Huckerby 2013) has objected to the language and references used by the US administration and human rights organisations which casts militant Islamists as "savages" and addresses them as "Muslim fundamentalists" (Akbar and Oza 2013, 158). The authors consider these to be secularist attempts to "link Muslim political activities to terrorist activities" (Akbar and Oza 2013, 164). They object to the "language and logic [that human/women's rights activists] leverage to articulate their critiques" (161) and worry about "the dangerous potential for convergences between human rights and "War on Terror" discourses" (155). The authors refer to the human casualties of the "WoT" as "Muslim men and communities targeted by Western governments in the "War on Terror"" (156) and also consider these Muslim men to be secondary victims of feminist human rights activists which they discuss in detail in their essay.[15]

The key problem with such challenges is with regard to the repackaging, where all the 'perpetrators' in the conflict in Afghanistan and Pakistan are by implication, non-believers, secularists and non-Muslim imperialists (including, presumably the Pakistan military) acting on behalf of the US, and only/all the militant-victims are considered to be Muslim *non-fundamentalists* or "communities". Certainly, no analyst of any ideological bearing in Pakistan refers to terrorists or members of militant organisations as those who engage in "Muslim political activities". Variably, they are seen as terrorists, extremists, militants or even freedom-fighters and anti-imperialists but the targets are not referred to as male politicians. More specifically, the Pakistani state and many Pakhtuns whose cities and villages have been besieged by the militant Taliban over the last decade, categorise them as insurgents and violators of the state and usurpers of their communities. This is not to suggest that the members of the banned *Tehreeq e Taliban* (even if they are called "non-state actors") do not qualify for human rights. On the contrary, human rights organisations in Pakistan have consistently upheld the legal rights of those who are considered anti-state or terrorists and rejected the parallel speedy, anti-terrorist courts system even long before 9/11. The paradoxical method of unpacking the "terrain" of "Muslim fundamentalism" and then immediately repacking a new landscape whereby, all shades of Islamists are swept under the generic and innocuous category of men who practice Muslim male politics is reductive. It also renders invisible all those

Muslim men who are normative politicians and representatives, tribal leaders and state officials and who are targeted specifically by the militants for their political support to the Pakistani state, and by other Islamists who target them in sectarian and political battles.

More relevant is that neither the Taliban nor the Pakistani state reference, dismiss, employ or reject the imaginary of human rights in any peace agreements, press-releases or propaganda. More interestingly, the self-acclaimed Muslim fundamentalists (and even non-fundamentalist, mainstream Islamists in Pakistan) are not in the least interested in the human rights of the militants or other victims of state abuse. Their exclusive political concern is invested only in stoking anti-American anger against the widespread perception of the latter's war on Islam and Muslims. Ironically, the only ones we can depend on for the preservation of the human rights of any sector would be the same handful of liberals and human rights/women's rights activists that scholars such as Toor (2012) vilify as "imperialist feminists" and who have stood (futilely, as in many, many other instances) for the principle of due process and human rights for terrorists and, who have advocated against special tribunals and anti-terrorist courts long before and after, 9/11.

The suggestion that Muslim fundamentalists are criticised or demonised only by liberal/secularists in Muslim contexts is a misplaced generalisation. Indeed, in Pakistan, an outpouring of condemnation of militant Islamists (such as the *Tehreeq e Taliban Pakistan*) has been from within the community of mainstream conservatives and Islamist groups who have quite crudely referred to them as savage monsters, anti-Islamic, non-Muslims and Bad Muslims ("Fifty Muslim Scholars Issue Fatwa Against Taliban," *Dawn*, Oct. 11, 2012; Ali Zain 2015, "4 Terrorist Groups That Condemned APS Terror Attack," *Daily Pakistan*, Dec. 16). Many Islamist groups, or who Akbar and Oza refer to as mislabelled "Muslim fundamentalists", are involved in sectarian bloodbaths where they condemn and kill members of opposing sects by subscribing to the same binary, as part of the same continuum and stemming from the same rationale – of eliminating Bad Muslims (e.g., *Ahmadi* and *Shia* minority Muslim sects). For most fundamentalists, the Bad Muslims and Christians/Jews/Hindus are worse offenders than the secularists, as evident in the code of Islamist competitiveness and political ethos. Several mainstream Islamists argue that militant Islamists misrepresent Islam, are foreigners, alien to "our" culture, US-constructs, and dangerous to Islam (Amir Zia 2013, "False Fault Lines," *The News*, May 6). There are reams of such available literature in the form of statements, journals, newsletters, media documents and official position papers often collated and strategically used by the government of Pakistan. It is strange then, that only liberal/secular feminists are held culpable for creating and perpetrating such a dehumanising and Otherising discourse of militant Islamists. The fact that the vaguely-defined, unelected, non-Constitutional, all-male *ulema,* or mainstream Islamists of Pakistan issue such regular condemnation of the Bad (militant) Muslim is particularly dangerous when we consider that the government of Pakistan solicits and instrumentalises this as the "official voice" of Islam and certainly gives no credence to the fairly un-influential and usually ignored, liberal voices.

In Pakistan, it has been only the non-governmental Human Rights Commission of Pakistan and some feminist groups that have advocated for the legal rights of terrorists even before 9/11. Further, it has been the (colonial) liberal rights discourse of the Rule of Law that has enabled Pakistan's judiciary to routinely and regularly release detainees suspected of terrorism both prior to and after the "WoT". No liberal group has ever challenged *habeus corpus* and in fact, Islamists or suspected terrorists have regularly invoked it for their own defence.[16] In that sense, the liberal principle that the state must be a guarantor of basic human rights, (regardless of the faith or crime of citizens) is observed more indiscriminately by liberal groups,[17] rather than any other community. In particular, fundamentalists or Islamists often selectively petition for liberal judicial rights for Muslim men but would deny them to Others (competing sects, minorities, women).

Even if feminists heed the call to deploy strategic silence, this is unlikely to appease Islamists or lead to a suspension or embargo on gender-based violence before, during, or after conflict. So, to suggest that feminists should not reify gender would imply that patriarchal politics must be prioritised, especially in times of conflict. There is no neutral in-between. Post-conflict patriarchies are not so easy to dismantle if they are allowed to gain momentum while the feminist project is suspended for the "larger cause"– a lesson that our post-colonial history has taught us well. Rather than abandoning or suspending feminist frameworks for Muslim contexts or where northern imperialist projects are being played out, it may be advisable to continue to prioritise gender. This is particularly so for cases of violence since, I argue, women should not have to bear the double burden or guilt for being raped, violated or restricted under any circumstances, pretext or context and then be denied the right to identify the perpetrator or seek justice for the violation.

More recently, Winter (2013) suggests that the confusion caused by postsecularists over notions of pietist agency or within political philosophies such as feminism may be "genuine, or disingenuously operated with the aim of making a political point or even silencing debate" (148). Moreover, Winter's questions are the same that I have been asking for several years about the "nature and extent of the constraints applied to the exercise of that agency" and "what political positions are being adopted by the women in question" (149). The call for feminist silence on human rights[18] abuses in Pakistan, regardless of the timing or context is tantamount to exonerating this historical and collusive continuity and is in line with what is common in conservative nationalist and Islamist rhetoric. It is a luxury that only the apolitical or detached observer can afford.

For feminists, this does not compensate for any crimes, particularly since women are primary targets of such male-defined abstractions and material gains. To distinguish between the motivations does, however, make it easier for the legal system and government policy to grapple with and resolve such conflict (however inadequately). Governments make laws to protect the state and citizens from acts of violence. The criminal justice system is meant to check the abuse of all violations and punish perpetrators after determining the victim, judging the damage, and applying the requisite sentence. But rationalising divine motivations makes it nearly impossible to bring crimes committed in the name of Islam into the legal net. It also negates the (liberal) principle of the indivisible right to life. Dividing or qualifying this basic right renders those perceived as "less Islamic" as more secular and so, less worthy of the right to live or be defended or receive justice. The singular commonality in this multi-dimensional drama is that all the actors, be they of religious, nationalist, cultural or state politics, routinely and consciously deploy the site of women's bodies as the stage on which to display their ideologies and over which they fight their material struggles. As carriers of both the virus and cure, as victims or agents, women also carry the seed of destruction and resurrection, war and peace. Since, violence against women settles men's scores and restores the pre-crime social order, any initial breach of male community codes requires her elimination, which then qualifies as the metaphorical, literal and justifiable end. So, when apologists for any crime engage in disassociating the crime from the criminal (which is quite a different exercise from theorising the reasons for the crime), they are guilty of such disembodiment. The evidence may be in the form of a dead body but it has been murdered by an abstraction – American hegemony, imperialism, Islamic freedom, militancy, Westernisation, class aspirations, honour, nationalism, secularism, women's rights. By not recognising the self-confessed murderer, such reasonings absolve the criminal and dissolve the crime. Different actors may use indiscriminate violence as a methodology but the process of rationalising them is different. The state uses the rationale that it is not punishing citizens but warring against forces oppositional to its (equally abstract claims of) sovereignty, honour, independence, and as custodian of Islam. Through such deflective exercises, in the end, we are left with multiple bodies and the obscured perpetrator.

'Liberal' is not a Class

It might be instructive for postsecularist scholars to look equally closely into the complexities of liberals – not just Islamists – in Pakistan. Such an exercise would reveal that all self-acclaimed liberals in Pakistan are not secularists and neither are they all enthusiastic supporters of drone attacks.[19] (It is also simplistic to believe that the drone attacks are not supported by the Pakistani military, which can be described as anything but subscriptive of liberal secularism). In fact, many liberals do not support *neo-liberal* economic policies that engage in US/IMF/WB funding for civilian projects or those that sustain Pakistan's bloated military budget – all of which, many Islamists may. It has become de rigueur to paint all Pakistani liberals as advocates for drone operations in Pakistan. It is a sweeping generalisation that has become fashionable amongst several scholars working on Islamist identities, in order to justify their critique of liberal-secularism. By extending the appraisal of the failures of secular projects in the Middle East to Pakistan, such scholars tend to lump together liberalism and secularism even though, many liberals in Pakistan do not support, advocate nor campaign for a secular state.[20] Many secularists (in the provinces of Balochistan and Khyber Pakhtunkhwa) are certainly not liberals, and all secularists or secularist aspirations are not "elite", as proposed by some left commentators (Akhtar 2016).[21]

In any case, the constant reference to General Musharraf's 'Enlightened Moderation' policy that he announced after his coup as proof of support by all liberal minded people, omits to mention the lack of reception, or substantive influence that the slogan held in real terms during his rule. It was understood as nothing more than an abstract justification for instituting himself as the appropriate buffer between the militants and corrupt civilian democratic leaders.[22] The international community (including some Indian liberal commentators) and some opportunists from the Pakistani political and cultural elite may have been thrilled by such statements but the General was always challenged and mocked for such abstractions in popular discourse and the opposition parties in the country at the time. In most cases, liberals in Pakistan do not "denounce the religiously political" as "unmitigated evil" in abstraction (Iqtidar 2012, 57) but usually despair over the political abuse of religion as a materialist power tool wielded by Islamists. Such mistrust has bred over many years and has been based on cases where Islamists have lobbied and assisted in the institutionalisation of discriminatory state laws and societal restrictions. Some of these include the aggressive pursuit and successful ex-communication and disenfranchisement of the Ahmadi sect; legislation of rigorous punishment for adultery and homosexuality; legal prevention of land reforms on the basis of Islam; reduction of women's worth in legal testimony and their *diyat* (compensation or blood money) compared to that of men's; resistance to reform the Blasphemy Law; and complicity towards a social vigilantism against minorities accused of committing blasphemy.[23] The fact that some of these laws and policies were passed by secular leaders who were pressurised to appease the religious lobbies is a criticism of liberal/secular politicians that is well documented by liberal feminists in Pakistan (Shaheed 2010). Undoing these at state levels is virtually impossible and resisted by Islamists.[24] Meanwhile, the reverberations of such laws at societal levels is evident in the accelerating acts of religious vigilantism.

The allegations that Pakistani liberals consider the "secular as *always* imperial" (Iqtidar 2012, 57, my italics) and therefore, do not condemn state terrorism against militants, is also inaccurate. Most political liberals have made careers out of condemning state terrorism, long before the drone operations. Even before that these activists have protested the state's treatment of the people and the military operations against East Pakistan, as well as in Balochistan province (where a separatist insurgency has simmered for decades). In return for such historical activism, these same liberals were/are accused of being RAW (Indian) agents, traitors and Westernised, precisely because of their challenges to the state's jihad policy in Kashmir and Afghanistan.[25] Specifically, these same liberals have even held a longstanding demand to disband the (colonial) Frontier Crimes Regulation (FCR) and bring the Federally Administered Tribal Areas (FATA) under the legal framework of the federation. The rationale is to avoid routine and unregulated tribunal punishments and human rights violations against its citizens under the prevailing tribal discourse.[26] All this was long before the "War on Terror". For those scholars who date their definition of terrorism from 9/11, the idea that drone operations/"WoT" are the first acts of "state terrorism" demonstrates that their consciousness of state formation begins with 9/11 and despite contrary claims, that theirs is a politically truncated project.

Interestingly, if we look a little more carefully, we will find the notion of rights itself is not necessarily rejected indiscriminately in

Muslim contexts and not as seamlessly as the postsecular critics would have us believe. In fact, if at first sight the resistance to a liberal, rights-based discourse by its opponents seems to be an outright denunciation and rejection, then a closer examination will reveal that it is also often *selectively* invoked by many (male) Islamists for their own defence. Very often, the vocabulary of several rights-based appeals by Islamist men in Pakistan is not directly referential to Islamic texts or traditions but instead, to the very liberal, Enlightenment inspired principles (such as due process, rule of law, right to legal representation, labour rights, freedom to worship, protection from racism, *habeus corpus*, legal safeguards against custodial torture etc.) that they purport to reject.

The duplicitous nature of US foreign policy which offered false pretexts of rescuing Afghan women to launch the "WoT" and the self-proclaimed 'successes', have all been consistently politically challenged by feminists in Pakistan. The targets for criticism in much of the new anthropology discussed above are specifically, *Western* liberal-secularist human rights/women's rights campaigners. Ultimately, however, this vilification is extended so as to include all advocates of liberal-secularism through the exercise of considerable creative license and selective historical suspension. The connection is circuitous, whereby the membership of some individual feminists who may be part of transnational networks becomes evidence of their fatal betrayal to all Muslim interests in their national contexts. The pursuit of international solidarity, research, campaigns, sharing of information of local resistance and documentation of the struggles of women against religious fundamentalism, as well as other obstacles towards social, political and economic equality for women and minorities in Muslim contexts is, apparently, to betray Muslim men. According to such logic, to be especially interested in the cause of women and minorities in Muslim contexts post-9/11 is to break ranks and betray not just the nation but Muslimness itself.

Campaigning against religio-political male activists qualifies as complicity in the "dehumanization of Muslims" (Akbar and Oza 2013, 173) and paints women who are committed to transnational feminisms as allies of US imperialism. This only applies to liberal feminists who belong to women's/human rights organisations. Islamic feminist groups, or Muslim women's networks and NGOs (*Musawah*, Sisters in Islam) are not included in such critiques. This is odd because members of several Muslim women's networks include activists who organise their activism against local patriarchal discriminatory practices (such as those perpetrated by Bad (?) Muslim men). Such men are identified by women members of these networks/organisations as obstructive to the path of their true

Islamic rights in Muslim contexts. According to such definition, Islamic feminists should also qualify as the "native informants" (Toor 2012, 157) and "comprador intellectuals" (Akbar and Oza 2013, 166) involved in exposing such historic and continuous sexism in Muslim contexts. Does Islamic feminism also qualify as dovetailing into and "aiding the imperial projects" (Akbar and Oza 2013, 166) by offering a "discursive terrain laid out by [offering themselves as] 'good Muslims'" and thereby, become "part of an uncritical and freely used parlance for justifying the state's violence and intervention" against male Muslim political activism? (166).

It is in historical specificity that the contest between liberals and Islamists may be founded – not in the broader moral competition of issuing statements of condemnation or support of drone operations as an indicator of some 'liberal versus Islamist' politics. Neither is it accurate to allege that all Pakistani liberals equate Islamists with terrorists or suicide bombing militants.[27] In fact, Musharraf's government in the past, as well as that of the Pakistan People's Party (both, purportedly liberal regimes), have repeatedly attempted to coerce the reluctant Islamists to condemn suicide bombings, not on the basis of Enlightenment ideals or secularist principles but emphatically, by invoking the notion that suicide bombings are *un-Islamic* and therefore, Islamic militancy is profane. Musharraf's liberals were constantly engaged in an effort to disentangle the knots between militant, and some hopeful alternative politics called "moderate" Islam.

Proposals for a Hybrid Feminism

Several ethical and pragmatic proposals have emerged as part of new feminist theory in response to the postsecularist critiques outlined above. These include the bid for a coalition of Islamic, secular and other feminisms in the form of "hybrid feminisms" (Ahmed-Ghosh 2008), or a "cosmopolitan feminism that outlines the tenets of a non-oppressive globally oriented feminism" (Reilly 2011, 25). Reilly's proposal for a feminist ontology which is formulated in mutually respectful dialogue has become harder to realise precisely because of the postsecularist interventions that have critiqued Enlightenment-inspired feminism and human rights.

Retro-Islamist scholarship has cemented the strategic worth of Islam as the exclusive alternative path to empowerment in countries such as Pakistan. By delegitimising women's rights as "Western" rights and by redefining agency, gender empowerment and advocating a place for religion in public service and social development, liberal-secular democracy has become associated with the project of imperialism and obstreperous to Muslim "ways of living meaningfully" (Mahmood 2005, xi). If, the very roots and plausibility of secularism have been delegitimised but religion, on the other hand, rehabilitated and its conservative, anti-women, anti-equality ethos has been *differently* rationalised, then what is the level playing field where this dialogue is to be conducted? It is practically impossible to find any post-9/11 scholarship on Muslim women that is not framed and preoccupied with their religious agency, rather than focused on their secular autonomy, class identities or feminist aspirations and successes.

The call for Muslim exceptionalism in the West (Amir-Moazami et al. 2011) also needs to be compared to the demands of liberals in Muslim-majority contexts. Based on their commitment to the secular principle of equal citizenry, Pakistani human rights activists demand that the policy and deliberate practice of exceptionalism be removed for religious minorities (HRCP annual reports, WAF press releases and several rights-based NGO publications and statements). However, in this case, the liberal demand for undoing exceptional treatment of religious minorities is not to afford them extra-legal status in a society that has overlooked their religious needs, nor to protect their religio-cultural sentiments. Instead, the liberal demand for anti-exceptionalism for religious minorities in Pakistan has been prompted by recognition of the need to defend them (and in fact, all citizens, including Muslim minority sects and women) from Pakistan's discriminatory Islamic provisions and laws. This demand is prompted by the recognition that rather than the benign indifference of a secular state (that on principle does not afford special recognition to religious beliefs, nor privileges the influence of one religion over others), the Islamic republic on the other hand, by law, deliberately excludes and actively discriminates against the non-Muslim communities as *exceptional* (lesser) citizens.

This means that rather than supporting legal and social exceptionalism for religious minorities (through separate laws, electorates, schools, alternate dispute resolutions or dress codes), liberal activists in Pakistan seek to integrate religious minorities into a secular domain through demands such as removing the separate electorate system, removing the requirement to declare one's religion in passports and official documents, and removing restrictions against inter-faith marriages. The liberals seek the active inclusion of minorities in order to qualify them for legal recognition and protection under the *secular Constitution* (prior to discriminatory amendments) but which are by definition, actively denied them under *Islamic state laws*. Currently, Pakistan has no *law* that affords rights or protection to religious minorities. To recognise the exceptionalism of religious minorities under these circumstances is to render them as legal and social Others and make them vulnerable in comparison to the status of majoritarian Muslims. The de facto disenfranchisement of minorities and women influences the demand for a de jure secular state.

The dialogue for democratisation across these divides is challenged by the requirements of credentials of the participating parties. If faith must be a criterion, then secularism stands disqualified even before participation – so, on what premise can the latter contribute to a dialogue? Further, the promotion of conservative desire as a legitimate by-product of Islamist thought and practice has furthered the concept of "patriarchy trading". The reification of Islamist practices that allows women some agency in return for their willing acceptance of patriarchy is a precarious precipice to put women on. Repeatedly, the experience of feminist alliances has shown that right wing politics manages to subsume and co-opt not just the tactics, vocabulary and strategies of feminism but even manages to subvert these for the most patriarchal ends.

At first, modernist feminists rethought the concept and symbol of the veil as more polysemic than the Orientalist and Western feminist understanding of it. The recommendation by Pakistani postsecularists to include religion as a significant vehicle for gender empowerment would now ostensibly extend to practices such as polygamy and unequal inheritance for Muslim women. Polygamy may well be a patriarchal practice but still, for many men and women, a desirous social arrangement, particularly since it often functions as a bargain that some (first wives) negotiate in order to gain domestic relief when second wives take over their duties. In practical terms, Islamists, conservative women and indeed, the Islamic Republic/state would uphold and even celebrate such arrangements. What possible contributions could liberal/secularists provide in a dialogue on such issues if neither patriarchy nor Islamic rationales are to be challenged according to the new proposals of engagement?

Some feminist safeguards, such as those proposed by Islamic feminism and as exemplified in the efforts of international networks including Sisters in Islam[28] and *Musawah*,[29] propose a two-tiered struggle – against secular patriarchies, as well as Muslim patriarchies. Certainly, it is beneficial to encourage debates and contestations within the religious political discourse in Muslim contexts, particularly between male and female ideologues on the issue and place of women's rights. However, such competitive struggles also tend to pit the perceived 'good Muslim woman' who adheres to the more literal, conservative visions of male orthodoxy against the challenging 'bad

Muslim woman'. But since, according to the new rules of feminist engagement, these conversations now cannot take place outside of the faith-based discourse, it sets up an impasse where Muslim women cannot represent themselves from any perspective other than that of their ascribed faith.

The proposals for a new feminism are useful in an epistemological sense but are not necessarily pertinent to materialist analyses. The critique of modernist feminism and of human rights activism in Pakistan has taken exception to the monopoly of "liberal-secular" Non-Governmental Organisations (NGOs) and their rights-based campaigns over the last thirty years. Although, NGOs have been the favourite ideological punching bag of the conservatives and liberals alike – albeit for different reasons – post-9/11 scholarship also targets the liberal agendas of these rights-based NGOs. Unlike the religio-nationalists, however, these scholars do not criticise libertarian-based development work simply for being Westernised attempts to subvert Islamic culture and the Muslim social order. Rather, they are reproached for excluding faith as a rational, viable motivational source for social and political development. Such proposals do not account for the various development organisations that have been reengineering their projects to include faith-based strategies in their programmes, in order to avail of the pool of funds reserved for such an approach to development in Pakistan (A.S. Zia 2011a). They do not account for the broader social influence and impact of this strategy of embedding "progressive Islam", even as it purports to be in service of interpreting gender relations and for an indigenous resolution of discriminatory practices. Also unresolved is the consequence of narrowing available choices for women by limiting the selection of empowerment strategies exclusively within a faith-based framework, and excluding other secular tools or strategic positioning that may be more effective in order to challenge patriarchal politics.

Summary

This chapter has identified the weaknesses in liberal resistance to religious militancy and faith-based conservatism but also challenges the allegations that Pakistani feminists invite imperialism by critiquing misogyny in Muslim contexts. It has cited examples of this scholarship that tends to prioritise a sympathetic analysis of the complexities of those who violate women's rights over strategies for justice for their victims. Attention has been drawn to how such criticism is indicative of a deliberate elision over the complexities involved in activist work and the mundane issues feminists have to deal with, broker over and negotiate with – whether these are with state enforcement agencies, political male resistance and/or customary practices. Many of the violators of rights often collude with or take refuge behind discriminatory Islamic laws and hegemonic readings of religion, which lends its patriarchal bias for such purposes. The call for feminist silence on human rights abuses in Pakistan, regardless of the timing or historical context is tantamount to exonerating this historical and collusive continuity and is in line with what is common in conservative nationalist and Islamist rhetoric.

Those scholars who endorse Islamists' agency and seek to redefine their complexities invalidate the legitimacy of liberal-feminist designs and question their success but seem not to hold Islamist women accountable by any measurement or criteria. The only defence seems to be that Islamist women do not have to aspire to rights or Western liberal frameworks of progress. Docility may be a form of contentment and a viable state of citizenry but when Islamist women actively pursue patriarchal, conservative, censorious and anti-women, anti-minority policies, then their agency should be examined for its effects and impact at the same time, rather than simply romanticised as different and non-Westernised. If Islamist women are supported in their promotion of an institutional, masculinist conservatism and this is rationalised as a viable course from the choices available to them (Iqtidar 2011b, Bano 2012b), then liberals should be considered equally within their right to resist the same. The reasoning would be that the opposition to liberal desires is an encroachment on their equally valid, localised, authentic aspirations chosen from the classical rational discourse.

Islamists embrace Western modernity and all its tools and products – from Islamic banking, cyber activism, Youtube *tabligh* (missionary work), Islamic portals for cell phone subscribers and hijab shampoos. When Islamists harness the probability of the market for worldly modern gains this is celebrated by their defenders. Surely, then, this should disqualify the criticism reserved for liberals in Pakistan and their (modern) ambitions, values, ideas and pursuits, regardless of their source in this globalised world. Either way, the reduction of political struggle to performativity, consumerism or inner empowerment is a serious shortcoming within both, liberal and Islamist analyses, as currently rehearsed in Pakistani scholarship on the subject of women and Islamic politics. The former is not political enough while the latter is limited and confined to a patriarchal framework.

Beyond Faith and Fatalism: Political Agency and Women's Secular Movements

The relationship between academic notions of agency and the political implications of such proposals with reference to pietist/Islamist women and their politics in Pakistan has been discussed prior. One key and contrasting example of working women's movements, the Lady Health Workers of Pakistan and their secular modes of activism, was discussed in Chapter 3. Further examples of working women's movements that demonstrate political rather than religious agency are now documented from secondary sources. These women have deployed agency for emancipatory ends, political power, using a liberal vocabulary, lay legal aid and secular means. These are referenced here to demonstrate that Muslim women in Islamic republics actively engage gendered agency towards secular ends, often successfully, and that piety and faith-based movements are not the only subject-formations that are available to them.

Saba Mahmood and her adherents are committed to the model of docile agency as a form of gendered Islamic virtue on a theoretical level and one that is permanently outside of the trope of liberal politics. The movements discussed challenge Mahmood's (2001) focus on Muslim women's agency as a "performance of gendered Islamic virtues" (203) by demonstrating that Muslim women also perform, aspire to and struggle towards gendered *secular or universalist* virtues often in resistance to religion and piety. These movements are complementary examples to the findings of other studies, such as the one conducted by Magnus Marsden (2008), of Chitrali women of north Pakistan who he found, "live vocal, risk-taking lives, and play an active and public role in their region's intellectual and political life" (407). Marsden notes that the price of privileging an emphasis on how Muslims embody subjectivities in relationship to Islamic traditions of self-discipline is the oversight of the complexity and significance of multiple and diverse modes of self-presentation and "being Muslim" (426). His study of Chitrali women's engagement and critical intellectual prowess in challenging Islamic virtuosity reveals a risky strategy undertaken by these women that is not defined by piety but in fact, challenges the authority of Islam's men of piety (418).

If liberal feminist politics has enabled anything in Pakistan, it has been to offer non-feminist women a channel of struggle and expectations of equal rights through activism that is not limited, facilitated or filtered through religious discourse. However, very often, they have been directly opposed by religious fundamentalism, Islamist politics, the Islamic state and, men across political divides. This has inspired an organisational resistance by women and various forms of this opposition have been channelled through liberal, secular and feminist methods to overcome conservative, faith-based and patriarchal obstacles.

The purpose of documenting these examples is simply to demonstrate how political activism in Muslim contexts often does not rely on religion/religious identities but plays a critical role for women's progress. Many of the issues that inform these movements engage with the broader challenges taken up by women's activism in Pakistan. These are discussed here in order to contextualise and contrast the practice of divine sourcing and peddling of religion with liberal and/or, secular paradigms in many Muslim states and societies and to examine the consequences. To foreclose the option and vantage of pursuing liberal/secular methods or ends through political or academic means is a serious omission. To slight or dismiss advocacy/advocates of liberal ideals or secularism in Muslim contexts is also to deny the possible benefits accrued to neutral citizens who may just be indifferent to faith and instead be invested in secular strategies and ends. Such endeavour may simply be motivated by the more compelling and rational means associated with material progress or identity-formation for them.

The chapter therefore begins with an example of the conceptual limitations of the 'docile agency' theory when it is extended beyond academia and applied in context and in 'play'. Following this, two nation-wide working women's movements are documented to emphasise working women's secular resistance, demonstrating how religious actors and patriarchal considerations directly impede women's progress in this regard.

Contested Expectations

In the 1980s, the women's movement in Pakistan excavated the hidden stories of women's lives and documented their struggles for equality despite the constraints of religious and cultural patriarchies (Mumtaz and Shaheed 1987; Khan 1992; Khan et al. (eds.) 1994). Subsequently (and for South Asia, under the influence of Subaltern Studies), the idea of women's "agency" under these restrictive conditions became more tempered with cultural flavours. Studies became more introspective with their attention turning to how women, even within oppressive structures, embodied means that helped in subverting obstacles or to changing their lives. As Michel Foucault became more influential in the academy and feminist thinking, the idea of agency as a dialectical effect of freedom and constraint suggested that agency always accompanied oppression. This thinking became apparent in feminist activism, which then called attention for the need to reconsider women who had faced violence as survivors – not victims. Simultaneously, a challenge to the emancipatory meaning attached to agency came by way of those survivors of violence who chose to return to abusive relationships or continued to value patriarchal institutions.

The concept of agency has also been re-evaluated with reference to women's choices regarding sex work, the media, glamour and the fashion industry as well as in the choice to veil. Such voluntary exercise of agency in order to maximise opportunities for a new generation of women threw a challenge to modernist feminists who were concerned about how such agency was blocking the transformative possibilities of any feminist gains, by the reinforcement of and benefit to patriarchy and capitalism. The responsive question became, should agency be limited to expression, performance, self-determination and narratives of the self and be redefined according to context, rather than as a means to emancipatory socialist and/or feminist ends?

The debates described in this book around the themes of faith and feminism have revolved around the pivot of "agency", too. For those who are more cautionary over the fetishisation of agency, scholars such as Sadia Abbas (2013) suggest that perhaps "'agency' has become the name of that which is exceptional, which exists in the crevices and interstices of the law" (28). In fact, Abbas suggests that agency seems to have become "a substitute for rights" and implicit in this suggestion that "it is *the* law which is always already (and apparently forever) given" (28). In the light of Islamic militancy that has raged in Pakistan following the waging of the "WoT" from 2001, the notion of Muslim women's agency with reference to Islam has encouraged quite specific gendered readings with reference to agency. Two different readings that demonstrate the ideological lens through which agency may be viewed are provided by postsecularist scholar, Humeira Iqtidar (2009), on the one hand, and those of US-based Professor, Sana Haroon (2011) and feminist researcher, Nazish Brohi (2012), on the other.

In 2009, some analysts were still arguing that there was no such force as the "Taliban" in conflict-ridden Swat. Instead, such views attributed such a misrepresentation of the *mujahideen* (engaged in jihad) to be the result of a media campaign bent on "distorting" the "complex reality in restive Pakistan" (Iqtidar 2009 online). At this time, the Taliban had not just claimed the identity and announced their organisation as the *Tehreeq e Taliban Pakistan* (TTP) but were also maintaining a healthy relationship with the media as a source for releasing regular press announcements through alternative but also, mainstream channels. Despite being declared a banned organisation by the Government of Pakistan since 2008, the TTP was also regularly given airtime on some TV channels to present their agendas directly.

The background to militancy in Swat valley in Khyber Pakhtunkhwa dates to the 1990s when it used to be a stronghold of the *Tehreeq e Nifaz e Sharia e Muhammad* (TNSM – Movement for the Enforcement of Sharia), created in the name of implementing Sharia in the district of Malakand. This internationally famed tourist resort turned into a site of armed militancy soon after the US overthrow of the Taliban regime in Afghanistan in 2001. Iqtidar (2009 online) insists that the call for supporting the Taliban in Afghanistan by leader of the TNSM, Sufi Muhammad, "received a lukewarm response from the Afghan Taliban leader Mullah Omar" (the latter released from a Pakistani prison in 2008 due to lack of evidence for his terrorist acts). However, most reports agree with the account that "thousands of TNSM followers crossed into Afghanistan who had been fighting alongside the Taliban against the U.S.-led Coalition. The TNSM lost most of its cadres during U.S. raids in Afghanistan and only a few survived, including Sufi Muhammad, the TNSM leader, and his son-in-law Mullah Fazlullah" (Brohi 2012, unpaged).

Soon after his take-over of Swat in 2006, Fazlullah established a Sharia court that operated the Taliban interpretation of Islamic law with particularly harsh sentences on suspected fornication and theft. A public morality squad was activated and Fazlullah became known as "mullah radio", since his main outreach tool was an illegal FM radio channel through which he preached regularly. In fact, it was through his radio sermons that the women of Swat first encountered his movement directly. Iqtidar (2009 online) argues that the motivation behind Fazlullah's campaign was not so much religious as much as it was to institute certain "mechanisms [albeit] misguided, open to abuse and problematic" that would bypass Pakistan's "heavily biased" judicial system and to ensure speedy justice for the people of the area. Interestingly, at this time, the entire country was witnessing a nation-wide Lawyers' Movement (2007–2009) for the restoration of the deposed Chief Justice and judicial independence of the lay courts. The movement nearly paralysed the country's courts for over a year and was marked with spectacular sit-ins, protest, constitutional debates and campaigns that raged across all the provinces in a unique movement. The country had not witnessed such a phenomenon since the Movement for the Restoration of Democracy of the 1980s. Aitzaz Ahsan, the lead lawyer and Parliamentarian who had spearheaded this movement, has consistently claimed that this was exemplary of a "peaceful and secular movement" (Chopan-Daud 2012). Ahsan is cited in the *Harvard Law Review* for claiming that "the broader aspect of the movement is the dream that has been placed in the eyes of people in the form of a transformed state" (HLR 2010, 1726). At no point over the two years of this movement was there a single call by the protestors and followers (despite the broad spectrum of political affiliation in the Pakistan Bar Association and a conservative judiciary) or by commentators and citizens, for Sharia justice or Islamic laws, modes or values as the driving motivation or ultimate end. There were no slogans, nor props nor references to religion during the entire movements across rural and urban Pakistan. All this is despite the enormous backlog of pending cases in Pakistan's "biased" judicial system and an overall despair over the inability of a corrupt and inefficient judiciary to dispense speedy justice to the poor (Rehman 2011, "Backlog of Over 1.35m Cases 'Haunts' the Judiciary," *Pakistan Today*, Aug. 30). Despite the consensual acceptance of the limitations and weaknesses of a weak lay justice system, this did not lead to a call for its replacement by an Islamic one. The slogan of the movement was, in fact, the demand for due application of (the liberal principle of) the 'Rule of Law'.

Several of these street protests held by the lawyers and members of civil society were targeted by suicide bombings as part of a series of such attacks by Islamic militants (and claimed by the Taliban) between 2007 and 2009. The argument is not whether the Lawyers' Movement was a target for militants or not, but rather the point here is that this challenges the proposal that the TNSM was a movement that emerged purely as a misguided but representative response to the demand for speedy justice. If anything, the singular religious motivations behind the TNSM demand was in stark contrast to the parallel nation-wide secular movement for judicial correction, which was in support of the lay courts and its officials and towards improved judicial equity.

Provoked and encouraged by the *Lal Masjid* siege in Islamabad in 2007 (see Chapter 4), Taliban commander, Mullah Fazlullah, declared war against the Pakistani security forces which led to armed clashes between Fazlullah's militia and the army. This was followed by the usual cycle of post-conflict peace deals.[1] In 2009, after a similar round of terrorist attacks and subsequent peace talks there were several warnings by commentators (and particularly, women's rights activists) that the accession of the *Nizam e Adl* (Regulations for Justice) or a separate justice system for the Malakand Division would be tantamount to "constitutional suicide" on the part of the state. Despite that, Pakistan's Parliament (with no debate) approved the peace deal with the TNSM in 2009.[2] Within days, the Taliban in Swat moved further, taking control of the local administration, police and schools.

Sufi Muhammad, who is often termed "a moderate", went on to declare that democracy and the legal system of Pakistan should be dismantled immediately since they were all "systems of infidels" (Farooq 2009, "MPs Who Opposed Nizam-e-Adl Are No Longer Muslims: Sufi," *Daily Times*, April 18). The Taliban in Swat quickly grew in force (estimated at more than eight thousand fighters), blew up approximately 122 girls' schools, implemented a Sharia which allowed for executions, floggings, and ruled against women leaving their homes and killed with impunity all those families that had earlier resisted them. Public hangings of prostitutes and barbers[3] were followed by a display of their bodies in public squares to serve as a warning of the fate of any future such transgression. These practices soon spread into the adjoining districts of Buner, Shangla, and Dir.

In contrast to the brutal reports of the actual Swat take-over by the Taliban, there is the blurry and somewhat romanticised secondary source analysis of the Swat conflict that posits Fazlullah as a kind of Che Guevara, leading a revolution that resonated with the historical peasant uprisings in the region. Despite the disclaimer that it would be "a stretch to see the TSNM [sic] in Swat as the heirs of these older peasant movements," still, this perspective is confident that "their legacy no doubt lingers in the restive region" (Iqtidar 2009 online). The works of Sana Haroon (2011) and Nazish Brohi (2012), on the other hand, are based on direct observation and research conducted in what Iqtidar calls a "restive" region, over the period of the conflict. The contrast in methodology and findings are not the concern, as much as what is emphasised in the comparative analyses.

Haroon's (2011 online) analysis of the social acceptance of the Taliban in parts of north-west Pakistan suggests that this depended on the "overlap between already existing gender norms and Taliban prescriptions." She goes on to argue that soon after the Taliban takeover,

> far from describing a system of passive capitulation before the agenda of the religious right wing, . . . conversations [with women for her research] bear testimony to the degree of recognition and awareness of the threat of brutality that the Taliban movement poses to women, and the ways in which it challenges traditional familial prerogatives through direct interference in domestic norms and relations. (Haroon 2011 online)

Haroon (2011) also references the historical connection between Islamist militancy and mainstream Islamists in noting that Sufi Muhammad was one time member of Pakistan's *Jamaat e Islami* and that under him, the TNSM "developed in parallel to the Taliban in Afghanistan." Unlike Iqtidar, she does not blur the nexus between mainstream Islamist and militant movements and also observes that in emulating the Taliban, Sufi Muhammad's intent was quite clearly to impose a specific form of Sharia. If we accept that Sufi Muhammad's interpretation of the Sharia was "misguided" – as Iqtidar puts it – then he was not the only one guilty of imprudence.[4]

The inability to make the distinction with the same clarity that Iqtidar offers in her definition, between Sharia as a broader imaginary and that of the quantifiable rigidity of Islamic law, eluded many women of Swat too – at least, initially. In the early years of Fazlullah's radio broadcasts, women gravitated towards his sermons and confessed that he inspired them with his spiritedness and which made them support his call for the implementation of Sharia across the country. Iqtidar considers this responsiveness to be proof of women's paradoxical embrace of public piety, despite the fact that the burden of this project falls on women. Brohi's (2012, unpaged) interviews suggest that in fact, Fazlullah's movement provided the women "a space in which they acquired social legitimacy for overriding the decision of men in their families." Iqtidar's definition of agency may be said to fall under Mahmood's (2005) definition of docile peitist agency, while Brohi's is more descriptive of a dormant, political and even feminist agency, awaiting a catalyst.

Brohi notes that her discussions with women supporters of Fazlullah (who were also councillors in the local government structure in 2003–2004) showed that most women did not, in fact, know what exactly Sharia law was. Brohi notes that the women councillors she interviewed had not read any literature on the Sharia and were not familiar with any Islamic scholars on the subject or the debates over interpretations. She notes that their demand for Sharia symbolised a stand-in for justice, development, progress and peace and that Fazlullah convinced them that the Sharia law provides for this in literal terms. For these women, Islamic history held the promise of economic prosperity and social cohesion for Muslims. This direct observation that documents the *economic and social expectations* associated with their agentive decision to initially support the Taliban, challenges the presumption that the women of Swat were blindly driven by faith to invite some entity called the 'Sharia', or under some prospective knowledge that they would be carrying its "burden" and without hopes for any temporal returns.

In contrast to Iqtidar's (2009) reading of the case of an alleged public flogging by the Taliban of a young woman which was caught on a cell phone video and widely circulated in 2009 (see Chapter 4), Haroon (2011) maintains that the Taliban's strategic combination of a complete ban of women in public spaces, along with their threat to slander any woman who defied their prohibitions, led to copy-cat attacks on women in other districts. Iqtidar's readings of the "sensationalisation" of this flogging case leads her to make the defensive and inaccurate claim that similar violations against women by secular, landed politicians do not receive as much media attention or outraged response by liberal groups. This is a completely false proposal. Just a few months before the flogging case, soon after a liberal civilian government came to power, two high profile cases involving the landed politicians of the ruling party were equally "sensationally" splashed across the media (for example, "Sherry Condemns Killing of Khairpur Girl," *DT*, Oct. 28, 2008; "Civil Society Protests Honour Killing of Women," *DT* 2008, Sept. 2; and Zakaria 2008, "Six Pakistani Women," *Daily Times*, Sept. 6). With reference to one of these cases of the alleged 'live burial' of girls who refused their arranged marriages, Pakistani women's groups lobbied, protested and came on TV channels demanding the removal of the cabinet minister responsible for the constituency since he defended such "traditions" and offered these as a justification for the crime.

To suggest that religious militancy is the only crime that is picked up by the media or liberal groups is a deliberate deflection. The spectacle of the flogging caught on video made the case more visual and so caused more outrage, as did the case where a young girl was allegedly mauled by dogs as part of retributive justice in Sindh. This defensiveness stems from a more common refrain used by the apologists of Islamists' politics of violence – that secular political forces are no better. Feminists, including myself, have persistently made this critique of not only liberal, secular men, but also of the state as an abuser of the political potential of women's bodies and also because such acts sanction a regulation of women's sexuality and all its manifestation. Interestingly, the Taliban themselves refuse the offer of historical context, socio-economic conditions or traditions as an excuse for their militancy. Perhaps it is time for scholars to go beyond the religious-politics-as-a-product-of-false-consciousness claim, particularly when they are critical of liberal readings that apply such theories regarding Islamist politics. It may also be appropriate to not always play the interlocutor for Islamist agency and instead, to also recognise the validity of the self-acclaimed and conscious motives and activism of religious militants, too.

Pakistani feminist researcher, Nazish Brohi (2012) observes that:

> The Swat conflict has also been of particular interest because of preliminary gendered readings: whereas the Pakistani Taliban curtailed women's rights, restricted their mobility, prohibited girls' education and in some cases, brutally assaulted women, evidence is often bandied about to show that women were partly responsible for this as they supported the Taliban movement not just by being a receptive audience but also by being active contributors through financial contributions. (unpaged)

Brohi conducted interviews with women in Swat in April 2011, two years after the military offensive against Fazlullah's militia ended. She found that in the years since the first interactions, the opinions of those women who had confessed their initial support for him had changed. The women were now opposed to the demands for Sharia and condemned Fazlullah and his militia. They spoke of the horrors and brutality they had witnessed against their family and community and said that "such ruthless tortures could not have been inspired by religion and that its invocation was a farce." They referred to Fazlullah as "the 'fitna' [chaos] who had brought 'azaab' [tribulations] onto them" (Brohi 2012). Brohi suggests that hindsight allowed women to process the motivation behind their earlier support and participation in Fazlullah's movement differently than they had done earlier. She notes that "through discussions among themselves, they were able to state in hindsight that a significant motivation for them was being given the public recognition as important actors – the notion of agency" (Brohi 2012 unpaged). She describes agency here as "the process of being addressed directly, the dignity of being an actor in their and their community's development was the fundamental reason women became involved." In his radio broadcasts, Fazlullah spoke to women directly and accredited them with agency. The interviewed women confessed about how their opinions were never solicited by the men in their families and communities. This made them feel irrelevant and marginalised from all decision-making and it was in this context that "Fazlullah created a discourse in which women were positioned as the most important decision-makers" (Brohi 2012).

Added to this was the promise of an increase in women's status in the future, since Fazlullah would announce the contributions to his cause that women had collected together in his radio broadcasts, as well as acknowledging individual contributions, whether of gold or money. Brohi argues that these women sought the prayers and blessings of one who they considered a religious leader, but also that "the status, acknowledgment of agency and recognition of their contribution to a wider cause" were equally compelling factors in their support (Brohi 2012). This circumvention of the approval of their husbands and families even led to a few divorces by their husbands who sent back money they earned from working in other countries as labourers.

In contrast to Iqtidar's readings of the allure of Fazlullah's offensive in Swat as representative of a response to the need for speedy justice, Brohi notes that it was the men she talked to who stated that the Swat Taliban's agenda of speedy dispensation of justice was among the main reasons they had been receptive to the militants. However, when she put this same question to the women, they pointed out that they had no connection with state institutions (such as law, police and judiciary) and that "justice issues for them were dealt *within the home*" (Brohi 2012, unpaged, emphasis added). According to these women, the explanation for this domestic injustice lay in the fact that they had no space or voice within their homes and communities. Fazlullah's rhetoric positioned women differently, as important actors with agency. By admission, these women's own ignorance on Sharia meant that even after the military offensive was over and Fazlullah and the Taliban were ousted from Swat, they were not sure whether his vision was in accord with Islamic law or not. However, Brohi records these women's collective testimony whereby they claimed that "even if such punishments and codes of conduct led to rewards in the afterlife, they no longer supported it or wanted it, because it led to an increase in their present suffering" (Brohi 2012).

Brohi argues for an unpacking of the appeal of collective political articulation of religion in contemporary society in Pakistan and suggests that "while faith addresses different individual needs – catharsis, therapy, divine guidance, approval, identity, hope in face of desperation . . . such. . . . faith-based political aspirations of groups and [] individual needs [often] dovetail into larger collective demands such as that for Sharia law" (Brohi 2012). In the case of the Swat women's initial support for Fazlullah's campaign and demand for Sharia, Brohi argues that this was reflective of the myriad issues women face and demands and aspirations they have, which would include social justice, economic prosperity, physical well-being, autonomy and agency.

This would suggest that the desires, motivation and resonance of such agency are in reference to pragmatic, secular needs rather than simply a reflection or expression of some aspiration for faith-based/spiritual transcendence. When it "became obvious that the militant movement proposing Sharia was not fulfilling these demands, the women withdrew their support – heavenly rewards notwith-standing" (Brohi 2012). The women did not aspire to study Islamic exegesis – just to improve in terms of quality of life. This is in contrast to the popular analyses that relate to people's demands for an increasing role of religion in politics in theocratic terms, or aspirations for religiosity.

The women councillors interviewed in the Brohi study reflected on their political actions and termed it "misplaced agency", based as they were on Fazlullah's sermons which promised them decision-making powers, property rights, and *haq mehr* [promissory gift or brideswealth]. He had also acknowledged them as stakeholders in the future and this, the women admit, led them to make the mistake of supporting him. In the light of her research, Brohi considers the analyses that emphasises the Swat women's initial support of the Taliban to be "simplistic assessments" of it being a case of women expressing agency with disastrous results and argues that instead, this support "represented something far more insidious and corrosive: the absence of women's sense of citizenship and control over their lives" (Brohi 2012). Like Haroon (2011), Brohi argues that this support in fact showcased how local patriarchies get endorsed and replicated by external actors, including by civil society organisations ostensibly supporting women, further closing off the minimal spaces available to women and leaving them with radical extremes as alternatives. Brohi argues that it is important to acknowledge women's agency under all conditions but that it must be differentiated from feminist agency and that "women's rights must be protected and given due considerations in mainstream governance concerns else, counterintuitive contexts will continue to emerge" (Brohi 2012).

The Rescue Narrative

The "WoT" has thrown up a wide-ranging set of criticism from a gendered perspective. Most prominent were Abu-Lughod's, "Do Muslim Women Really Need Saving?" (2002), Hirschkind and Mahmood's, "Feminism, Taliban and the Politics of Counter-Insurgency" (2002) and later, Hunt and Rygiel's book *Engendering the War on Terror* (2006). Avatar Brah and Ann Phoenix (2004) called for recognising the dangers of homogenising the category of 'woman', in this case, the oppressed Muslim Woman, and how the "WoT" had reinforced the divisions between different groups of women and privileged some while oppressing others.

Much of this literature has looked to return the gaze on (international and domestic) governing elites and exposes the falsity of the rescue narrative woven around victimised Muslim women. Some activist-scholars have even critiqued the convenient link made between women's advancement and a post-war reconstruction that has been based on a neo-liberal economic agenda. This was the one that promised Afghan women benefits of some trickle down economics as low paid workers, producing traditional goods for the global market. Deniz Kandiyoti (2009 online) scrutinises how neo-liberal economics and cultural essentialism have informed the "WoT" narrative and resulted in what she calls, "pragmatic activism". She argues that such cultural essentialism of the Afghan Muslim woman has informed gender targeted development agendas in Afghanistan. The results of such essentialism have also been observed in their influence over many USAID-funded NGO projects in Afghanistan and Pakistan and which have encouraged an instrumentalisation of Islam in development programmes in both countries.

All the caution advised in this post-9/11 literature is with reference to military interventions that serve imperial interests under the guise of humanitarian and liberatory rhetoric and are invaluable. There is however, a tendency in some of the anti-war literature to privilege anti-imperialist anxiety over gendered readings of local patriarchies. This makes any defence of women's human rights that may be "coterminous with efforts to critique misogynist "Muslim extremism"" (Akbar and Oza 2013, 166) a casualty. The affiliated call for a hiatus in prioritising gender because of its availability for the justification of imperialist adventures, argues that routine and unexceptional systems of violence and injustice may be recognised but not attended to until the 'telos' of "after imperialism, after racism, after the end of pain, of death, perhaps when we are restored to some pre-lapsarian future" (Abbas 2014, 58).

Secular feminists in Pakistan face double jeopardy in the new anthropological turn in the field and interest on women and Islam. On the one hand, some of the post-9/11 theses outlined above, privilege imperialism and Islamophobia over local patriarchies and therefore, accuse Muslim liberal feminists of encouraging and aligning themselves with imperialist adventures by virtue of their campaigns and activism against local patriarchal abuse. This is especially the case because the intersections of cultural and religious practices are so intricately intertwined and mutually beneficial. On the other hand, liberal feminists are confronted by a new Islamic feminist discourse that refuses to view women as victims of culture and/or religion, and subverts oppressive social practices by redefining them as enabling instead. Wilful conformity with patriarchal traditions and practices is read as an act of free will. Women's activism and exercise of agency *within* the framework of patriarchy is recognised and celebrated as long as it remains within the prescribed limits of male-defined cultural and religious boundaries. Occasionally, these limits may be challenged through pietist practises but political transformation of the structures of power that define gender relations is not a feasible goal or aspiration for Muslim women. The academic work that corresponds with such narratives enables a reconsideration of what counts as 'political' through a redefinition of agency, liberty and freedoms by depending on a rejection of Western liberalism and secularism.

Less addressed in this new literature is how agency can be a slippery commodity. Women who may feel empowered by either pietist or faith-based movements may very well experience disempowerment from the same source – as did the women of Swat. Feminists in Pakistan have tracked and critiqued secular male politics not just on its own terms but in fact, for colluding with religio-political groups and parties and agreeing on a ban that disallowed women in northwest Pakistan from voting in national polls, based on tribal tradition which does not recognise women's enfranchisement. Recognition of women's agency with all its contradictions and paradoxes and which may reject liberal empowerment is not a revelation to women in Muslim contexts, despite the excitement that such 'leaked' revelation may have caused in Western academia. For feminists and activists in countries such as Pakistan, it is the instrumentalisation of this agency that is far more relevant and particularly, how its expression through the partners of conservatism and religion displaces liberal and secular aspirations and possibilities.

Necessarily, sourcing and peddling divinity, however contested, trumps liberal/secular paradigms in many Muslim states and societies. To foreclose the latter framings further is an injustice, not just to the advocates of the secular politics but also to those who may be indifferent to faith. To deny liberal politics as an option for men and women in Muslim contexts is to deny them the right to authentic citizenry in accordance with their equally "complex lived realities" and their experiences and "subjectivities", living as they do, under theocratic orthodoxies.

Women in Organised Politics

Women activists' expectation of the Pakistani state to act as a neutral arbiter of competing interests is tempered by the realisation that it is also often complicit in, and even an initiator of anti-women practices. Therefore, in 2000, the Devolution of Power Plan, (subsequently the Local Government Ordinance, LGO 2001) introduced under Musharraf, seemed to be a perfect opportunity for women to become directly absorbed and influential at all tiers of political decision-making in the country. Under the LGO, Musharraf introduced the reservation of 33 percent seats of women in all three tiers of local government. A further 17 percent representation for women was reserved in national and provincial assemblies. These women were to be elected through a proportional representation system. The initial scepticism about women not being willing to form a political cadre was largely put to rest with the nomination of 67,000 women in the first local body election under devolution in 2001. The reservations enabled 36,105 women to enter formal politics at the local government level in the first round in 2002. Of these, 126 women were elected on seats reserved for minorities and 16 as *Nazims* (Mayors) and/or *Naib Nazims* (Deputy Mayors) in different councils. For the 2005 local government elections, the overall numbers of seats were reduced at union council levels and so a reduced number of 28,550 women returned to local government through the reservation system.

Some well-grounded critiques have emerged about these women's state of preparedness of taking on the challenge of electoral politics at the local and national levels, including concerns over the advantages of women from political families or those who were said to have benefitted from and therefore, remained proxies of male politicians. There were also concerns expressed about the lack of class- or gender-consciousness among the new women representatives. Some even cautioned that women's legally mandated inclusion in political processes must also be read in conjunction with the context of General Musharraf's 'liberal' military rule, whereby women had become among the leading metaphors for an enlightened, moderate Pakistani state and its 'soft' image. However, the 33 percent reservation of seats for women came in a context of a wider historical effort of state feminism. These included unprecedented legislative quotas, government-wide reform initiatives (including several donor-supported programmes such as the Gender Reform Action Plan) and changes in certain discriminatory laws like the *Hudood* Ordinances, as well as the outlawing of some customary forms of violence against women. The unintended consequences of such 'managed' empowerment became evident in the experiences of the Women Councillors' Network and the activities of its members over the next decade.

The formation of the Women Councillors' Network (WCN) has been termed a unique experience in the political history of Pakistan. The majority of women councillors were first time entrants into electoral politics and indeed, into public service, and many came with limited educational background, political exposure and skills. The politics of opening up political space for women in the local government, through the reservation of seats by the authoritarian military regime had a contradictory meaning and impact. Also, the institutional context of the local government was male-dominated. Women councillors faced tremendous patriarchal resistance in claiming their legitimate right and space to perform their roles effectively in local governance.

Due to strong institutional resistance at the local level, women councillors quickly realised that the only way forward to counter public patriarchy was through their collective voice and will. Pattan Development Organisation, which is a left-leaning NGO and managed by one of the leading feminist activists in Pakistan, played an early role in supporting women councillors on their idea to form a collective forum in order to have an independent power base. Over the last decade, Pattan has guided these councillors in establishing a cross-party women councillors network (WCN) and facilitated them through tremendous capacity building support to assume a leadership role (F. Bari 2009).

The WCN is the only nationwide, membership-based and democratically elected network in the country that has effectively aggregated and articulated women's interest in the local government. The WCN had played a remarkable role in helping women at the local level and raising their concerns within and outside local government institutions. The documentation of the history of activism of the WCN clearly demonstrates the "voice agency of women councillors and their ability to make cracks in the system despite all socio-cultural, political and institutional challenges to their participation and representation in public life" (S. Bari 2010). The experience of the WCN is the story of courage, commitment and collective will. Their proven ability to push institutional boundaries and to create space for their own agenda through mobilisation and organisation of women, provides for rich learning and even celebration. The WCN demonstrated that networking amongst the socially excluded and marginalised and encouraging them to raise a collective voice was the kind of agency and action that proved to be one of the most important pathways to women's political empowerment. Over time, these councillors began to link patriarchal obstructions with state policies (which included the discriminatory Islamic laws and procedures in cases of violence against women) and they protested against the absence of state interest or policies for women's social, political or economic equality.

Between 2001 and 2005, these councillors were found demonstrating and lobbying for rights which spilled beyond the direct concerns of their local councils but were still linked to women's issues. The ambition was to influence the national discourse on women's issues. In contrast to such political possibilities, the experiences of women councillors in the conflict-ridden areas of north-west Pakistan (see above) serve as a direct comment on the limitations of women's political agency when religious and cultural patriarchies overlap and operate under imperial and domestic collusive militarisation of a society. Although on ideological terms the religious parties that formed the *Muttahida Majlis Amal* (MMA) in 2002 opposed the notion of women's services in public office, they did support the increase of reserved seats for women in the national and provincial legislative assemblies. However, after the 2002 local body elections and prior to the following one in 2005, religious parties ruling the province of (now) Khyber Pakhtunkhwa convened a meeting where an election agreement was signed by the representatives of different parties to keep women away from contesting the polls. In Swabi, Mardan and Dir districts, women were not just prevented from filling their nomination paper but from even casting votes. In the Malakand division, religious leaders gathered to declare that the *Nikah* (solemnisation of marriage), *Namaaz-e-Janaza* (funeral prayers) and all other religious rites of any women candidates and/or, woman voter would be boycotted (S. Bano 2009). Some women councillors in Dir were prevented from carrying out their duties and the male relatives of these women would attend council sessions on their behalf.

The contrast of the documented experiences and achievements of the women councillors (which went beyond just the delivery of basic services to their communities with a specific focus on women's needs) should be read against the backdrop of a combined cultural and religious patriarchal resistance to their participation and work through the entire process. This resistance however, was not just the normative expression of patriarchies associated with tribal cultures and theocratic governance systems. Much of the backlash against any progress, mobility and achievements that could have been facilitated through the increased devolution of decision-making and effective improvements at the grass-root council levels came by way of virulent campaigns of Islamic militants against women, minorities and their perceived 'secular' modes of life, particularly in the northern areas of Pakistan. This is not to suggest that there were not limitations and serious flaws in the local government structure, including bureaucratic hurdles, financial mismanagement and considerable political reluctance to devolve actual powers to local representatives. Or indeed, that there were no obstacles by way of non-faith-based patriarchal attitudes. However, for women councillors in particular, the growing threats that came by way of the narrative of militancy that grew in strength under the governance of the Islamist governments in Khyber Pakhtunkhwa peaked in 2007. By this time, preventing women from voting in Lower Dir, Kohistan, Battagram, Upper Dir, Swabi and Mardan in the 2005 by elections, as well as prohibition from contesting the reserved seat for women in Kohistan and other areas in the Khyber Pakhthunkhwa province, were lesser concerns. By this time, Maulana Fazlullah had already unleashed his campaign against basic medical services in the Swat region and also declared that educating girls in state schools was un-Islamic. The threat campaign issued to teachers of girls' schools was not dissimilar to that instituted against the health workers (Chapter 3), where threatening letters warning individual targets were sent to the identified schools and homes of faculty members.

It is easy to dismiss the "extremist" Islamists by pretending that such radical practices took place in what was otherwise normalcy, or as a post-dated expression of some anti-imperialist momentum. However, the political environment of Khyber Pakhtunkhwa enabled the embedding of militancy to occur firmly and unchecked under the rule of the Islamists who governed the province at the time. During their rule, the range of Islamist parties that made up the MMA were competitively dedicated to promoting their political Islamisation programme in the province where they formed government. In exchange for their collaboration with General Musharraf, they earned the freedom to change the very political and cultural landscape of the province. This was not only through the political access given to them by Musharraf to operate as a legitimate government in the province, but through an aggressive campaign to change its very social (previously secular) fabric.

The MMA government delivered no development but did implant a conducive theocratic environment that was ripe for the more radical force that was the *Tehreeq e Taliban Pakistan*. It was always naïve to hope that censure from the supposed "moderate" mainstream religious parties would somehow counter the Taliban offensive, thereafter. Subsequently, the federal government's appeals to the mainstream religious leaders to declare that suicide bombing and prohibiting girls' education was not the preferable way to legitimately pursue the Islamic agenda, was simply an eye wash. After assuming power in Khyber Pakhtunkhwa, the cultural agenda of the Islamist political parties had focused on issues such as prescribing prohibitive and restrictive gender roles, a morality police, gender segregation, shutting down of women's shelters, attacks on NGOs under the suspicion of being spy agencies, ban on music and film and policies that stressed the domestication of women and dress/appearance codes, even for men. The elected Islamist parties were complicit in campaigns pitted against female enfranchisement and the drive for the systematic removal of women from all public visibility (including female forms such as mannequins). The intolerance for entertainment such as music and movies for being 'un-Islamic' logically led to the destruction by militants of CD shops and attacks against women artists and activists.

It is imperative to understand that these Islamist parties do not simply follow some archaic agenda but are very much the product of a modernist politics, and so are pursuing their vision accordingly. Those who would deny the nexus between mainstream Islamists and those termed "fundamentalists" or "extremists" on many issues, particularly on the role and place of women, would be well advised to study the period of the MMA government (2002–2008). The government's policy of appealing to the "moderate" Islamists simply extends them credence as the legitimate voices for the cause of an 'authentic' Islam as opposed to the allegedly perverted version practised by the Taliban. However, the political reality is that conservatism, whether in the form of religion or politics will challenge and can easily displace tolerant, liberal and moderate values unless the state enforces its own liberal identity categorically and if civil society organises its secular resistance with less ambiguity.

Less discussed is the post-conflict or post-militancy vision for religious politics. Even as religious militancy is declared as defeated and routed after 2014, how will this curb the future political articulation of religion in the absence of any secular alternative? There is little or no possibility that some moderate, reformist, socio-religious formula is going to undo the effects of either the militant or mainstream Islamist policies, given the thin line between moderate, conservative

and extreme interpretations of religion that has come to define politics in Pakistan. Specifically, their consensus over the role and status
of women implies that this will remain of particular concern to
women's rights activists. It is for these reasons that women's rights
activists continue to lobby for the revival of the local body government
that was disbanded[5]after 2008 because this cadre symbolised and
offered secular resistance to extreme expression of religio-politics. The
process also revealed the non-theocratic, prosaic but critical, material-
based political concerns of women at community levels. This is not to
suggest that some uniform feminist agenda is being pursued through
these councillors but the politicisation of women and the potential to
influence local politics and patriarchal obstacles is certainly being
enhanced.

The Okara Peasant Movement

One such movement that is exemplary of scholarly oversight has been
the women's corp of the Okara Peasant Movement of 1999. This
movement began as a confrontation between the peasant tenant
farmers and the administration of Okara Military Farms and the adja-
cent Renala Military Farms in Punjab. The trigger of the conflict was
over the attempt to change the status of sharecropping tenant farmers
and convert them to contract renters, instead. Women's direct entry in
the conflict began in Okara in 1999–2000 but soon spread to other
parts of Pakistan's agricultural-rich province, Punjab (Saigol 2010;
Mumtaz and Mumtaz 2012).

The population of the peasant farmers in Okara is a mix of Muslims
and Christians. The latter were settled as tenants by the missionaries,
dating to the time of the colonial British Administration. The tenants
have farmed the lands on the basis of share-cropping and at the time
of the surfacing of the conflict in 2000, were actually receiving one-
third to one-fourth of the share of the produce rather than the half
share that is presumed under the *battai* (share) system. The tenants
were not allowed to build permanent brick houses or to extract mud
for repair and maintenance. They needed prior permission for
weddings and funerals, for entertaining guests, and to build schools or
roads. There have been struggles for ownership rights going as far
back as 1928, with various court cases in between, most of which have
been pending.

Under the new scheme, the peasant tenants feared they would
become contract wage labourers for a set period of time, at a fixed
amount of cash rent to be paid annually. In addition, they would be

required to grow fodder for the military farm animals to be sold to the military, at rates decided by the latter. Originally, the lease period was specified as three years and later, increased to seven years when faced by stiff resistance from the tenants. These proposed new arrangements threatened the peasants who felt vulnerable and open to eviction on short notice. One study noted that this change "would also strip the peasant tenants of the protection that they enjoyed under the Punjab Tenancy Act 1887, which among other things, gave the first right of purchase to those who had tilled the land for more than two generations for over 20 years, whenever the land is sold or leased" (Mumtaz and Mumtaz 2012, 141). The attempt to change these (colonial) arrangements was met with widespread resentment from the farmers and the first large public demonstration was staged in Okara, in October 2000, outside the office of the District Coordination Officer.

Rubina Saigol (2010), who has conducted an in-depth study on the role of women peasants in the Okara movement, argues that it was the fear of eviction and loss of the only means of livelihood that led them to agitate for their ownership rights. The slogan the peasants coined that summed up their resolve and their refusal to sign such a contract was *"malkiyat ya maut"* (ownership or death). So began what is believed to be one of the biggest civil disobedience movements in the recent history of the Punjab in which a million tenant farmers rose up in revolt against the most powerful economic and political institution in Pakistan – the military. Saigol notes the reaction of the military as one of shock and incredulity over how "one of the most powerless and dispossessed sections of the country had revolted against the State's awesome machinery of coercion" and that the military reacted by "using all the instruments of state repression and control that it has in its deadly arsenal – the law courts, police and Rangers" (Saigol 2010, 30).

On August 8, 2000, women's involvement was prompted by the arrests and harassment of men by police and Rangers. Saigol (2010) notes that most early activists were either wives or mothers and sisters of male leaders/arrested members, or women with relatively greater mobility. As men were routinely picked up by the police and arrested, "it was the women who responded by arming themselves with *thapas* (thick sticks flattened at one end used for washing clothes) and pots and pans blocking police parties . . . Soon these women's groups came to be known as the 'thapa force'" (Mumtaz and Mumtaz 2012, 143).

Women's confrontation with the police and Rangers continued and the Deputy Director of the Military Farms denied them permission to pick the firewood that the peasants had collected, as part of a general harassment campaign and as punitive action for their revolt. Mumtaz and Mumtaz (2012) note in a report of the movement that in June 2002, thousands of villagers encircled the police station while women lay down before police vans, refusing to move until their leaders were freed – which they were, the same day. Mumtaz and Mumtaz also recount a similar incident when the Rangers force confiscated a tractor-trolley and the peasant women managed to win it back from them. The authors note how women were part of the hunger strikes and sit-ins and travelled from village to village and to the cities, while also attending court hearings and addressing seminars and press conferences. They recall how many women were injured due to police action and firing and at least one died. The authors record how the women peasants they interviewed recalled the reaction of a police inspector who would taunt the men in the movement by admitting that "you [peasants] are harvesting wheat only because of the thapa force" (cited in Mumtaz and Mumtaz 2012, 144).

The newly formed *Anjuman-e-Mazareen Party* (AMP) inducted women into the organisation as card-carrying members and formed "women's wings" at the village and district levels. Women are members and office bearers in the Punjab committee of this party and represent the organisation at national and international fora. Several studies note that despite the greater mobility and confidence, as well as increased capacity to confront state forces, the women members admitted to not having a voice in AMP's decisions and were critical of the lack of sharing of information about AMP budgets and expenditures (Saigol 2010; Mumtaz and Mumtaz 2012). The collective initiative to resist the victimisation of the community and its shared memory, the legitimacy accorded to women's entry in the struggle, and the respect from men it has earned for their contributions leads Mumtaz and Mumtaz (2012) to conclude that this is a significant step towards women's emancipation, signaled by their willingness to come out of their segregation and challenge the state (147). As seen in this movement, they also challenged patriarchal expectations, customs, and traditions and rose above any male-prescribed religious norms and with no theocratic guidance.

Rubina Saigol notes that the tenant struggle in Punjab is a unique example of unprecedented unity across religious divides. She documents that about 40 percent of the tenant farmers in Okara and some 30 percent in Khanewal belonged to the Christian community while the rest are Muslims. She observes how these two communities appeared to have worked in "a unity seldom witnessed in Pakistan's deeply divided society" (Saigol 2010, 46). She also points out that the tenants she interviewed reported that the efforts by the military owners to drive a wedge between the Christian and Muslim farmers failed because "they decided to work together for a common cause based on shared material interests" and that "they knew that they could only succeed if they stood together and united" (47). Saigol cites the views of her interviewees, which underline the importance of the traditional links across religious lines:

> Muslims and Christians decided that they would drink from the same cup, eat from the same plate. We will not be divided. Economically the Christians are at the same level as the Muslims. There is no religious prejudice. The Maulvis tried to break us apart on religious basis. For generations we have lived together and attended marriages at each others' houses and celebrated both *Eid* [Muslim religious celebration] and Christmas. We ate and drank together. We were accused of being foreign agents by the agencies only because we are Christians. (Interview with Younis Iqbal, July 8, 2004, cited in Saigol 2010, 47)

Saigol reveals how the intelligence and security agencies used the religious difference as an excuse to accuse the tenants of "playing into the hands of foreign agencies" (47). She also observes how the "Kissan Board [Farmers' Board] created by the *Jamaat-e-Islami* also tried to play a role in reaching an accord with the government, but the peasants were careful to avoid contact with a party premised on religious lines" (47). She notes that the two religious communities prayed together for the success of the movement and despite adversities were determined to stick together. Conceding the importance of a common material interest based on the relation to the land, Saigol suggests that "when survival is at stake, religion can take a back seat in human affairs" (47).

Also noteworthy is a damning report by Human Rights Watch (HRW, July 2004) on the role of the military in this confrontation. It led the Inter-Services Public Relations Spokesman, Major General Shaukat Sultan, to contest the report (stemming from the usual, nationalist anxiety over the ubiquitous threat of the imperialist intentions of international human rights organisations and local NGOs) by arguing that the report amounted to "interference" in the country's internal matters ("Army Spurns HRW Report on Okara Military Farms," *The News*, July 22, 2004). As an aside, there have since been repeat aspersions cast over the work of Human Rights Watch in Pakistan. At one point, following a virulent campaign against a report issued by the HRW on the situation in Balochistan province, in 2012, an English language newspaper printed the address and telephone contact of the HRW director, Pakistan, in what was seen to be a thinly veiled encouragement of vigilante response to his 'betrayal' to the country (Noorani 2012, "HRW Presented One-sided View on Balochistan to US panel," *The News*, Feb. 21).

Feminist analysis over the tangible translation of peasant women's agency from its public expression into their domestic lives remains cautious. However, the link between public empowerment and domestic realisation is clear in Saigol's (2010) observation that

> in spite of the women's involvement in the movement primarily as protectors of their male kin, it seems that a certain level of agency has been generated through the process of collective participation. This sense of personal agency goes beyond merely fighting the State in defence of male kin. It appears that women in Khanewal have taken collective stands against domestic violence. (76)

Saigol's interview with Aqeela Naz (secretary of the AMP) reveals that previously the beatings of women at the hands of male kin were considered private family matters. After women's collective action as the *thapa* brigade, domestic violence became a community matter.[6] According to Naz's testimony, the women's wing members of the AMP are called when a beating occurs and they help resolve the dispute and warn the men. As a result, there has allegedly been a lessening of domestic physical abuse. Saigol cites Naz's claim that

> we have suddenly realized how strong and powerful we can be. In the past, the men thought it beneath their dignity to even talk to us. Now they seek our opinion on all matters related to the current issue. The women collect and organize the funds for the movement. They decide how the money will be spent. So there is decision-making power. But the senior positions in the AMP all belong to the men. (Naz in an interview May 27, 2004, cited in Saigol 2010, 76–77)

Saigol also documents the experiences of personal empowerment of the peasant women that range from confidence in public speaking to a desire to work as a collective force on gender violence beyond their communities. Saigol concedes that "although the loosening of domestic controls extended only to working with the AMP, it brought a new sense of power and an awareness of personal agency" (78). On the question of religious divides, Saigol cites the observations of the general secretary of the women's wing of the AMP:

> The [State] Agencies tried to divide us by telling the Muslims that the Christians just wanted to serve their own interests. There was a

mosque in one of our villages and a few of its bricks broke away and fell during one of the rallies. The Law Enforcing Agencies quickly told the Muslims that a Christian peasant woman's foot had kicked down the bricks of the mosque. This was meant to incite a religious riot and break us apart. One of the Muslim peasant women quickly came forward and said that it was her foot that had accidentally struck the mosque during the tussle and lathi-charge [baton beating]. So they were unable to provoke a religious riot. (Naz, cited in Saigol 2010, 83)

Saigol reads the privileging of class links and "a feeling of sisterhood" (83) to be the factor that led to the prevention of religious division at that moment in time. She observes that this class-based unity across religious lines, at the height of the struggle was "unique and unprecedented in Pakistan's history" (83). She also recounts the inter-faith activities that bound the peasants together in oppression and struggle. Saigol does acknowledge though, how some feminist analysis is cautious with regard to the permanence of such temporary bonding across religious divides.

Interesting also, has been the role of NGO involvement and donor support to this movement but which is read from different perspectives. Mumtaz and Mumtaz recall that the struggle received strong support from civil society organisations, national and international humanitarian organisations and the media. Besides moral support, free legal aid, accommodation during court appearances, and financial help, there was considerable media coverage, seminars, press conferences that gave widespread prominence and currency to the issue and invited attention of international media as well as diplomats. According to these researchers, "the ensuing public debate served to strengthen the peasants' resolve to remain steadfast and not buckle under pressure" (2012, 142).

On the other hand, Saigol observes, "once donor money came in the differences of class and religion surfaced" (82). The reasons she cites are that the Christians are somewhat better educated and belong to a slightly better off class than the Muslim peasants. Saigol notes how a large number of Christians were able to assume leadership roles on account of their status and that this did cause some resentment among a section of the Muslim peasantry. She notes that from the perspective of an oppressed religious minority, the Christian community believed that the donor money from foreign countries would assist in their struggle. However, Saigol notes that this made the Muslim peasantry feel excluded. She argues that such differences "were further fanned and exploited by the law enforcing agencies to divide the movement and weaken it" (Saigol 2010, 82). Saigol concludes that although the peasant women across the religious divide denied any differences, it seems that if it came to a choice, they would be more likely to choose their own communities rather than bind together on the basis of gender. The reason cited is the pull of collective identities that supercede individual ones on the basis of gender, since the former is a system on which women's survival is often dependent. Saigol observes that since a large part of the peasant women's involvement was to protect their male kin, it was not conceivable that they would bond with other women regardless of religious difference. For all these reasons, it was also pertinent that for all their empowerment and inter-faith good will, the peasant women from either faith never entertained nor raised the feminist demand for women's autonomous right to ownership of the land but rather, were always just directing their struggle for the collective instead.[7]

Summary

The experiences of two working women's movements of the women councillors and peasant women that gathered momentum under the "WoT" period in Pakistan have been summarised. Unlike the direct encounter of the Lady Health Workers (Chapter 3) with religious mili-tancy,[8] the movements outlined above illustrate the resistance of working women under normative conditions of patriarchy and reli-gious politics. It is seen that the material and meaningful translation of agency, voice and changing consciousness for working women is only possible through oppositional resistance that is based on non-theocratic strategies rather than docile or pietist patience or virtue. Rather than archiving the details of these movements, only the selec-tive aspects of these movements were discussed to demonstrate the importance of resistance and opposition to the collusive forces of reli-gion and patriarchy that operate systemically at state and social levels. Further, repeatedly and under the most promising and hopeful of conditions and expressions of women's agency is the reminder of its limitations and the need therefore, that it must be differentiated from feminist autonomy.

Conclusion

Feminism and Faith-based Politics

This book has emerged from scholarly readings, observations, experiences, participation and involvement in a broad range of debates and direct activism within the women's movement in Pakistan. The purpose of documenting these has not been to construct binaries, competitiveness or lend to cleavages between Islamist women's and feminist agendas in Pakistan. It has been to unapologetically confirm that these political dualities exist in Pakistan— legitimately so – and to highlight the points of departure in these agendas. One of the reasons that I have consistently referred to a body of post-9/11 anthropological works on gendered religious identities in Pakistan as postsecularist is because these studies imply that women reside not in the Islamic Republic but in some post-Islamic state and that legitimate women's rights and empowerment must be committed towards some post-secular end.

Discussion and political engagements between Islamist women and secular feminists, in my experience, do not make them uncomfortable with these "binaries", and their respective political points of departures do not cause as much anxiety as perceived in recent post-9/11 scholarship. It is also inaccurate to suggest that one group consistently demonises or sharpens its political teeth against the other. To disagree with each other's politics does not have to translate into delegitimisation, provided the political position is accurately treated and based on substance rather than suspicions over associations and abstract conspiracy over motives. Rather, the terms of engagement have become far more sophisticated in the post-Zia years and this has been due to the compulsions of (albeit, interrupted) democratic requirements of women leaders who wish to seem representative of The Pakistani Woman, as well as of modernity, public service, and globalisation.

The point here is not to make a case that Enlightenment, modernity and secularism are the literal panacea for Pakistani secular feminists. Rather, the argument offered is that the patriarchal collusion of religion and local customs and the actors who enable these make it unviable to rely on either of these as sources of emancipatory or progressive politics. It is possible that universalist human rights and women's rights guidelines that are premised on liberal/secular principles may not be desirable alternatives unless filtered through some kind of critical lens, either. However, patriarchal political hegemonies in Pakistan (and practically everywhere else) are sourced predominantly in religion and customary masculinist codes and so, a liberal/secular resistance simply offers a strategic interruption to the way these tools of control are used. Such an oppositional standpoint is not poised to operate as a political supremacist bulldozer in order to open the floodgates of Westoxification. Those critics who keep pretending that religion and local cultural codes are not the immediate sources that limit women's progress or freedoms and who argue that women may be comforted by introspective spirituality and should negotiate with the tools available only within their domestic and communal locations, are missing the points being raised by Islamist women, as well as secular feminists.

The idea that the historical symbolism of Muslim women's contributions in Islamic history and postcolonial nationalisms can be a useful influence in the process of the empowerment of women is an investment that has unravelled in contemporary Pakistan in terms of actual political worth. The notion that all forms of empowerment, including enhanced visibility in public spaces, can be translated and linked to women's tangible rights is misplaced. This is an argument that is especially favoured amongst moderates, who promote the reductionist notion that if women can be veiled and enter public space/service, then this figurative worth will eventually convert or lead to improved rights. Instead, in the experience of Pakistan, the worth of secular strategies has outweighed religious symbolism – such that right-wing Islamists have learned to apply secular approaches in order to achieve their Islamist (mostly anti-feminist) ends. The faith-based, or pragmatic politics of Islamist politics in Pakistan (including participation and contributions by Islamist women) has not yielded any evidence that could be attributed towards an improvement in the status of women's material, symbolic or policy worth in the country or indeed, global indices.

In any case, the central point challenges the hope that re-interpretive, faith-based strategies (often advocated by some modernist feminists too) will accrue continuous incremental change. This has not come to fruition in Pakistan. Neither is it adequate to argue that it is not religious politics but really something called "liberal-secularism" that is the source of all political damage in Muslim societies. Instead, it has been in the political subversion of Islamic law and reversion to the universalist and "secular spirit" of the Constitution that has allowed an expansion of material and legal rights for women in the last decade. This is true of both the Family Laws of 1961, promulgated by General Ayub Khan and the Women's Protection Act of 2006, enacted under General Musharraf and a host of pro-women legislation that has recently been passed by the civilian legislature in Pakistan, often in the direct defiance of the CII and Islamist political pressure (see Chapter 2). Women's increased mobility and prominent presence in public spaces is visible in the high number of women at universities across the country, their participation in non-traditional occupations and as senior officials in state offices, as well as in representing the country in sports and the arts which were once banned or taboo for women under the period of General Zia ul Haq. These are some evident examples of non-pietiest achievements and markers of secular autonomy.

Given the limited agenda of Islamist women politicians, despite their much-discovered agency and the targeted discrediting of secular feminism in post-9/11 scholarship, the impasse in the progress of women's rights in Pakistan remains suspended between the two limiting narratives of faith-based re-interpretive empowerment and, gradual, symbolic liberal reform. Feminists in Pakistan have for decades framed their activism within a gender-based understanding of patriarchal violence and campaigned against faith-based violence against women but equally so, against honour crimes, acid-throwing, rape and 'secular' violence, too. They have also resisted the conservative dictates of religious political groups and protested about their silence over violence against women in the domestic and public realms.

However, since 9/11, considerable international scholarship tends to view all events in Pakistan through the singular lens of the "War on Terror". This tempts scholars such as Nivi Manchanda (2012 online) to argue for a specific attention to epistemic violence that the region has been subjected to rather than the "individual agency underscoring such acts of violence." While liberal/secular feminists in Muslim contexts are accused of propping up binaries of the secular versus religious, the critics themselves reify and critique such feminists and their politics as the binary Others of pietiest women and their "interiorised politics" and, in the view of Manchanda (2012), Akbar and Oza (2013) and Toor (2012), even as the Others of militant Muslim men and their politics. This defensive prescription only surfaces in response to crimes committed by religious militants or in the name of religion.

The difference between this appeal and Pakistani feminist analysis is that while understanding the cultural and political context, feminist activists do not subscribe to cultural or geo-political specificity as an excuse to exonerate the crime. While recognising and locating the contextual roots and material basis of patriarchal violence and noting its links to masculinist imperialism, feminists also seek to hold accountable the actors and expressions of such violence. Most of the founders of feminist movements in Pakistan affiliate themselves with, or have been part of a leftist political leaning. To suggest that they are not aware of the history or imperialist trappings that have produced forces such as the Taliban is a deliberate oversight. The accusation that feminists cunningly set up binaries by propping up all Islamists as evil and themselves (women/victims) as secular innocents, serves only to assist a new generation of academics to position themselves as "objective" commentators on the reinvention of Islamic politics in Pakistan. However, this is a politically and historically truncated project. By focusing only on the post-9/11 era, the politics of religion and its instrumentalisation by organised groups and the state is cast in the dustbin of history.

It is this kind of commentary that imagines that the resistance to polio vaccination has peaked because a fake vaccination campaign was staged as part of a CIA dragnet operation to hunt and kill Osama Bin Laden, in 2011 (Shah 2011, "CIA Organised Fake Vaccination Drive to Get Osama bin Laden's Family DNA," *The Guardian*, July 11). The Bin Laden raid and capture in northern Pakistan has definitely contributed to a different kind of political mistrust of the routine health campaign and is unconscionable. But it does not explain or condone the historic and simultaneous oppositional strategies and violence meted out against women community workers by religious clergy and/or militants. The collusion of patriarchal partnerships as expressed through the narrative of religious fundamentalism and sustained through conservatism is historic and continuous. It is an unfair expectation to think feminists are likely to apply the prescription for silence or tempered activism when violent acts are urged, sanctioned and supported by mainstream clerics or indeed, the state.

Female mobility, knowledge of sexuality, and financial independence is a threat for most men in Pakistan. So the in-roads made by the hundreds of thousands of women serving communities that have little or no access to very basic healthcare, education or decision-making cannot be underestimated. The work of women health workers, teachers and community social workers has met with resistance from large landowners, as well as local clergymen, but the state has been instrumental (via a practical, non-theocratic policy) in extending legal and other support to the women workers. The resilience and political agency of these working/class women also makes remarkable documentation – whether it is over minimum wage or security of their lives and livelihoods, as well as of their children and communities.

To suggest that Pakistani feminists are compromised liberals from the outset is another misgiving that has become a recent mantra of some diasporic postsecularist scholars. However, the political trajectory of secular feminist politics reveals all the signs of idealistic hope for a socialist feminist transformation of the state and society. Amongst them, there were some members who had initially envisioned the possibility of developing a vernacular of secularisation through discursive traditions and Quranic hermeneutics. The merits –or otherwise – of such strategies were always debated in feminist groups. Today, the secular feminist project has been whittled down due to a pragmatic realisation of the haemorrhaging of liberal/secular resistance in the face of armed religious militancy, organised religious politics, the influence of societal piety that has the ability to destabilise communities in the form of flash vigilantism, and a State that offers little or no secular reform and sustains an opaque relationship with jihadist outfits. Hence, the reason that the women's movement seems today to be limited in its liberal political formation is precisely because it has not pursued an adversarial campaign against Islamic laws or groups, as it used to under the Islamisation period of the 1980s.

Under genuine threats to their lives, some feminists and women politicians who are identifiably liberal and/or secular require around-the-clock security guards and this has affected their political stances and curtailed their political energies and influence, even as they remain personally courageous. Moreover, the notion that liberal/secular politics are either a bourgeois interest or have 'failed' in Pakistan needs to be challenged in view of the working-class interests and movements described above. These new political identities are directing themselves against the collective constitution of the (male) community and are pressurising the state to fulfill their material demands. This is a moment of transition, and the fact that these demands are outside of the religious pale or beyond pietist subjectivity is crucial towards the construction of what Sinha (2011) calls "the agonistic liberal universalism of women *qua* women as the paradigmatic [Pakistani] citizen" (86). This is an important point because it signals or gestures a resignification of how liberal/secular feminist politics can still be engaged in challenging both traditional and neo-liberal hegemonies or authoritarianism.

Those advocating an anti-modernity, anti-enlightenment, non-liberal, supposedly alternative Muslim politics need to acknowledge in their scholarship that in practical terms, feminism and human rights activism is being successfully silenced in Pakistan. If there is a contest between feminism and faith-based politics, it is quite clear which is the front-runner. The contention is simply that ultimately, no matter how much is invested into excavating the worth of reinvented, faith-based identities as a postcolonial and post-9/11 alterity, ultimately the losers are still the women of Pakistan. The efforts to paint liberal/secular rights-based activism as imperial and Western resonate with domestic conservative politics that focus on denying the struggle for equal rights for women and minorities by activists in Pakistan. The goals and methods of such activism sometimes align with, and at others deviate from classical European liberalism. These academic and political efforts to delegitimise and obscure the historical benefits that such liberal rights gave to a generation of Pakistani women allow such critics to offer piety and religious rights as unproven alternatives. By doing so, this project potentially interrupts the possibility of an alternative genealogy of the universal secular female citizen-subject in the future. By recalling women's rights from the universal and thrusting these back to the 'inner' religious community, such scholars ignore how these communities were themselves colonial constructs of imperial India and to whom the welfare of women was constantly conceded by the colonial state (including, for example, on the Child Marriage Restraint Act of 1929).

Why the religious realm should be privileged as an alternative to imperial Western liberalism is both mystifying and encouraging of historical fallacious myth. Why feminists should be cautioned against identifying the particular violations of women's rights within these communities is even more disturbing. Universalist movements allow women with shared political agendas to critically reimagine their (individualised or collective) citizenry beyond the limits of male-based community or collective identities. If such partial ruptures are permitted – without the suspicion of scholars critical of secular feminism or the violent prevention from male politics that is threatened by liberal freedoms for women – then a potentially filtered universality of rights for women may emerge from within the experiences of Pakistani women. To foreclose these on the basis of theoretical whims, defensiveness of religious patriarchies or to presume they are never local and always external and imposed is to ignore the liberal/secular agency or contextualised desires of many, many women.

Pakistani Liberalism/Secularism

More than any organisational definition, such as a separation of church and state or the autonomy of governance and religious institutions, secularism, for the section of the women's movement that is committed to it, has come to mean an expectation of public institutions to maintain a minimal neutrality or reference to religion, particularly in matters relating to women's and minorities' equal rights. At the very least, secularism for them pivots around the concept of advocating a pluralism of beliefs and for resisting a hegemonic, majoritarian Islamism from driving laws, social relations or state policies. It also means resisting religious justifications that reinforce class, gender and sectarian discrimination as well as those that target minorities.

Just as for other societies, many secular practices may be intersectional, contradictory and diverse. The competitive spirit of Islamists in the tussle for state power and social domination does not qualify as contributive to this secularisation since Islamists may believe in electoral democracy, but refute the legal and constitutional base of the principles of liberty and equality that inform these in Pakistan. So, the accountability process for such groups and parties would require a different form of measurement – non-liberal, non-secular and therefore, one that is based on inequality, hierarchy, limits of freedoms and contested Islamic norms. At the moment, the hypothetical proposals that suggest that Islamist politics contribute towards a process of healthy differentiation is based on an imaginary not a substantive framework, such as the Constitution. The most striking feature of secularism as it may be observed in Pakistan is that the exercise of secular identities take succour from and in return, sustain a secular domain, despite the lack of secular institutions especially at state levels (except perhaps, the contested and multi-amended Constitution).

These secular identities are not always or routinely in contest with something called 'Islam' or religious violence, but faith-based politics are a permanently available 'divine' resource in male-dominant communities, as well as in the layers of State juridical and political discourse. Feminists recognise the potential of this resource as an oppositional and patriarchal force to the realisation of their equal rights and opportunities. Religion is a resource that far exceeds its availability as a tool of emancipation or material equality, couched as it is in the multiple layers of masculinist and capitalist power politics. This realisation is based on historical and contiguous contextual political observations and not necessarily motivated by some inherent "secular hate" for Islam by feminists. To foreclose any rights-based emerging discourse and focus exclusively on women's protection and potential within the religious fold is to deny the expansion and conversions of any non faith-based changes into direct political rights for women. It is to deny expression to the diverse demands coming from a variety of movements and organisations that are not motivated nor focussed on religion or faith.

To enable a condition where such expressions and desires may legitimately be recognised and permitted, there has to be a vocabulary or modes which are allowed to be 'free' from religion, removed from the strictures and patriarchal bias of religions. Mufti (2004) argues that secular criticism contains within it "a critique of the hope for the hereafter, of religious opiate, of the religious impulse per se" but that it is also scrutinises its own "tainted history" (4, 3). However, the value of secular criticism is that it calls for "a constant unsettling and an ongoing and never-ending effort at critique" which must be embedded in the social fabric rather than simply give in to transcendental narratives (3).

The secular women's movement in Pakistan has to resolve two broad issues. First, they need to reinforce that theirs is a political position that cannot and should not be delegitimised by being measured against the same contested academic definitions or understandings of secularism as in some Western contexts. In Pakistan, a secularist identity is associated with the political demand for the separation of religion from the policies of the State, the rescinding of the State's patronage of informal (often, banned) religious politics and militant organisations, and the dismantling of a formal parallel Islamic legal system, with all its attendant clerical authorities and supportive institutions. For feminists, this is an easier position to adopt, as many of them do not shy away from the terms or politics of feminism, socialism or secularism despite their "Western" connotations. Rather than dispose of the term "secular" altogether, the idea is to define a citizenry and forms of social justice that are based on indivisible equality and to ensure that all state discourse upholds its commitment towards these – without discrimination or exceptionalism on the basis of gender, class or religion.Second, there is an urgent need to recognise that neither the modernist nor the postsecularist approach will curb radical and extremist religio-political activism or expression, as seen in the escalation of faith-based violence all over Pakistan. In fact, postsecularist scholarship is more likely to become rationalised and subsumed within radical discourse even as the former looks to legitimise itself as a viable political alternative to Western rights and justice for Pakistan. Women's own experiences of such radicalisation suggest that under such circumstances hope for equal rights or even reform is near impossible. For Pakistan, such secular criticism, sentiments, expressions and politics have to be permitted to have some bearing on public institutions, jurisprudence and social modes and relations. This is particularly true if the state embraces a religious identity with no ambivalence or ambiguity. No one understands this more than women, the working classes and the feminists of Pakistan.

Notes

Introduction

1. Afghanistan and Nigeria are the other two. After a round of fresh military operations launched in 2014 against militants in Pakistan and a concerted new ("no children missed") vaccination campaign directed by the government, polio cases have dropped to just 13 registered in 2016 and 4 in 2017. Source; National Emergency Action Plan for Polio Eradication (NEAP) 2016–2017, Government of Pakistan, http://www.endpolio.com.pk/polioin-pakistan.

2. The Lady Health Workers Programme (LHWP) is a government-run project that employs over 110,000 trained female community workers involved in delivering basic health services at doorsteps in communities. The programme was founded in 1994 by the government of the (late) Prime Minister, Benazir Bhutto. LHWs cater to pre and postnatal health care requirements and are often inducted into the government's polio vaccination programmes.

3. Conversation with President of the LHW Association, Bushra Arain and colleagues, Karachi, 2013 at a Women's Action Forum meeting. Arain has led the nation-wide movement for minimum wage and regularisation of the Lady Health Workers. The LHWs have sustained protest campaigns for four years now in this regard and more recently, for security against the threats of murders of their colleagues who are involved in administering polio vaccinations.

4. See below and Chapter 2 for details of this scholarship.

5. For a historical record, see Mumtaz and Shaheed (1987), Saigol (2013) and some of the ASR publications cited in the bibliography. There is little academic work on the more recent theories or activism of the women's movements in Pakistan.

6. Specifically, this is a genre of travel writing by colonialist women about their visits to imperial harems. Later, however, this refers to a genre of writing by women who belonged to imperial palaces and homes in the Ottoman Empire, but also other Middle Eastern contexts. These writings challenged the stereotypes of harem women as ignorant, sexualised odalisques. For an excellent review on such literature, see Reina Lewis 2004.

7. General Zia ul Haq (1977–88) sought to legitimise his military coup of 1977 and his subsequent rule under the pretext of Islamising Pakistan's law and society.

8 Self-appointed male preachers, outside the scholarship associated with Islamic learning. Historically such scholars have no legitimacy within the larger religious discourse but exert an important cultural influence within communities. During General Zia ul Haq's rule (1977–88), *maulvis/mullahs* practically gained state sanction to operate as vigilantes particularly in enforcing the state prescription of *chador and chardevari* (the veil and the household) for women.

9 I refer to this category broadly, with reference to the works of those Pakistani scholars and activists and the scholarship they are producing in the post-9/11 period and who are involved in the deconstruction of 'metanarratives' on Islam. While critical of postcolonial modernity and Enlightenment-driven women's/human rights activism in Pakistan, several such scholars are often found to be invested in the project of rehabilitating and propping up Islamist identity as a viable political and sociable alternative to the presumed spuriousness and failure of the former's "liberal-secular" framing. The specific scholars are listed throughout the book.

10 Others include Pakistani doctoral students or scholars who rely heavily on the works of postcolonial scholars and subaltern studies in their theses which are thematically wrapped around the "War on Terror" in Pakistan. For example, see Arsalan Khan http://muse.union.edu/anthropology/2015/07/arsalan-khan/, Noaman G. Ali's thesis work in Political Science, University of Toronto, Canada, and Tabinda M. Khan's thesis work, Columbia University, USA http://itu.edu.pk/faculty-itu/tabinda-mahfooz-khan/, to list a few.

11 I refer to Islamist women not as a binary distinction from Muslim women but rather in recognition of the former's political persuasion, consciousness or activism. I also note that amongst Islamist women (and men), some recognise the Pakistani state and constitution, while others contest the legitimacy of both. I do, however, use the term as inclusive of those women who lead and associate with pietist or mosque movements in recognition of their self-defined subjectivity or agency, which I consider political.

12 A colloquial reference to the channeling of political activism into paid, donor-funded employment in Non-Governmental Organisations. This is often critiqued for diluting the radical edge of direct and street political activity into more palatable liberal formulations of training, workshops, dialogues and report writings.

Chapter 1

1 The categorisations are far more limited and simply reference those considered relevant to the discussion of the impact of such scholarship on the interplay of faith and feminism in Pakistan.

2 The range of this scholarship is rich and has a social scientific bent including, the works of Afshar 1988; Ahmed 1993; Al-Hibri 1982; Brah 1993; Esposito 1982; Kandiyoti 1991; Mernissi 1987, 1991a, 1991b;

Papanek 1973, 1991; Sadaawi 1980; Tucker 1986; Yamani 1996, as just a few examples. For an explanation about how the categorisation of topics and disciplines of the study of women and Islam, particularly with reference to literary studies, is a 'modern' endeavor, see Mary Loyoun in Joseph 2013.

3   An international solidarity association formed in France in 1985, WLUML monitors laws affecting women in Muslim communities, publicises injustices and links activists and academics in an ambitious, Muslim personal law reform project.

4   Sisters in Islam is a "Muslim Women's NGO" formed since 1987 in Malaysia and is committed to promoting an understanding of Islam along the principles of justice, equality and freedom within a democratic nation-state. The organisation focuses on a variety of issues with a special focus on Family Laws and Quranic studies. http://www.sistersin-islam.org.my/.

5   *Karamah* (Dignity in Arabic) is a Washington based, non profit organisation of Muslim Women Lawyers for Human Rights, which works on the rights of Muslim women under Islamic and civil law. *Musawah* (equality in Arabic) is another organisation and global network (launched in 2009 at a meeting in Malaysia) that works on issues of equality and justice in the Muslim family.

6   In Pakistan, for example, while some may advocate the strategies associated with Islamic feminism, there is no organised Islamist or feminist group that identifies itself as "Islamic feminist."

7   Many of these observations are based on my participation and dialogue at the Third Islamic Feminist Conference held in Barcelona, Spain (24–27 Oct., 2008), as well as studies and debates on Islamic feminism in various other contexts.

8   This is not to suggest Islamic feminists are not active in Muslim states, rather that they are not politically organised in the form of political parties or independent of mainstream, male-dominated organisations.

9   See the discussion on Al-Huda and Jamia Hafsa in Chapter 4.

10 Some of Hassan's influential works include, "The Role and Responsibilities of Women in the Legal and Ritual Tradition of Islam" (1980); "On Human Rights and the Quranic Perspective" (1982); "An Islamic Perspective" (1990); and "Challenging the Stereotypes of Fundamentalism: An Islamic Feminist Perspective" (2001).

11 A list of ASR publications may be found at http://www.spinifexpress.com.au/fasiapub/pakistan/asr.htm

12 Islamic laws promulgated in 1979. For a critical reading of these laws, see Jahangir and Jilani 1990; A.S. Zia 1994.

13 WAF refused to recognise or legitimise the Council, although this constitutional body continues to advise the government on the unsuitability of those laws that may potentially contravene Islamic provisions.

14 In Pakistan, the contest for state power by religio-political groups had tremendous advantage during the religio-military dictatorship of

General Zia ul Haq (1977–1988). These forces colluded with various misogynist forces to Islamise the country by making women the main signifiers (and hence, casualties) of this project.

15 Women Living Under Muslim Laws is an international solidarity network formed in 1984 that provides information, support and a collective space for women whose lives are shaped, conditioned or governed by laws and customs said to derive from Islam. http://wluml.org/english/index.shtml

16 A project record can be found on the website of the British government's Department for International Development, http://r4d.dfid.gov.uk/Project/60091/.

Chapter 2

1 These range from expensive week-long courses (such as the ones offered by the London Middle East Institute at School of Oriental and African Studies, UK) to annual conferences such as The Islamic Feminism Congress which is regularly held in Europe, or the Islamic World International Conferences in the USA.

2 See Introduction for reference to such scholarship for Pakistan. For a more historic discussion of the introduction of the term "postsecular" in philosophy particularly, its association with Jürgen Habermas and within a post-9/11 context, see Winter 2013. For another recent discussion, see Mufti 2013.

3 This included re-writing the Universal Declaration of Human Rights from a feminist perspective and streamlining the Convention for the Elimination of Discrimination Against Women (CEDAW), not to make it more culturally specific but to make it more feminist (Lahore chapter of WAF, 1993).

4 I have used the term "post-9/11" in my writings over the past few years to date the turn in scholarship on religion and women but Bronwyn Winter (2013) coins the term, "post-9/11ism" as a "shortcut to describe the political context in which women generally and feminists in particular are operating" (149).

5 I use the term broadly in this book to refer to social liberalism or progressive liberalism – one that seeks to balance individual liberty and social justice. I recognise the overlap of this with classical liberalism in that it endorses a market economy and the role of government in addressing economic and social issues including poverty, health and education. Under social liberalism, the good of the community is viewed as harmonious with the freedom of the individual and its policies have been widely adopted in much of the capitalist world. I also note that the term "social liberalism" is often used interchangeably with modern or new liberalism to differentiate it from old or classical liberalism. Most liberal feminists in Pakistan would subscribe to this definition, whereas, Marxist feminists usually depart from this view by way of their resistance to capitalist modes of economies. My own bias is towards a Marxist feminist politics.

6   I use 'jihad' loosely, as used in the Pakistani lexicon to refer to holy struggle and with recognition that this varies in interpretation and invocation, which can range from the idea of jihad as a form of struggle for personal improvement, to 'defensive' war, to armed insurgency against an infidel enemy state (including in some cases, the Pakistani state) and non-believers.

7   For an insightful and informative critique of the some of the new literature on Pakistan by a respected Pakistani left scholar and social scientist, see S. Akbar Zaidi's (2012b) review essay. He reviews the recent works of Anatol Leivan, Humeira Iqtidar and Saadia Toor, among others. The headings that Zaidi uses to categorise these works include, "Journalistic Account," "Amateur Anthropology," "Running Out of Ideas," "Wishful Thinking," and "Concocted History."

8   See Introduction.

9   One example from a score of seminars and courses would be this one on "Reframing the 'Islamic turn' amongst young British Muslims," School of Oriental and African Studies and University of East London, UK, 2007. http://www.soas.ac.uk/centresoffice/events/framingmuslims/11dec2007 -seminar-reframing-the-islamic-turn-amongst-young-british- muslims.html. Last accessed December 2015.

10 The campaign, generally referred to as "women's rights are human rights," sought successfully to redress weaknesses in the conventional framework of international human rights law. These weaknesses derive from: (1) the state-centred nature of international law; (2) the enduring emphasis in human rights discourse and practice on civil and political rights (i.e., "public" rights), and (3) deference to the family as a private domain.

11 Sinha acknowledges the validity of the criticism of the legislative inefficacy of the Child Marriage Restraint law but stresses that her point is not to debate this. Rather, her interest lies in the "symbolic and rhetorical implications of its passage" (100). In other words, the Act afforded an opportunity for the mobilisation of women across communities towards an imaginary of an Indian subject-citizenry and for rights as shaped by their own agency and a liberal universalism.

12 Sinha observes that this moment of universalist possibility was ultimately a "Pyrrhic victory" (91), not in terms of a failed attempt to graft a liberal universalist option onto the body politic of India but rather, due to the crisis posed by women's conflicting role in the political reforms of 1935. In the suffrage debate, disaffected Muslim women broke away from the majority position and chose to support the main Muslim political parties for reserved seats and separate electorates on a communal basis – seeing the unitary position to be in the interests of Hindus. The colonial 'solution' was to accede reserved seats for communal or special interest groups thereby reinstating communal patriarchies and foreclosing the moment of opportunity for women's citizenship to be framed in a (futur-

istic) universalist perspective of rights, rather than as symbols of competing community collectives.

13 The Anti-Honour Killing Laws (Criminal Amendment Bill) 2015; The Anti-Rape Laws (Criminal Amendment Bill) 2015; The Acid Control and Acid Crime Prevention Act, 2011; Prevention of Anti-Women Practices Act, 2011; The Protection against Harassment of Women at the Workplace Act, 2010; The Criminal Law Amendment Act, 2010; Protection of Women (Criminal Laws Amendment) Act, 2006; The Sindh Domestic Violence Prevention and Protection Act, 2013; The Sindh Child Marriages Restraint Act, 2013 (raising the legal age to 18 years), are a few examples. Most of these have been opposed by Islamist political parties and groups during the passage of debate in the legislative process, including by the state's Council of Islamic Ideology.

14 The Objectives Resolution (1949) was a guiding principle and preamble to the Constitution of Pakistan but was made a substantive part of the Constitution itself, through General Zia ul Haq's 8th Amendment of 1985 under Article 2A. The resolution's premise reads as; "Whereas sovereignty over the entire universe belongs to Allah Almighty alone and the authority which He has delegated to the State of Pakistan, through its people for being exercised within the limits prescribed by Him is a sacred trust."

15 Citing article 14, Shahla Zia argued under case law that the Constitution recognises almost all the guarantees of the United Nations Universal Declaration of Human Rights, including the right to life and liberty, to privacy of home, and to human dignity, which is "unparalleled and could be found only in few Constitutions of the world" (PLD 1994, SC 693d).

16 Farzana Shaikh (2011) reviews and considers the flaws of Iqtidar's thesis to be a result of her over-reliance on Talal Asad's "Humpty Dumpty-like definition of secularism." Shaikh is critical of Iqtidar's fantasy-based, "intellectual endeavor aimed at shoring up a discourse of resistance against 'the West' and its attendant evils – in this case, secularism," rather than a concern to understand Pakistan "in the light of its own history."

17 *Muttahida Majlis e Amal* was a six-party alliance of Islamist political parties that won the elections in 2002 (in a 'deal' brokered with General Musharraf) and formed government in the North West Frontier Province that borders with Afghanistan (renamed Khyber Pakhtunkhwa in 2008).

18 Renamed to Khyber Pakhtunkhwa in 2008.

19 These include the 2005 Local Bodies elections in Lower Dir and in a by-election in Malakand.

20 The MMA rule in the Frontier Province based itself on a moral imperative to provide social order through vigilantism and remove all visible markers of womanhood from the public and relegate it to the private realm. The hegemonistic intent of religious political parties and their affiliate charitable organisations is clearly political rather than merely academic.

21 Presumably, feminists in Muslim contexts do not engage in "Muslim political activities" even though they may be Muslims.

22 Afshari (2012) considers the readings of Iran from a cultural relativist position to be ethnographical explorations that "lead to a scholarly demand for a retooling of human rights discourse and practice" (545). His conclusion is, however, that such explorations do not provide any meaningful guidelines or practical value to human rights monitors. For Afshari, such re-readings of Islamic regimes with their recommendations for "tempered universalism" or "chastened universalism" are merely reflective of an "anti-imperialist narrative [that] mixes discourse analysis – in a Foucauldian sense of legitimizing power and "truth" – with the defensive Third Wordlist nationalism of 1960s vintage" (539). His research challenges those who consider the Iranian or any other Islamic Republic as being absolved of human rights abuses just because these regimes reject the definition and framing of universal human rights. Afshari challenges the conclusion that violations of human rights in Muslim contexts are incidental, or only responsive to Western imperialist occupations, threats and anxieties. His findings bear important lessons for those who suppose that Iran's citizens have passively and homogenously embraced new sites for rights.

23 In many ways, the interrogation of the secularisation project is a much easier task for scholars whose work focuses on the Middle Eastern context, where secular regimes have been associated with (sometimes brutal) projects of Westernising the nation or secularising the state and/or, liberalising society. Some feminist scholars (Jad 2011) make a more nuanced and critical distinction in the trajectory of Arab secularism and argue that it is important for analysis to focus *not on the origins* but "the forms of life secularism articulates, the powers it releases or disables. It then becomes increasingly clear that Arabic secularism resulted in crushing the very structure of the notion of citizenship and the figure of the secular citizen subject itself" (41). Jad observes that Islam was incorporated as a defining feature of Arab secularism to distinguish it from other (for example, socialist) secularisms and that it became part of state defined nationalism as a symbol of loyalty and religious orthodoxy. This nuanced reading suggests that it is the Islamic secularist project rather than secularism that has been the cause of such erosion of the notion, as well as the subject of citizenship in the Arab context.

24 Javed Ahmed Ghamdi is a leading Islamic scholar of Pakistan who used to be a member of the *Jamaat e Islami* but left to form his own institute in Lahore (*Al-Mawrid*) from which he published many tracts. He was identified and promoted as a jurisconsult by President General Musharraf as part of his 'Enlightened Moderation' programme for Pakistan. Sadaf Aziz (2011) reads Ghamdi's career as part of religious managerialism in Pakistan prompted as part of a post-9/11 liberal imperialist project, while Samina Yasmeen (2013) supports his contributions and attributes his popularity due to his ability to tap into the wide

response to his campaign for a "passive secularism" in Pakistan. Ghamdi had to flee the country after several threats and eventually left, after one of his office-bearers was shot in the face by unidentified detractors. Ghamdi had a widely popular following, both in terms of media outreach and amongst the youth, in particular.

25 Amna Akbar and Rupal Oza (2013) suggest that their critique is not to "forsake secularist, feminist, or human rights frameworks" but merely to engage with the morals and ethics in deploying them (154). However, their critique is aimed only at women/feminists and not at male liberals or secularists in Muslim contexts and focuses on men as victims of feminist activism. Simultaneously, their critique does not comment on the recent construct of terms such as "liberal secular fascism" which is used by neo-conservatives and Islamists who condemn any rights-based movements or campaigns. Nor is there any discussion of the use of the term "secular fundamentalists" by other feminists such as Ziba Mir-Hosseini (2011, 71). This selective critique suggests that fundamentalist groups, Islamists, or believers of varying political bearing are passive recipients/victims in the construct of such binaries or labeling.

Chapter 3

1 For a useful discussion on empowerment for the Indian context, see Batliwala 2010.

2 Twice Prime Minister of Pakistan, Benazir Bhutto was assassinated allegedly by a religious extremist in 2008 while a social media activist (Sabeen Mahmud) was assassinated in 2015 by a religious radical because she promoted free speech and liberal ideals. Threats made to human rights activists and "NGO women" are quite common and a murder attempt was made in 2012 on the life of the 15 year old girl, Malala Yousufzai, who defied the Taliban's warnings against secular education for girls in Swat, Pakistan.

3 For details, see the Benazir Income Support Programme, Government of Pakistan, http://www.bisp.gov.pk/.

4 Unlike some welfare and charity programmes, the criteria for receiving BISP funds does not include being widowed or unemployed but is simply a supplemental cash transfer. The recipients are often working (in the informal sector) but their 'poverty scores' are very high.

5 Section 1(3), NO.PAS/Legis-B-23/2013-The Sindh Industrial Relations Bill, 2013. http://www.pas.gov.pk/uploads/acts/Sindh%20Act%20No.XXIX%20of%202013.pdf.

6 Khan (2007) observes how in Pakistan, "a political critique of women's employment issues is absent from the current literature and is sorely missed. Further, Pakistan lacks a strong community of feminist economists and researchers in other disciplines who can apply explicit feminist analyses to the subject at hand" (28).

7 Those sections of the Pakistan Penal Code which relate to offences of murder and manslaughter were replaced in 1990 by the *Qisas* and *Diyat*

Ordinance which redefines the offence and its punishment in Islamic terms. *Qisas* is equal punishment for the crime committed and *Diyat* is compensation payable to the victims or their legal heirs. The compensation for women is calculated at a lesser worth in comparison to men.

8　I have no idea what goals number four and five of the Millennium Development Goals (MDGs) are but Arain, a lower middle-class woman from a small city in Sindh, is clearly well-versed in such "liberal" developmental terms and has no compunction referring to them for fear of cultural impropriety.

9　Khairunnisa Memon, a Lady Health Supervisor (LHS) and the provincial head of the All Pakistan Lady Health Workers Employees Association reported this at a meeting with WAF Karachi, April 2012.

10　Address To The Islamic Scholars' Consultation by, Dr. Ala Alwan, Regional Director, World Health Organisation, Eastern Mediterranean Region, Cairo, Egypt, 6–7 March 2013.

11　Palejo was referring to the widely publicised case of Raymond Davis, a CIA agent who had murdered two men in Lahore in January 2011. Through some bizarre legal machinations, Davis was exonerated after the payment of blood money to the victims' families as retribution (according to a provision in the Islamic law of *Qisas* and *Diyat*), in return for which he was freed and flown out to the US after a 'fast-track' closed judicial hearing.

Chapter 4

1　In 2008, Pakistan topped the list of countries with the highest number of casualties due to suicide bombings executed, ahead of Iraq and Afghanistan. See "Demographics of Suicide Terrorism," *Dawn*, Aug. 5, 2010 http://www.dawn.com/news/844531/demographics-of-suicide-terrorism. For more detailed analysis on suicide bombings in Pakistan, see Naqvi et al. (2011).

2　In some commentary, the *Jamia Hafsa madrasa*/seminary female students have been portrayed as 'militia' but this is inaccurate. These women were radical in their vigilante campaigns that attempted to shut down video and music shops that they considered 'un-Islamic', as well as in their brief 'capture' and warnings to the head of an alleged prostitution ring in the capital city of Islamabad. However, these women were not armed (except with sticks) and their links to any militant group is ambiguous, at best. In a state siege (2007) of their *madrasa* connected to the *Lal Masjid* (Red Mosque), they claimed many female students were killed in a shoot out likened to the Waco siege in the USA. The Pakistani state denies any female casualties and there is no reported evidence of this claim.

3　I use certain terms to refer to the identities of religious groups in the way they are loosely used in Pakistan's lexicon. Usually, "fundamentalism" is used to describe the political world-view of those (religio-political groups) who resist any innovative divergence (*Bid'aat*) from original Islam or adherence to Islamic jurisprudence and is committed to rigid social asceticism. I also acknowledge the contradictions, splits and overlaps within self-professed and cross-definitional fundamentalisms. The extremists or militant Islamists fall outside of this purview and include those who seek to subvert the Pakistani state (i.e., *Tehreeq e Taliban Pakistan* (TTP) and associated networks of Al-Qaeda). The 'jihadists' can vary from those who recognise the state as a platform to promote an agenda of pan-Islamism (*Hizbul Tahrir* – banned in Pakistan) and/or who locate their (armed) struggle for the freedom of oppressed Muslims regionally/globally (*Lashkar e Tayyaba* – also a banned militant outfit). Yet other religious groups politic around their sectarian identities and are locked in communal jostle for control, influence and often, real estate, such as mosques and *madrasas* (e.g., *Sipah e Sahabah*, operating under the pseudonym, *Ahle e Sunnat Wal Jamaat*). Compared to fundamentalism, the term 'Islamism' refers to a political agenda that is relatively recent and part of a post 9–11 vocabulary rather than one that refers to any indigenous revivalism or resurgent movements.

4   Militancy and religious extremism in Pakistan is most often associated with the Afghan Taliban and its franchise forms in Pakistan (*Tehreeq e Taliban Pakistan*) and is presented by the State as a "foreign import".

5   Although Pakistan's legal system observes Islamic Laws, under Pakistan's penal code there is no provision for stoning, amputation or whipping.

6   Subsequently, the alleged victim, Chand Bibi, was reported to have denied the flogging in Pakistan's Supreme Court, which had issued an inquiry into the case. This led to further speculation in the media over whether she was coerced to deny this punishment or whether the video was a 'fake'. Feminist activists in Pakistan later interviewed Chand Bibi in Swat confirming that she was whipped. These feminists have succeeded in getting her employment outside of Swat where she had been socially isolated and since she personally requested anonymity.

7   Similar analysis found under blogs or sites such as Globalsecurity.org, http://www.globalsecurity.org/military/world/war/nwfp-1937.htm.

8   By memorialisation here, I do not refer to the written word. Feminist collective memories are often still narrated in oral tradition and so, remain limited in circulation. For a discussion on lack of scholarship in Pakistan, see Zaidi 2002. One feminist reading of this event may be seen in a newspaper article by Brohi 2010.

9   Hauner (1981) records Faqir Ipi's vehement opposition to Pakistan and alliance with other opposing tribal leaders in 1946–47. Also, see Alan Warren 2000 and Sana Haroon 2007. Such narratives can be found in the political rhetoric of Pakhtun nationalists even today.

10 The trajectory of a "new-style" fundamentalism in the early years of the Taliban formation is discussed in Rashid (2000). This process continues with far more symbolism and vehement expression in tribal Pakistan, often tipping into urban settlements too, as in Swat.

11 "Faqir of Ipi," *Khyber.org*, Sept. 16, 2005. http://www.khyber. org/people/a/Faqir_of_Ipi.shtml.

12   Spivak clarifies she is not offering this as "a plea for some violent Hindu sisterhood of self-destruction" (Spivak 2010, 281).

13   The motivation fuelling the majority of suicide bombings is attributed to revenge by tribal insurgents against the Pakistani state, which the militants consider to be a collaborator in the US-led War on Terror and occupation of Afghanistan. In this case, the female suicide bomber was thought to be executing active revenge on behalf of her tribe against the state's officials, that is, security personnel at the World Food Programme camp.

14   For more on female suicide bombings in Pakistan, see A.S. Zia 2011. For the application of Mahmood's theory of agency to female suicide bombings, see Yadlin 2006.

15   Spellings vary.

16   Ahmed Rashid (2003) describes jihadi militants in Afghanistan as those who engage in militancy so as to impose a new Islamic order by adopting the Sharia or Islamic order, not for the purpose of pursuing justice or any social benefits but as a means to regulate personal behaviour and a regime that sustains itself through punitive rule.

17   One example can be found in the argument made by Farida Shaheed 2010. For a detailed analysis of the denial of agency to right-wing women, see Amina Jamal 2005.

18   In particular, Iqtidar's research looks at the agentive potential of women members of the Islamist welfare organisation, *Jamaat ud Dawa*, known to be the charitable cover of the banned jihadist group, *Laskhar e Tayyaba*. This corroborates the argument made elsewhere in this publication that Islamist organisations may be liberating sanctuaries for some women members while sapping their agency simultaneously.

19   Dr Siddiqui, a US-based neuroscientist of Pakistani origin was wanted by the FBI between 2003 until her capture and extradition in 2008, when the Pakistani government handed her over to the US. There, following a court trial, she was incarcerated as a terrorist suspect and subsequently indicted and sentenced to life imprisonment in an American facility for shooting a US marine in Afghanistan.

20   There are a wide range of websites for the Aafia Siddiqui cause and a selection of images which reveal the associative symbolism of nationalism, religion and masculinity revolving around the campaign can be found at:
     http://www.google.com/images?client=safari&rls=en&q= Aafia+siddiqi&oe=UTF-8&um=1&ie=UTF-8&source=univ&ei= hKJSTcWSHoLMrQfvwMn-Bw&sa=X&oi=image_result_group& ct=title&resnum=6&ved=0CFoQsAQwBQ&biw=1353&bih=589

21   Dahir, the last Hindu ruler of the Indian subcontinent was ruling from Sindh (now part of Pakistan) where he lost the battle waged by the Arab conqueror, Muhammed Bin Qasim for the Muslim Ummayad caliphate in 712 AD. The rescue of enslaved and kidnapped women as Qasim invaded Sindh, particularly along the coastline where Karachi now sits,

has formed an important part of folklore, which recalls him as the saviour of Muslim women.

22 I have referred to these movements as "political nunneries" or outposts of "segregated, artificial, stateless, social suspension . . . where women can interpret Islamic texts, educate and empower themselves, within religious discourse" (A.S. Zia 2009a, 44).

23 The philosophical and ideological base for the activism of the Muslim League party in pre-partition India towards a two state solution, whereby a predominant separate Muslim nation (Pakistan) would stand independent of Hindu majoritarian India.

Chapter 5

1 Abul Ala Maududi [Abū'l-Alā Mawdūdī], (1903–1979) founder of *Jamaat e Islami* (1941).

2 The examples used by the leader in this statement are deliberate. Many Islamist men resist the use of razors in order to groom beards as a *sunnat* or Islamist requirement and as such, would consider shaving a secular practice. Militants in northern Pakistan have consistently bombed barbershops and threaten men who do not grow beards. The condemnation of commercials that use female models to sell shaving razors for men fuses a disapproval of the dual evils of women's sexuality *and* the lay practice of shaving.

3 The declaration of such an event was made at the World Assembly for the Protection of the Hijab in London, organised in reaction to the banning of the veil in France in 2003. It is observed on the 4th of September.

4 The Islamic law that criminalised adultery was part of the *Hudood* Ordinances promulgated by President of Pakistan, General Zia ul Haq in 1979. It was amended in 2006 under General Musharraf's regime and contested by Islamists in the Federal Shariat Court. The amended form remains law under the Women's Protection Act, which has introduced reforms such as distinguishing rape from adultery and which was previously blurred under the Islamic law/*Hudood* Ordinances.

5 Islamist women had protested against the excesses of the implementation of this law in public protests during Zia ul Haq's regime, alongside other liberal women's groups such as the Women's Action Forum. However, they would part ways when the latter demanded the repeal of all religious laws.

6 The case for a complete rejection of any reforms to this (and other Islamic laws) may be found in the *Jamaat e Islami* publication, "Hudood Laws and NGO's [sic]; Facts Behind the Propaganda," Institute of Women and Family Studies, (JI), Mimeo, Undated, publisher uncited, Lahore.

7 By which I mean the empowering possibilities of women's private, ritualistic religiosity was often advocated as a successful feminist strategy that gave women comfort in an otherwise male-dominated articulation of formal religion. This religious imaginary was distinguished from the

male defined Islam as found in the public forms and which depended on patriarchal interpretations of religious laws and codes.

8   One of the largest such endeavour was spearheaded by the British Government's development agency, DFID. A projects record can be found on the website of the British government's Department for International Development, http://r4d.dfid.gov.uk/Project/60091/. Similarly, USAID assistance by various departments from the government of the United States has funded countless *madrasa* reform projects (USAID 2010) and gendered ones such as, Behind the Veil (USAID 2008). Many more examples exist which promote the communitarian logic of Islam as an entry point for development projects and rational method of gender empowerment for Muslims.

9   Dr. Muhammad Khalid Masud, a Pakistani Islamic scholar acclaimed internationally and former head of the Council of Islamic Ideology (Pakistan), agrees with this term I use to describe clergy for hire. He observes that "Western countries as well as the Government of Pakistan begun seeking the Ulama's cooperation in their development policies, particularly relating to public health and female education" (Masud, in Weiss and Khattak (eds.) 2012, 192). However, Masud maintains that there is no evidence to show "if the Ulama's interventions were successful in improving public health issues, reducing the rate of population growth, or lowering maternal and infant mortality" (188). Masud suggests that, "since the Ulama still maintains its reservations toward development policies, attempts to enlist the Ulama's cooperation have strengthened its authority at the cost of development targets. Such recognition of the Ulama's influence has further politicized both religion and development in Pakistan" (192).

10   One of the leading organisations that has been involved in such projects is Shirkat Gah (Lahore), which is also the regional headquarters for Women Living Under Muslim Laws.

11   It is unclear why, after such a conclusion by the lead consultant, an expensive research study was still carried out under this category, insistent on finding development opportunities and partnerships with religious organisations and in the paradigm of something called "faith-based".

12   Bano has also been lead contributor in the Religions and Development Research Programme (RaD) funded by the British International Development Fund, DFID, in Pakistan and which was carried out by the public sector Universities of Birmingham and Bath, England, in collaboration with the private, Lahore University of Management Sciences (Pakistan). See bibliography for a list of projects.

13   *Jamaat ud Dawa* (JuD) is one of the largest missionary-based welfare organisations founded in Lahore in 1985 by Hafiz Saeed. It is commonly known as the charity cover for the banned terrorist/jihadist group, *Lashkar e Tayyaba* (LT or LeT). The welfare-jihadist nexus is further corporatised such that leaders of such organisations are often leased out

or appointed on secondment to other franchises. In the case of JuD, the example may be cited of the *Tehrik e Hurmat Rasool* (Movement for the Reverence of the Prophet) for which the convenor also belongs to the leadership of the JuD.

14 Some of the popular literature produced by the *Jamaat ud Dawa's* publishing house, *Dar ul Andalus* (House of Spain) include, "Hindu-Origin Customs and Traditions Among Muslims" and "Why Women Will Be in Majority in Hell?" See Waqar Gillani 2012, "Knowledge Bank," *The News on Sunday*, April 15.

15 Iqtidar considers this process of deprivatisation as leading to the secularisation of Pakistani society (by Islamists), while I maintain that this is the definition of the process of Islamisation.

16 This is different from Iqtidar's suggestion that it is a matter of perception and that Islamist parties may be oppressive for some, yet liberating for others. In fact, these organisations instrumentalise faith-based politics or afford agency to liberate and oppress at the same time. The agenda of Islamists permits (what Iqtidar reads as) "liberation" only if the 'freed agent' accepts an overall discriminatory or unequal framework (for women, minorities and landless classes).

17 For other examples within Muslim-majority countries, see Janine Moussa 2011.

18 A recent casualty has been the Women's Protection Act of 2006, http://www.pakistani.org/pakistan/legislation/2006/wpb.html, which was enacted in response to a 25-year campaign to repeal the discriminatory *Zina*/Adultery Ordinance. Pakistan has a dual judicial system that includes a referential Islamic court, the Federal Shariat Court, which adjudicates on legislation to ensure it is coterminous with Islamic laws. In December 2010, the FSC upheld challenges petitioned against the Women's Protection Act that had been passed under Musharraf's rule ("Certain Clauses of WPA 'Repugnant': FSC," *The Nation*, Dec. 23, 2010. http://www.nation.com.pk/pakistan-news-newspaper-daily-english-online/Politics/23-Dec-2010/Certain-clauses-of-WPA-repugnant-FSC). The FSC judgment sees some clauses as contraventions of Islamic law and is an example of one recent reversal of liberal reform.

19 The case of Davis was a widely publicised one, as he was a CIA agent who executed two young men who were allegedly chasing him on a motorbike in a busy *bazaar* in Lahore city in 2011. After 6 weeks of one of the speediest murder trials in Pakistan's legal history, Davis was pardoned by the legal heirs of the victims in a surreptitious court hearing and, according to Islamic law, in exchange for an astronomical amount of blood money (speculated in the press as donated by the Saudi government). So secretive was the closing of this deal that the counsel representing the heirs was not allowed in court during the signing of the bargain. On 17th March 2011, when the media broke the news of the acquittal and immediate flight of Davis out of the country on a private plane, the public response was one of infuriated moral indignation. For

a feminist critique of this outrage, see A.S. Zia 2011. For more on the case, see Declan Walsh 2011, "Raymond Davis Trial Underway in Pakistan," *The Guardian*, Feb 25 http://www.theguardian.com/world/2011/feb/25/raymond-davis-trial-starts-pakistan.

20 *Difaa e Pakistan Council* (Defend Pakistan Council), is one recent conglomeration of jihadist, Islamist and conservative parties, see Cyril Almeida 2011, "Rally in Lahore Sends Alarm Bells Ringing," *Dawn*, Dec. 21 http://dawn.com/2011/12/21/rally-in-lahore-sends-alarm-bells-ringing/. In 2012, nuclear scientist Dr. Qadeer Khan founded a political party called, *Tehreeq e Tahfuz Pakistan* (Movement for Protection of Pakistan).

Chapter 6

1 This is not to suggest that women artists and singers are new to any of Pakistani multi-ethnic contexts but that the Taliban's actual and symbolic footprint after 2004 spread a culture of asceticism under which artists were persecuted and threatened against performing what the militants consider "anti-Islamic" practices.

2 Some of these headlines were as follow; "Pakistan Fashion Week Begins by Models Baring Navel," *Thaindian News*, Nov. 4, 2009 http://www.thaindian.com/newsportal/south-asia/pakistan-fashion-week-begins-with-models-exposing-navels_100270312.html; "Pakistan Fashion Week Symbolic Blow to Taliban," *Fox News*, Nov. 7, 2009 http://www.foxnews.com/story/2009/11/07/pakistan-fashion-week-symbolic-blow-to-taliban.html; Chris Allbritton 2009, "Anti-terrorist Fashion; Pakistani Fashionistas Defy Taliban with Non-Islamic Dress," *The Telegraph*, Nov. 5, http://www.telegraph.co.uk/news/worldnews/asia/pakistan/6504709/Pakistan-fashion-week-defies-Taliban-with-non-Islamic-dress.html. Several media outlets quoted the CEO of Pakistan Fashion Week calling the event a "gesture of defiance against the Taliban" (Amy Oddel 2009, "Pakistan Fashion Week a 'Gesture of Defiance to the Taliban'," *nymag.com*, Nov. 9 http://www.huffington-post.com/2009/11/07/pakistan-fashion-week-def_n_349539.html; Saeed Shah 2009, "Pakistan's Fashion Week Bares Country's Frothy Side," *Mclatchy DC*, Nov. 4 http://www.mcclatchydc.com/2009/11/04/78363/pakistans-fashion-week-bares-countrys.html).

3 The reference here is to the *Maidan e Faizan* event organised by *Dawat e Islami* in Karachi in 2006, where a reported 29 women and children died partly because rescue teams of men were not allowed to enter the women's section due to Islamists' restrictions on gender mixing, see Ahmed 2006, "The Politics of Nishtar Park Massacre," *Daily Times*, May 16.

4 Iqtidar 2009; Manchanda 2012.

5 In 2013, the chief of *Jamaat e Islami*, Munawar Hasan made a public statement declaring the Taliban to be true Muslims who were worthy of "Islamic martyrdom" of a more meritorious variety than the soldiers of

the Pakistan army fighting them ("Controversial Remarks: Army Demands Apology," *Express Tribune*, Nov. 17, 2013).

6 This was the case in the murder of Governor Salmaan Taseer by his body guard in 2011 which was justified by Islamist commentators on the pretext that the Governor was *wajib ul qatl* (liable to murder) for supporting the case of an underprivileged Christian woman accused of blasphemy, "Sunni Tehreek Rejects Capital Punishment to Mumtaz Qadri," *Dawn*, Oct. 1, 2011, https://www.dawn.com/news/663094/sunni-tehreek-rejects-capital-punishment-to-mumtaz-qadri.

7 The controversy continued when Malala was nominated for the Nobel Peace Prize in 2013, and again when she went on to win it the following year. For a discussion on the reactions, see A.S. Zia 2014a.

8 Manchanda 2012; Toor 2012; Akbar and Oza 2013.

9 One example is a critical essay regarding the nexus of Pakistani and Western feminisms as reflective of what Saadia Toor terms, "Imperialist Feminism Redux," in an essay that is committed to exposing the "nativists" who posit secularism as "the necessary prerequisite for achieving equal rights for women" (Toor 2012, 149).

10 Even the examples Toor (2011) cites to differentiate between Islamisation from "above" (state-enforced) and "below" (societal) are inapplicable to Pakistan or are at best, redundant. Pakistan has experienced both simultaneously and if the dress-code for women in universities was not imposed by the state (Toor's criteria as a comparative indicator of Islamisation in Egypt), such has been the success of Islamisation of society that the majority of women attending universities in Pakistan do in fact, now observe the veil – an entirely unprecedented factor up until the 1980s.

11 One recent example was the resistance by leading male members of the conservative ruling party of the Pakistan Muslim League (Q) (which was headed by General Musharraf) and the Islamists who refused to support the Women's Protection Bill (2006) arguing that reforming the much-abused and discriminatory *Zina* (Adultery law) would turn Pakistan into a "free sex zone". Ironically, it was the liberal Pakistan People's Party that sat in opposition but supported the government's bill on principle and this allowed the law, despite the resistance, to be reformed after nearly 30 years of activists' campaigns.

12 For an interesting comparison, see Gayatri Spivak's critique of Gilles Deleuze's statement; "A theory is like a box of tools. Nothing to do with the signifier." Spivak says in response and in reference to the prescribed severance between theory and signifiers that "it is when signifiers are left to look after themselves that verbal slippages happen," cited in Morris (ed.) 2010, 28.

13 On another matter, in 2008 the CII objected to the use of the term "gender equality' by the government body, the National Commission on the Status of Women, terming it a "vague", "un-Islamic" and "absurd" term and an impractical concept given the distinct differences in

"anatomy and mental capacities" between men and women. The CII also objected to the listed criteria for membership to this Commission saying that instead, there should only be members who are knowledgeable of Islamic teachings ("'Gender Equality' Vague, "Un-islamic" Term, Says CII" *Dawn*, Dec. 17, 2008). http://www.dawn.com/news/334648/gender-equality-vague-un-islamic-term-says-cii.

14   For more on this debate see Allison 2013a and 2013b.

15   The unverified claim that Akbar and Oza make regarding the killing of the wife of the Taliban commander, Baitullah Mehsud, and that she was seen as a "justified subject of targeted killing" and considered (presumably by unnamed human rights advocates) "a necessary casualty" in a drone attack that killed them both, is total speculation and sourced as such (172). The only public opinion about the incident in Pakistan was the one circulating in conservative Urdu language media and which reported (to my mind, equally speculatively) that Mehsud was making a conjugal visit to the second wife with whom he had contracted marriage after having four daughters from his first wife. The report concluded that it was in the hope of conceiving a son that Mehsud went to his second wife's house and it was during this meeting that both were killed in a drone attack.

16   A recent example has been the attempt by the conservative Pakistan Muslim League (N) in 2013 to lift the moratorium on the death penalty in Pakistan, which had been enforced by the previous (liberal) government of the Pakistan People's Party (2008–2013). Several indicted terrorists on death row belonging to the militant group of the *Tehreeq e Taliban Pakistan*, otherwise in favour of capital punishment, threatened to respond aggressively if the government lifted the moratorium under the circumstances. The moratorium continued under the new conservative government but the decision was defended as one that was not in response to the Taliban's demand but due to economic pressure by the European Union to not lift it. This sparked a debate over the convenience of deploying liberal policies to accommodate and appease militant Islamists and convicted terrorists. (The moratorium was lifted in 2015 after the Taliban assassination of 144 school children and faculty members at a school in Peshawar).

17   One cannot speak of the private individual stands of liberals or secularists or for that matter, feminists, in the same way that the critics prefer to label in absolutist terms all those who espouse liberalism and/or secularism as some unstratified class.

18   Manchanda, Toor, Pratt, Akbar and Oza, and other contributors in Satterthwaite and Huckerby, mentioned above and listed in bibliography, and several scholars/contributors to online magazine, Tanqeed.org.

19   The evidence cited by critics of liberals/secularists is the perceived lack of their activism against drone operations by the US in Pakistan (Iqtidar 2012) and Kasuri 2012, "The Hypocrisy of Pakistan's Self-declared

Liberals," *Express Tribune*, Nov. 23. For a response, see Shehrbano 2014, "Fear of Liberal Politics," *The News*, March 14.

20 Perhaps the best exemplar of such confused political amalgams is cricketer-turned-politician, Imran Khan, who, despite being conservative in political bent, has been condemned for his self-acclaimed liberalism by the Taliban ("Taliban to Discuss Pakistan's Khan March," *Al Jazeera*, August 9, 2012). Khan often finds himself in agreement with the Islamic political parties even as he leads an independent political party. In 2006, as member of Parliament, while the Islamists boycotted the session in protest, Khan, along with the conservative Pakistan Muslim League (Nawaz group), abstained in the Parliamentary vote to reform the *Zina* Ordinance (Adultery law). It was due to the votes of the opposition party of the Pakistan People's Party (PPP) that the Musharraf government managed to pass the Women's Protection Bill.

21 See A.S. Zia 2017, "The Secular Myth," *Dawn*, May 24. https://www.dawn.com/news/1334995/the-secular-myth.

22 The references to such doubts can be found in many critical reports by Pakistanis writing for foreign journals and international agencies and newspapers including, the International Crisis Group, the New York Times, Amnesty International. Also, local NGOs and activist groups in their reports, monographs and particularly, newspapers are replete with such criticism of Musharraf's 'hoax' for international consumption.

23 This colonial (Western) law, successively 'Islamised' over the years, sits well with Islamists as it serves as a useful tool of religio-political leverage in contemporary Pakistan.

24 In 2009, the ruling (liberal) Pakistan People's Party passed the controversial Nizam e Adl which effectively surrendered judicial authority to the militant group, *Tehreeq e Nifaz e Sharia Muhammad* (TNSM–Movement for Sharia Justice), in the Malakand Division as part of a peace deal brokered with them. The TNSM instituted Qazi (Islamic) courts for 'swift Islamic justice' in place of the lay courts that run the judicial system of Pakistan. The peace deal broke down a month later and a military operation ensued against the militants but the government has not repealed the new 'swift' justice system. Liberal women's groups called this deal "constitutional suicide" by the Parliament where there was no debate nor dissenting voices on record, with the single exception of woman Parliamentarian, Sherry Rehman. The myth of an elite liberal resistance to the power of religiosity in Pakistan is overestimated in post-secularist scholarship.

25 It is unclear whether Pakistani anthropological scholars such as Iqtidar would consider or define the training of jihadists by Pakistan's military and their engagement as proxies in wars against these countries as "state terrorism".

26 The Human Rights Commission of Pakistan (HRCP) has also maintained a log that is released in every annual report (prior to and) since the launch of the "WoT", on human rights violations during counter-

insurgency operations and warned against the impact of extra-judicial killings in this context.

27 The Human Rights Commission of Pakistan, often a target of Islamist hostility for its liberal stands, has consistently upheld the legal and human rights of terrorist suspects and lobbied against Anti-Terrorist Courts as extra-judicial and against principles of the human right to due legal process.

28 Sisters in Islam is a 'Muslim Women's NGO' formed since 1987 in Malaysia.

29 *Musawah* (equality in Arabic) is another organisation and global network (launched in 2009 at a meeting in Malaysia) that works on issues of equality and justice in the Muslim family.

Chapter 7

1 One of the points of negotiations conceded by the Islamist-led provincial government, the *Muttahida Majlis-e-Amal*, was to allow Mullah Fazlullah's radio broadcasts to continue in return for his agreement to support the polio vaccination campaign and terminate militant training facilities.

2 In the peace negotiations, the Taliban in Swat agreed to cease attacks on Pakistani security forces and government installations and to dismantle militia and deny shelter to foreign militants. In return, the Pakistani government agreed to release Swat militants from jail, to implement Sharia in the entire region, to establish an Islamic university in Imam Dehri and, to withdraw troops from the Swat region. Subsequently, neither of the parties fulfilled their parts of the agreement and a military operation was launched against the militants.

3 The Taliban consider maintaining beards an Islamic obligation and that shaving these amounts to un-Islamic behaviour.

4 Iqtidar suggests that the TNSM (*Tehreeq e Nifaz e Sharia e Muhammad*) translates into, 'Movement for Implementation of Mohammaden Law' although the 'S' in the acronym stands for Sharia and not law. Iqtidar's attempt is to dislodge Sufi Muhammad's agenda as problematic by claiming that he substitutes "Law" for "Sharia" which reveals his leaning towards a rigid set of Islamic laws rather than "Sharia" which, according to Iqtidar, is a "broad[er] set of guidelines allowing greater subjectivity and contextualisation to the individual judge than "law" does" (Iqtidar 2009 online). Why Sufi Mohammad's interpretation of the Sharia should be seen as "problematic" and narrow compared to other interpretations is irrelevant because it was not he but a cadre of madrasa qualified Islamic judges or Qazis, who were instituted as part of Sufi's justice movement and who continue to adjudicate on cases in Swat today. The texts of these judgments have yet to be studied (see Kamal 2010).

5 After the 2013 national elections, local bodies were restored but elec-

tions were staggered across the provinces. Women councillors remain active where elected.

6   Saigol (2010, 76) cites Bina Agarwal's (1996) observations on the Tebhaga peasant uprising in India, where the female participants objected to wife beating and "the women argued that if the men and women are together fighting in the battle for Tebhaga against a common enemy 'how then was it possible for one soldier to beat the other after returning home?'"

7   There was some talk that the Khanewal-based women of AMP had formed an appendage organisation called the Peasant Women's Society in 2008. By 2011, the society was operating in seven districts of Punjab, including Okara. Their main demand is for land rights for landless women peasants to be given from state land. The Okara struggle resurfaced in 2015–16.

8   Although, many women councillors in Swat were also targeted by the Taliban in the same way the health workers were.

Bibliography

Abbas, Sadia (2014) *At Freedom's Limit: Islam and the Postcolonial Predicament*. Fordham University Press.

—— (2013) "The Echo Chamber of Freedom: The Muslim Woman and the Pretext of Agency." *boundary 2* 40 (1): 155–189.

Abu-Lughod, Lila (2002) "Do Muslim Women Really Need Saving? Anthropological Reflections on Cultural Relativism and Its Others." *American Anthropologist New Series* 104 (3): 783–790.

—— (2013) *Do Muslim Women Need Saving?* Cambridge, MA: Harvard University Press.

Afshar, Haleh (1998) *Islam and Feminisms: An Iranian Case-Study*. New York: St. Martin's Press.

—— (1996) "Islam and Feminism: An Analysis of Political Strategies." In *Feminism and Islam: Legal and Literary Perspectives*, edited by M. Yamani. New York: Ithaca Press.

Afshari, Reza (2012) "Iran: An Anthropologist Engaging the Human Rights Discourse and Practice." *Human Rights Quarterly* 34 (2): 507–545.

Afzal-Khan, Fawzia (2008) "What Lies Beneath: Dispatch from the Front Lines of the Burqa Brigade." *Social Identities* 14 (1): 3–11.

Agarwal, Bina (1996) "A Field of One's Own; Gender and Land Rights in South Asia." *Land Economics* 72 (2) May: 269–273.

Ahmad, Irfan (2009) *Islamism and Democracy in India: The Transformation of Jamaat e Islami*. New Jersey: Princeton University Press.

Ahmad, Nausheen (1998) "The Superior Judiciary: Implementation of Law and Impact on Women." In *Shaping Women's Lives: Law, Practices and Strategies in Pakistan*, edited by F. Shaheed, S.A.Warraich, C. Balchin, and A. Gazdar. Lahore, Pakistan: Shirkat Gah.

Ahmad, Sadaf (2009) *Transforming Faith; The Story of Al-Huda and Islamic Revivalism Among Urban Pakistani Women*. New York: Syracuse University Press.

Ahmed, Khaled (2006) "The Politics of Nishtar Park Massacre." *Daily Times*, May 16. http://www.dailytimes.com.pk/default.asp?page=2006%5C05%5C16%5Cstory_16-5-2006_pg3_3 (last accessed December 2015).

Ahmed, Leila (1993) *Women and Gender in Islam: Historical Roots of a Modern Debate*. New Haven: Yale University Press.

Ahmed-Ghosh, Huma (2008) "Dilemmas of Islamic and Secular Feminists and Feminisms." *Journal of International Women's Studies* 9 (3): 99–116.

Akbar, Amna, and Oza, Rupal (2013) "'Muslim Fundamentalism' and Human Rights in an Age of Terror and Empire." In *Gender, National Security, and Counter-Terrorism: Human Rights Perspectives*, edited by M.L. Satterthwaite, and J.C. Huckerby. Routledge.

Akhtar, Aasim Sajjad (2016) "Dreams of a Secular Republic: Elite Alienation in Post-Zia Pakistan." *Journal of Contemporary Asia* 46(4): 641–658.

Al-Hibri, Azizah (1982) "A Study of Islamic Herstory: Or How Did We Ever Get Into This Mess?" *Women's Studies International Forum* 5 (2): 207–219.

Al Jazeera (2012) "Taliban to Discuss Pakistan's Khan March," August 9. http://www.aljazeera.com/news/asia/2012/08/2012891471380547.html.

Ali, Shaheen Sardar (2006) *Conceptualising Islamic Law, CEDAW and Women's Human Rights in Plural Legal Settings: A Comparative Analysis of Application of CEDAW in Bangladesh, India and Pakistan*. Report. New Delhi: UNIFEM.

Ali, Shaheen Sardar, and Naz, Rukshunda (1998) "Marriage, Dower and Divorce: Superior Courts and Case Law in Pakistan." In *Shaping Women's Lives: Law, Practices and Strategies in Pakistan*, edited by F. Shaheed, S. A.Warraich, C. Balchin, and A. Gazdar. Lahore, Pakistan: Shirkat Gah.

Allison, Katherine (2013a) "American Occidentalism and the Agential Muslim Woman." *Review of International Studies* 39 (3): 665–684.

—— (2013b) "Feminism and 10 Years of the War on Terror." *Critical Studies on Terrorism* 6 (2): 320–322.

Almeida, Cyril (2011) "Rally in Lahore Sends Alarm Bells Ringing." *Dawn*, December 21. http://dawn.com/2011/12/21/rally-in-lahore-sends-alarm-bells-ringing/.

Alwan, Ala Dr. (2013) "Address To The Islamic Scholars' Consultation." Cairo, Egypt, 6–7 March. http://applications.emro.who.int/docs/RD_Speech_Mesg_2013_EN_14849.pdf.

Amir-Moazami, Schirin, Jacobsen, Christine M, and Malik, Maleiha (2011) "Islam and Gender in Europe: Subjectivities, Politics and Piety." *Feminist Review* 98 (1): 1–8.

An-Na'im, Abdullahi Ahmed (2008) *Islam and the Secular State: Negotiating the Future of Shari'a*. Cambridge, MA: Harvard University Press.

—— (1990) *Toward an Islamic Reformation: Civil Liberties, Human Rights, and International Law*. Syracuse, NY: Syracuse University Press.

—— (2001) "Human Rights in the Arab World: A Regional Perspective." *Human Rights Quarterly* 23(3): 701.

Appiah, Kwame Anthony (1991) "Is the Post- in Postmodernism the Post- in Postcolonial?" *Critical Inquiry* 17 (2): 336–357.

Asad, Talal (2003) *Formations of the Secular: Christianity, Islam, Modernity*. Stanford, CA: Stanford University Press.

Asad, Talal, Brown, Wendy, Butler, Judith, and Mahmood, Saba (2009) *Is*

Critique Secular? Blasphemy, Injury, and Free Speech: Berkley: Townsend Centre for Humanities: Distributed by University of California Press.

Aziz, Sadaf (2005) "Beyond Petition and Redress: Mixed Legality and Consent in Marriage in Pakistan." *Bayan* IV: 55–70. Simorgh Publication: Lahore.

—— (2011) "Making a Sovereign State: Javed Ghamidi and 'Enlightened Moderation'." *Modern Asian Studies* 45 (3): 597–629.

Azzam, Maha (1996) "Gender and the Politics of Religion in the Middle-East." In *Feminism and Islam: Legal and Literary Perspectives,* edited by M. Yamani. New York: Ithaca Press.

Baabar, Mariana (2009) "Swat the System." *Outlook India*, April 20. http://keepingcount.wordpress.com/2009/04/11/flogging-in-swat-pakistan/.

Badran, Margot (2011) "From Islamic Feminism to a Muslim Holistic Feminism." *IDS Bulletin* 42(1): 78–87.

Badran, Margot, and Cooke, Miriam (Eds.) (2004) *Opening the Gates: An Anthology of Arab Feminist Writing.* Bloomington: Indiana University Press.

Balchin, Cassandra (2011) "Avoiding Some Deadly Sins: Oxfam Learnings and Analysis About Religion, Culture, Diversity, and Development." Oxfam Discussion Papers. Oxfam GB.

Bannerji, Himani, Mojab, Shahrzad, and Whitehead, Judith (2001) *Of Property and Propriety: The Role of Gender and Class in Imperialism and Nationalism.* Toronto: University of Toronto Press.

—— (2010) "Of Property and Propriety: The Role of Gender and Class in Imperialism and Nationalism: A Decade Later." *Comparative Studies of South Asia, Africa and the Middle East* 30 (2): 262–271.

Bannerji, Himani (2000) "Projects of Hegemony: Towards a Critique of Subaltern Studies' 'Resolution of the Women's Question.'" *Economic and Political Weekly* 35(11) March 11–17: 902–920.

Bano, Masooda (2005) "Review of 'The Charitable Crescent: Politics of Aid in the Muslim World' by Jonathan Benthall and Jerome Bellion-Jourdan, London, I. B.Tauris, 2003." *Journal of Islamic Studies* 16 (3): 383–386.

—— (2007) "Contesting Ideologies and Struggle for Authority: State-Madrasa Engagement in Pakistan." Working Paper 55. University of Birmingham and DFID: Religions and Development Research Programme, UK. http://epapers.bham.ac.uk/1566/1/Bano_Pakistan.pdf.

—— (2009a) "Rethinking Madrasa Reform in Pakistan." Religions and Development Research Programme: Policy Brief 1. https://assets.publishing.service.gov.uk/media/57a08b71ed915d622 c000ca7/Policy_Brief_1_2009.pdf

—— (2009b) "Marker of Identity: Religious Political Parties and Development Work – The Case of Jama'at-i-Islami in Pakistan and Bangladesh." Working Paper 34. University of Birmingham and DFID. Religions and Development Research Programme, UK.

https://assets.publishing.service.gov.uk/media/57a08b8a40f0b652
dd000d2c/wp34.pdf

—— (2010a) "Madrasas as Partners in Education Provision: The South Asian Experience." *Development in Practice* 20 (4–5): 554–566.

—— (2010b) "Female Madrasas in Pakistan: A Response to Modernity." Working Paper 45. University of Birmingham and DFID: Religions and Development Research Programme, UK. https://assets.publishing.service. gov.uk/media/57a08b1ded915d622c000aed/working_paper_45.pdf.

—— (2012a) *Breakdown in Pakistan: How Aid is Eroding Institutions for Collective Action.* Stanford, CA: Stanford University Press.

—— (2012b) *The Rational Believer; Choices and Decisions in the Madrasas of Pakistan.* Ithaca: Cornell University Press.

Bano, Saira (2009) "Women in Parliament in Pakistan: Problems and Potential Solutions." *Women's Studies Journal* 23 (1): 19–35.

Bari, Farzana (2009) "Role and Performance Assessment of Pakistani Women Parliamentarians 2002–2007." Monograph. Pattan: Islamabad.

Bari, Farzana, and Khattak, Saba Gul (2001) "Power Configurations in Public and Private Arenas: The Women's Movement's Response." In *Power and Civil Society in Pakistan*, edited by A. M. Weiss and S. Z. Gilani. Pakistan: Oxford University Press.

Bari, Sarwar (2010) "An Unfinished Struggle: The Tale of the Women Councillors' Network." Monograph. Pattan: Islamabad.

Barlas, Asma (2002) *"Believing Women" in Islam: Unreading Patriarchal Interpretations of the Qur'an.* Austin: University of Texas Press.

Bartolovich, Crystal, and Lazarus, Neil (Eds.) (2002) *Marxism, Modernity and Postcolonial Studies.* Cambridge: Cambridge University Press.

Basu, Amrita and Jeffery, Patricia (Eds.) (1999) *Resisting the Sacred and Secular: Women's Activism and Politicised Religion in South Asia.* India: Kali.

Batliwala, Srilatha (2007) "Taking the Power Out of Empowerment – An Experiential Account." *Development In Practice* 17 (4–5): 557–565.

Bautista, Julius (2008) "The Meta-theory of Piety: Reflections on the Work of Saba Mahmood." *Contemporary Islam* 2: 75–83.

BBC News (2006) "Pakistan Votes to Amend Rape Laws," November 15. http://news.bbc.co.uk/2/hi/south_asia/6148590.stm.

Benthall, Jonathan, and Bellion-Jourdan, Jerome (2003) *The Charitable Crescent: Politics of Aid in the Muslim World.* I.B. Tauris: London.

Bhasin, Kamla, Khan, Nighat S., and Kumar, Ritu (Eds.) (1994) *Against All Odds: Essays on Women, Religion, and Development from India and Pakistan.* India: Kali.

Bhatti, M. Waqar (2013) "Unicef Publishes Fatwas in Favour of Polio Vaccination." *The News*, March 14. http://www.thenews.com.pk/Todays-News-4-165123-Unicef-publishes-fatwas-...%E2%80%8E.

Bokhari, Farhan and Johnson, Jo (2007) "Pakistani Forces Kill Red Mosque Cleric." *Financial Times*, July 10.

Boubekeur, Amel (2004) "Female Religious Professionals in France."

International Institute for the Study of Islam in the Modern World Newsletter 14.

Brah, Avtar (1993) "'Race' and 'Culture' in the Gendering of Labour Markets: South Asian Young Muslim Women and the Labour Market." *Journal of Ethnic and Migration Studies* 19 (3): 441–458.

Brohi, Nazish (2006) "The MMA Offensive; Three Years in Power 2003–2005." Monograph. Islamabad: Action Aid.

—— (2010) "The Inheritance of Loss?" *Daily Times*, January 29. http://www.dailytimes.com.pk/default.asp?page=2010%5C01%5C29%5Cstory_29-1-2010_pg3_6 – (last accessed, December 2015).

—— (2012) "The Swat Retrospective: Collective Reflections on the Taliban Encounter and the Consequent Conflict by Women in Communities Across Swat District." Unpublished paper.

Brown, Wendy (2011) "Thinking in Time: An Epilogue on Ethics and Politics." In *The Question of Gender: Joan W Scott's Critical Feminism*, edited by J. Butler and E. Weed. Bloomington: Indiana University Press.

Butler, Judith (2003) *Precarious Life: The Powers of Mourning and Violence.* London: Verso.

—— (2008) "Sexual Politics, Torture, and Secular Time." *British Journal of Sociology* 59 (1): 1–23.

Calhoun, Craig, Juergensmeyer, Mark, and Anterwerpen, Jonathan Van (Eds.) (2011) *Rethinking Secularism.* New York: Oxford University Press.

Carey, Daniel, and Festa, Lynn (Eds.) (2009) *The Postcolonial Enlightenment: Eighteenth-Century Colonialism and Postcolonial Theory.* New York: Oxford University Press.

Carmit Karin, Yefet (2011) "The Constitution and Female-Initiated Divorce in Pakistan: Western Liberalism In Islamic Garb." *Harvard Journal of Law and Gender* 34: 553–615.

Casanova, José (1994) *Public Religions in the Modern World.* Chicago: University of Chicago Press.

—— (2009) "Religion, Politics and Gender Equality: Public Religions Revisited." In 'A Debate on the Public Role of Religion and its Social and Gender Implications.' UNRISD Gender and Development Programme, paper no. 5. Geneva.

Chakrabarty, Dipesh (2000) *Provincializing Europe: Postcolonial Thought and Historical Difference.* New Jersey: Princeton University Press.

Chatterjee, Partha (1982) "More on Modes of Power and the Peasantry." In *Subaltern Studies: Writings on South Asian History and Society II* (311–49), edited by R. Guha. Delhi: New York: Oxford University Press.

—— (1990) "The Nationalist Resolution of the Women's Question." In *Recasting Women: Essays in Colonial History,* edited by K. Sangari and S. Vaid. New Brunswick: Rutgers University Press.

—— (2007) "Postcolonialism and the New Imperialism." In *The Present as History: Critical Perspectives on Global Power*, by N. Shaikh. New York: Columbia University Press.

Cheema, Iftikhar, Farhat, Maham, Hunt, Simon, Javeed, Sarah, Keck,

Katharina, and O'Leary, Sean (2015) 'Benazir Income Support Programme: Second Impact Evaluation Report.' Oxford Policy Management. http://www.bisp.gov.pk/Others/2ndImpactEvaluation.pdf.

Cheema, Moeen H., and Akbar, Shahzad (2010) "Liberal Fundamentalism?" *The News*, January 7. https://www.thenews.com.pk/archive/print/215205-liberal-fundamentalism?

Cheema, Moeen H. and Mustafa, Abdul-Rahman (2008–2009) "From the Hudood Ordinances to the Protection of Women Act: Islamic Critiques of the Hudood Laws of Pakistan." *UCLA Journal of Islamic and Near Eastern Law* 8: 1–48.

Chopan-Daud, Malaiz (2012) "The Pakistan Lawyers' Movement: Setting a Course for Genuine Democracy?" *openDemocracy*, March 6. http://www.opendemocracy.net/opensecurity/malaiz-chopan-daud/pakistan-lawyers-movement-setting-course-for-genuine-democracy.

Conway, Gordon (1997) "Islamophobia: Its Features and Dangers: a Consultation Paper." Runnymede Trust Commission on British Muslims and Islamophobia: Runnymede Trust.

Collins, Andrea A. (2016) "'Empowerment' as Efficiency and Participation: Gender in Responsible Agricultural Investment Principles." *International Feminist Journal of Politics*. Published online 5 August, 2016.

Cornwall, Andrea and Rivas, Althea-Maria (2015) "From 'Gender Equality' and 'Women's Empowerment' to Global Justice: Reclaiming a Transformative Agenda for Gender and Development." *Third World Quarterly* 36 (2): 396–415.

Dabashi, Hamid (2011) *Brown Skin, White Masks*. Pluto Press.

Daily Times (2009) "Religious Scholars Denounce Whipping of Girl by Taliban," April 4. http://www.dailytimes.com.pk/default.asp?page=2009%5C04%5C04%5Cstory_4-4-2009_pg7_30 (last accessed December 2015).

Das, Veena (1996) *Critical Events: An Anthropological Perspective on Contemporary India*. New Delhi: Oxford University Press.

Dawn (2008) "Pak Hindus Rally to Support Jamaatud Dawa," December 17. http://archives.dawn.com/2008/12/17/nat4.htm, http://archives.dawn.com/archives/125499.

Dawn (2009) "Flogging of Girl in Swat Widely Condemned," April 5. http://archives.dawn.com/archives/133954

Dawn (2010) "Anti-Polio Campaign Faces Threats of Boycott," February 9. http://dawn.com/news/519244/anti-polio-campaign-faces-threats-of-boycott

Dawn (2010) "Woman Suicide Bomber Strikes at WFP Centre; 45 Killed," December 25. http://www.dawn.com/news/593552/explosion-in-bajaur-agencies-khar-head-quarter-several-injured.

Dawn (2011) "Women's Rights Amendments to Nikahnama Proposed," March 31. http://www.dawn.com/2011/03/31/womens-rights-amendments-to-nikahnama-proposed/.

Dawn (2012) "Madonna Slams Taliban, Dedicates Song to Malala at

Concert," October 11. http://dawn.com/2012/10/11/madonna-slams-taliban-dedicates-song-to-malala-at-concert/.

Dawn (2012) "Fifty Muslim Scholars Issue Fatwa Against Taliban," October 11. https://www.dawn.com/news/755908.

Dawn (2013) "Who's Sadiq and Ameen?" April 5. http://www.dawn.com/news/800478/whos-sadiq-and-ameen.

Deb, Basuli (2012) "Transnational Politics and Feminist Inquiries in the Middle East: An Interview with Lila Abu-Lughod." *Postcolonial Text* 7(1): 1–12.

Deneulin, Severine with Bano, Masooda (2009) *Religion in Development: Rewriting the Secular Script*. Zed Books.

Devji, Faisal (2005) *Landscapes of the Jihad: Militancy, Morality, Modernity*. Ithaca: Cornell University Press.

—— (2008) "Red Mosque." *Public Culture* 20(1): 19–26.

Eagleton, Terry (1999) "In the Gaudy Supermarket." Review of A Critique of Post-Colonial Reason: Toward a History of the Vanishing Present, by Gayatri Chakravorty Spivak. *London Review of Books* 21 (10): 3–6.

Ebrahim, Zofeen (2011) "Pakistan: Health Workers Without Maternity Leave." *Inter Press Service*, April 27. http://www.ipsnews.net/2011/04/pakistan-health-workers-without-maternity-leave/.

Esposito, John Louis (1982) *Women in Muslim Family Law*. Syracuse: Syracuse University Press.

Farooq, Ghulam (2009) "MPs Who Opposed Nizam-e-Adl Are No Longer Muslims: Sufi." *Daily Times*, April 18. http://archives.dailytimes.com.pk/national/18-Apr-2009/mps-who-opposed-nizam-e-adl-are-no-longer-muslims-sufi (last accessed December 2015).

Ferguson, Michaele L. (2005) "'W' Stands for Women: Feminism and Security Rhetoric in the Post-9/11 Bush Administration." *Politics and Gender* 1(1): 9–38.

Ghanea, Nazila (2007) "'Phobias' and 'Isms': Recognition of Difference or the Slippery Slope of Particularism?" In *Does God Believe in Human Rights? Essays on Religion and Human Rights*, edited by N. Ghanea, A. Stephens, and R. Walden. Leiden: Martinus Nijhoff.

Gillani, Waqar (2012) "Knowledge Bank." *The News on Sunday*, April 15 (last accessed, December 2015).

Gillani, Waqar, and Sengupta, Somini (2009) "Pakistan Court Orders Release of Militant Suspected of Ties to Mumbai Attacks." *New York Times*, June 2. http://www.nytimes.com/2009/06/03/world/asia/03lahore.html?ref=lashkaretaiba

Global Polio Eradication Initiative Newsletter (2013), March 7. http://polio-eradication.org/tabid/488/iid/279/Default.aspx.

Gökariksel, Banu, and McLarney, Ellen (2010) "Muslim Women, Consumer Capitalism, and the Islamic Culture Industry." *Journal of Middle East Women's Studies* 6 (3): 1–18.

Goldenberg, Suzanne, and Shah, Saeed (2008) "Mystery of 'Ghost of Bagram' – Victim of Torture or Captured in a Shootout?" *The Guardian*, August 6.

https://www.theguardian.com/world/2008/aug/06/pakistan.afghanistan.

Gourgouris, Stathis (2008a) "Detranscendentalizing the Secular." *Public Culture* 20(3): 437–445.

—— (2008b) "Antisecularist Failures: A Counterresponse to Saba Mahmood." *Public Culture* 20(3): 453–459.

Grewal, Inderpal, and Kaplan, Caren (Eds.) (1994) *Scattered Hegemonies: Postmodernity and Transnational Feminist Practices*. Minneapolis: University of Minnesota Press.

Gruber, Aya (2013) "Neofeminism." *Houston Law Review* 50 (5): 1325–1390.

Grünenfelder, Julia (2013a) "Discourses of Gender Identities and Gender Roles in Pakistan: Women and Non-domestic Work in Political Representations." *Women's Studies International Forum* 40: 68–77.

—— (2013b) "Negotiating Gender Relations: Muslim Women and Formal Employment in Pakistan's Rural Development Sector." *Gender, Work & Organization* 20 (6): 599–615.

Guha, Ranajit (1983) *Elementary Aspects of Peasant Insurgency in Colonial India*. New Delhi: Oxford University Press.

Hafez, Sherine (2011) *An Islam of Her Own: Reconsidering Religion and Secularism in Women's Islamic Movements*. New York; London: New York University Press.

Haider, Nadya (2000) "Islamic Legal Reform: The Case Of Pakistan And Family Law." *Yale Journal of Law & Feminism* 2 (2) Article 5: 287–341.

Hajjar, Lisa (2004) "Religion, State Power, and Domestic Violence in Muslim Societies: A Framework for Comparative Analysis." *Law and Social Inquiry* 29 (1): 1–38.

Hardiman, David (1981) *Peasant Nationalists of Gujarat: Kheda District, 1917–1934*. Delhi; New York: Oxford University Press.

Haroon, Sana (2007) *Frontier of Faith: Islam, in the Indo-Afghan Borderland*. New York: Columbia University Press.

—— (2011) "Pakistan: the Taliban's Successful Marriage of Dogma and Custom." *openDemocracy*, February 14. http://www.opendemocracy.net/5050/sana-haroon/pakistan-talibans-successful-marriage-of-dogma-and-custom. –

Haq, Farhat (2007) "Militarism and Motherhood: The Women of the Lashkar-i-Tayyabia in Pakistan." *Signs: Journal of Women in Culture and Society* 32 (4): 1023–1046.

Hartsock, Nancy (1987) "Rethinking Modernism, Majority Versus Minority Theories." *Cultural Critique* 7:187–312.

Harvard Law Review (2010) "Notes: The Pakistani Lawyers' Movement And The Popular Currency Of Judicial Power." *HLR* 123: 1705–1726.

Harvey, David (1990) *The Conditions of Postmodernity: An Enquiry into the Origins of Cultural Change*. Blackwell.

Hasan, Ali Dayan (2005) "Pakistan's Moderates are Beaten in Public." *New York Times*, June 15. http://www.nytimes.com/2005/06/14/opinion/14iht-edhasan.html.

Hashemi, Syed M., Schuler, Sidney Ruth, and Riley, Ann P. (1996) "Rural Credit Programs and Women's Empowerment in Bangladesh." *World Development* 24 (4): 635–653.

Hashmi, Salima (1995) "Creativity and the Women's Movement." In *A Celebration of Women; Essays and Abstracts from the Women's Studies Conference,* edited by N.S. Khan, R. Saigol, A.S. Zia. Lahore: ASR Resource Centre.

Hassan, Riffat (1980) "The Role and Responsibilities of Women in the Legal and Ritual Tradition of Islam." Paper presented at a bi-annual meeting of a Trialogue of Jewish-Christian-Muslim Scholars at the Joseph and Rose Kennedy Institute of Ethics, Washington, DC., October 14.

—— (1982) "On Human Rights and the Quranic Perspective." In *Human Rights in Religious Traditions,* edited by A. Swidler. New York: Pilgrim Press.

—— (1990) "An Islamic Perspective." In *Women, Religion and Sexuality,* edited by J. Becher. Geneva: WCC Publications.

—— (2001) "Challenging the Stereotypes of Fundamentalism: An Islamic Feminist Perspective." *Muslim World* 91 (1/2): 5–6.

—— (2002) "Islam and Human Rights in Pakistan: A Critical Analysis of the Positions of Three Contemporary Women." Unpublished paper. http://www.mediamonitor.net/riffathassan1.html.

Hatem, Mervat (1998) "Secular and Islamist Discourses on Modernity in Egypt and Evolution of the Postcolonial Nation-State." In *Islam, Gender, and Social Change,* edited by Y. Haddad and J.L. Esposito. New York: Oxford University Press.

—— (1986) "The Enduring Alliance of Nationalism and Patriarchy in Muslim Personal Status Laws: The Case of Modern Egypt." *Feminist Issues* 6 (1): 19–43.

Hauner, Milan (1981) "One Man against the Empire: The Faqir of Ipi and the British in Central Asia on the Eve of and during the Second World War." *Journal of Contemporary History* 16 (1): 183–212.

Hedges, Chris (2009) *Empire of Illusion: The End of Literacy and The Triumph of Spectacle.* Vintage: Canada.

—— (2010) *Death of the Liberal Class.* Knopf: Canada.

Hirschkind, Charles and Mahmood, Saba (2002) "Feminism, the Taliban, and Politics of Counter-Insurgency." *Anthropological Quarterly* 75 (2) 339–54.

Hudood Laws and NGOs; Facts Behind the Propaganda. Undated Monograph. Institute of Women and Family Studies, Jamaat e Islami. Lahore: Publisher uncited.

Human Rights Commission of Pakistan, Annual Report (2006) *State of Human Rights in 2005.* Maktaba Jadeed Press: Pakistan.

Human Rights Watch (2004) *Soiled Hands: The Pakistan Army's Repression of the Punjab Farmers' Movement.* Report 16 (1) July. http://www.hrw.org/reports/2004/pakistan0704/pakistan0704.pdf.

Hunt, Krista and Rygiel, Kim (Eds.) (2006) *(En)gendering the War on Terror: War Stories and Camouflaged Politics*. England: Ashgate.

Ikramullah, Shaista Suhrawardy (1998) *From Purdah to Parliament*. Pakistan: Oxford University Press (first published 1963).

Iqbal, Nasir (2005) "CII Okays Draft Bill to Stop Marriage with Quran." *Dawn*, June 17. http://archives.dawn.com/2005/06/17/nat6.htm.

Iqbal, Nasira (1992) *Law of Qisas and Diyat: A Critique*. Monograph. Lahore: ASR Resource Centre.

Iqtidar, Humeira (2009) "Who Are the Taliban in Swat?" *openDemocracy*, April 30. http://www.opendemocracy.net/article/email/who-are-the-taliban-in-swat.

—— (2011a) *Secularizing Islamists? Jamaat-i-Islami and Jama`at-ud-Da`wa in Urban Pakistan*. Chicago; London: Chicago University Press.

—— (2011b) "Secularism Beyond the State: the 'State' and the 'Market' in Islamist Imagination." *Modern Asian Studies* 45 (3): 535–564.

—— (2012) "Secularism and Secularization; Untying the Knots." *Economic and Political Weekly* 47 (35) September 1: 50–58.

Jad, Islah (2011) "Islamism and Secularism: Between State Instrumentalisation and Opposition Islamic Movements." *IDS Bulletin* 42 (1): 41–46.

Jafri, Owais (2012) "Pakistan Constitution Should Make Hijab Compulsory: JI." *Express Tribune*, September 2. http://tribune.com.pk/story/430181/pakistan-constitution-should-make-hijab-compulsory-ji/.

Jahangir, Asma (1998) "The Origins of the MFLO: Reflections for Activism." In *Shaping Women's Lives: Law, Practices and Strategies in Pakistan*, edited by F. Shaheed, S.A. Warraich, C. Balchin, and A. Gazdar. Lahore: Shirkat Gah.

Jahangir, Asma and Jilani, Hina (1990) *The Hudood Ordinances; A Divine Sanction?* Lahore: Rohtas Books.

Jalal, Ayesha (1991) "The Convenience of Subservience: Women and the State of Pakistan." In *Women, Islam and the State*, edited by D. Kandiyoti. London: Macmillan.

—— (2000) 'South Asia.' *Encyclopedia of Nationalisms*. Academic Press. http://www.tufts.edu/~ajalal01/Articles/encyclopedia.nationalism.pdf

—— (2008) *Partisans of Allah: Jihad in South Asia*. Cambridge, MA: Harvard University Press.

Jamal, Amina (2005) "'Feminist 'Selves' and Feminism's 'Others'; Feminist Representations of Jamaat-e-Islami Women in Pakistan." *Feminist Review* 81: 52–73.

—— (2005) "Transnational Feminism as Critical Practice; A Reading of Feminist Discourses in Pakistan." *Meridians* 5 (2): 57–82.

—— (2009) "Gendered Islam and Modernity in the Nation-Spaces; Women's Modernism in the Jamaat-e-Islami of Pakistan." *Feminist Review* 91 (1): 9–28.

—— (2013) *Jamaat-e-Islami Women in Pakistan: Vanguard of a New Modernity?* New York: Syracuse University Press.

Jayawardena, Kumari (1996) *Feminism and Nationalism in the Third World.* London: Zed Books.

Jeffery, Patricia (1999) "Agency, Activism and Agendas." In *Resisting the Sacred and Secular; Women's Activism and Politicised Religion in South Asia,* edited by A. Basu and P. Jeffery. India: Kali.

Jejeebhoy, Shireen J., and Sathar, Zeba A. (2001) "Women's Autonomy in India and Pakistan: The Influence of Religion and Region." *Population And Development Review* 27(4): 687–712.

Joseph, Suad (General Ed.), and Marilyn Booth et al. (Associate Eds.) (2013) *Women and Islamic Cultures: Disciplinary Paradigms and Approaches, 2003–2013.* Leiden; Boston: Brill.

Kabeer, Naila (1994) *Reversed Realities: Gender Hierarchies in Development Thought.* London: Verso.

—— (2012) "Empowerment, Citizenship and Gender Justice: A Contribution to Locally Grounded Theories of Change in Women's Lives." *Ethics and Social Welfare* 6 (3): 216–232.

Kalmbach, Hilary, and Bano, Masooda (Eds.) (2011a) *Women, Leadership, and Mosques: Changes in Contemporary Islamic Authority.* Leiden: Brill.

—— (2011b) "The Spread of Female Islamic Leadership." *openDemocracy,* November 21. http://www.opendemocracy.net/5050/masooda-bano-hilary-kalmbach/spread-of-female-islamic-leadership.

Kamal, Seemin (2010) "Nizam E Adl Inside Out: A Study of Nizam-E-Adl in the Light of the Constitution, Women's Policies and the Perceptions of Pakistani Society." Report for the National Commission on the Status of Women. Islamabad: Government of Pakistan. http://www.ncsw.gov.pk/publications.

Kamalkhani, Zehra (1998) *Women's Islam: Religious Practice among Women in Today's Iran.* London: Kegan Paul International.

Kandiyoti, Deniz (Ed.) (1991a) *Women, Islam and the State.* London: Macmillan.

—— (1991b) "Identity and Its Discontents: Women and the Nation." *Millennium: Journal of International Studies* 20 (3): 429–43.

—— (1991c) "Islam and Patriarchy: A Comparative Perspective." In *Women in Middle Eastern History: Shifting Boundaries in Sex and Gender,* edited by N. R. Keddie and B. Baron. New Haven; London: Yale University Press.

—— (1995) "Reflections on Gender in Muslim Societies: From Nairobi to Beijing." In *Faith and Freedom: Women's Human Rights in the Muslim World,* edited by M. Afkhami. Syracuse, NY: Syracuse University Press.

—— (1996) "Islam and Feminism: A Misplaced Polarity." *Women Against Fundamentalism* 8: 10–13.

—— (2009) "Gender in Afghanistan: Pragmatic Activism." *openDemocracy,* November 2. http://www.opendemocracy.net/deniz-kandiyoti/gender-in-afghanistan-pragmatic-activism.

Karmi, Ghada (1991) 'Women, Islam and Patriarchalism." In *Feminism and Islam: Legal and Literary Perspectives,* edited by M. Yamani. New York; London: New York University Press.

Kasuri, Ifsundiar (2012) "The Hypocrisy of Pakistan's Self-declared Liberals." *Express Tribune*, November 23. http://tribune.com.pk /story/470237/the-hypocrisy-of-pakistans-self-declared-liberals/.

Kazi, Shahnaz (1999) "Gender Inequalities and Development in Pakistan." In *50 Years of Pakistan's Economy: Traditional Topics and Contemporary Concerns*, edited by S. R. Khan. Karachi: Oxford University Press.

Keating, Christine, Rasmussen, Claire, and Rishi, Pooja (2010) "The Rationality of Empowerment: Microcredit, Accumulation by Dispossession, and the Gendered Economy." *Signs: Journal of Women in Culture and Society* 36 (1): 153–176.

Keddie, Nikki R. (2003) "Secularism and its Discontents." *Daedalus* 132 (3): 14–30.

Khan, Ayesha (2007) "Women And Paid Work In Pakistan: Pathways of Women's Empowerment South Asia Research Programme." Pakistan Scoping Paper. The Collective for Social Science Research. Karachi.

—— (2008) "Women's Empowerment And The Lady Health Worker Programme In Pakistan." Paper for The Collective for Social Science Research. Karachi.

—— (2011) "Lady Health Workers and Social Change." *Economic and Political Weekly* 46 (30) July 23: 28–31.

Khan, Nighat Said (1992) *Voices Within; Dialogues With Women on Islam*. Lahore: ASR Resource Centre.

—— (1999) "Up Against the State: The Women's Movement in Pakistan – Implications for the Global Women's Movement." Dame Nita Barrow Lecture. Toronto.

Khan, Nighat Said, Saigol, Rubina, and Zia, Afiya Shehrbano (Eds.) (1994) *Locating the Self: Perspectives on Women and Multiple Identities*. Lahore: ASR Resource Centre.

—— (1995) *A Celebration of Women; Essays and Abstracts from the Women's Studies Conference*. Lahore: ASR Resource Centre.

Khan, Omar Asghar (2001) "Critical Engagements: NGOs and the State." In *Power and Civil Society in Pakistan*, edited by A.M. Weiss, and S.Z. Gilani. Pakistan: Oxford University Press.

Khan, Seema, and Ladbury, Sarah (2008) "Increased Religiosity Among Women in Muslim Majority Countries." Issues Paper. UK Department for International Development (DFID) Study for Governance and Social Development Resource Centre (GSDRC). http://www.gsdrc.org/docs/ open/eirs1.pdf.

Khan, Shahnaz (2006) *Zina, Transformational Feminism and the Moral Regulation of Pakistani Women*. Pakistan: Oxford University Press; University of British Columbia.

Khattak, Saba Gul (1994) "A Reinterpretation of the State and Statist Discourse in Pakistan (1977–1988)." In *Locating the Self: Perspectives on Women and Multiple Identities*, edited by N.S. Khan, R. Saigol, and A.S. Zia. Lahore: ASR Resource Centre.

Khattak, Saba Gul, Habib, Kiran, and Khan, Foqia Sadiq (2008) "Women and Human Security in South Asia: The Cases of Bangladesh and Pakistan." A Paper for Sustainable Development Policy Institute, Islamabad.

Kirmani, Nida (2011) "Interactions between Religion, the State and Civil Society in Pakistan: Some Implications for Development." Working Paper 65. University of Birmingham and DFID: Religions and Development Research Programme, UK. http://r4d.dfid.gov.uk/Output/186534/Default.aspx.

Lateef, Shahida (1990) *Muslim Women in India: Political and Private Realities 1890s-1980s*. London: Zed Books.

Lau, Martin (2005) *The Role of Islam in the Legal System of Pakistan*. London-Leiden Series on Law, Administration and Development (Book 9). Brill/Nijhoff.

Lewis, Reina (2004) *Rethinking Orientalism: Women, Travel, and the Ottoman Harem*. UK: I.B. Tauris & Co. Ltd.; New Jersey: Rutgers University Press.

Lewis, Reina, and Mills, Sara (Eds.) (2003) *Feminist Postcolonial Theory; A Reader*. New York: Routledge.

Loomba, Ania (1988) *Colonialism/Postcolonialism (The New Critical Idiom)*. London; New York: Routledge.

—— (2003) "Dead Women Tell No Tales: Issues of Female Subjectivity, Subaltern Agency and Tradition in Colonial and Postcolonial Writings on Widow Immolation in India." In R. Lewis and S. Mills (Eds.) (2003) *Feminist Postcolonial Theory; A Reader*. New York: Routledge.

Mahmood, Saba (2001) "Feminist Theory, Embodiment, and the Docile Agent: Some Reflections on the Egyptian Islamic Revival." *Cultural Anthropology* 16 (2): 202–236.

—— (2003) "Questioning Liberalism, Too: A Response to 'Islam and the Challenge of Democracy.'" *Boston Review: A Political and Literary Forum* [online] April 3. Reprinted as, "Is Liberalism Islam's Only Answer?" In *Islam and the Challenge to Democracy*, edited by J. Cohen and D. Chasman (2004). New Jersey: Princeton University Press.

—— (2005) *Politics of Piety; The Islamic Revival and the Feminist Subject*. New Jersey: Princeton University Press.

—— (2006) "Secularism, Hermeneutics, and Empire: The Politics of Islamic Reformation." *Public Culture* 18 (2): 323–347.

—— (2008a) "Secular Imperatives?" *Public Culture* 20 (3): 461–465.

—— (2008b) "Is Critique Secular? A Symposium at UC Berkley." *Public Culture* (20) 3: 447–452.

Maira, Sunaina (2009) "'Good' and 'Bad' Muslim Citizens: Feminists, Terrorists, and US Orientalisms." *Feminist Studies* 35(3): 631–656.

Malhotra, Anju and Mather, Mark (1997) "Do Schooling and Work Empower Women in Developing Countries? Gender and Domestic Decisions in Sri Lanka." *Sociological Forum* 12(4): 599–630.

Mamdani, Mahmood (2004) *Good Muslim, Bad Muslim: America, the Cold War, and the Roots of Terror*. New York: Pantheon.

Manchanda, Nivi (2012) "Out of Nowhere? The Taliban and Malala." *openDemocracy*, November 7. https://www.opendemocracy.net/opensecurity/nivi-manchanda/out-of-nowhere-taliban-and-malala.

Marsden, Magnus (2008) "Women, Politics and Islamism in Northern Pakistan." *Modern Asian Studies* 42 (2–3): 405–429.

Marx, Karl, and Engels, Friedrich (1848) "Bourgeois and Proletarians." In *The Communist Manifesto*. (Reprint 1988) London: Signet Classics.

Masud, Muhammad Khalid (2012) "Religion and Development Challenges in Pakistan." In *Development Challenges Confronting Pakistan*, edited by A.M. Weiss and S.G. Khattak. USA: Kumarian Press.

Mayer, Ann Elizabeth (1995) *Islam and Human Rights: Tradition and Politics*. Westview Press.

McLaren, Margaret A. (2002) *Feminism, Foucault, and Embodied Subjectivity*. New York: State University of New York Press.

McNeil Jr., Donald G. (2013) "Pakistan Battles Polio, and Its People's Mistrust." *New York Times*, July 21. http://www.nytimes.com/2013/07/22/health/pakistan-fights-for-ground-in-war-on-polio.html.

Mendieta, Eduardo, and Vanantwerpen, Jonathan (Eds.) (2011) *The Power of Religion in the Public Sphere*. New York: Columbia University Press.

Mernissi, Fatima (1987) *Beyond the Veil: Male-Female Dynamics in Modern Muslim Society*. Bloomington: Indiana University Press.

—— (1991a) *Women and Islam: A Historical and Theological Enquiry*. Oxford: Blackwell.

—— (1991b) *The Veil and the Male Elite: A Feminist Interpretation of Women's Rights in Islam*. Reading, MA: Addison-Wesley.

—— (1997) *The Forgotten Queens of Islam*. Minneapolis: University Of Minnesota Press.

Metcalf, Barbara D. (1990) *Perfecting Women: Maulana Ashraf `Ali Thanawi's Bihishti Zewar. A Partial Translation with Commentary*. Berkeley: University of California Press.

—— (1996) "Islam and Women; The Case of the Tablighi Jama'at'." *Stanford Electronic Humanities Review* 5 (1): 51.

—— (2004) *Islamic Contestations: Essays on Muslims in India and Pakistan*. New Delhi: Oxford University Press.

Mir-Hosseini, Ziba (1999) *Islam and Gender: The Religious Debate in Contemporary Iran*. New Jersey: Princeton University Press.

—— (2011) "Beyond 'Islam' vs 'Feminism'." *IDS Bulletin* 42 (1): 67–77.

Moallem, Minoo (1999) "Transnationalism, Feminism and Fundamentalism." In *Between Woman and Nation*, edited by C. Kaplan, N. Alarcon, and M. Moallem. Durham, NC: Duke University Press.

Modirzadeh, Naz K. (2006) "Taking Islamic Law Seriously: INGOs and the Battle for Muslim Hearts and Minds." *Harvard Human Rights Journal* 19: 191–233.

Moghadam, Valentine M. (2000) "Hidden from History? Women Workers in Modern Iran." *Iranian Studies* 33 (3/4): 377–401.

—— (2004) "Women's Economic Participation in the Middle East: What

Difference Has the Neoliberal Policy Turn Made?" *Journal of Middle East Women's Studies* 1 (1): 110–46.

—— (2003) *Modernizing Women: Gender and Social Change in the Middle East.* Boulder: Lynne Rienner.

—— (2005) *Globalizing Women: Transnational Feminist Networks.* Baltimore: Johns Hopkins University Press.

Moghissi, Haideh (1999) *Feminism and Islamic Fundamentalism: The Limits of Postmodern Analysis.* London: Zed Books.

Mohanty, Chandra Talpade (1988) "Under Western Eyes: Feminist Scholarship and Colonial Discourses." *Feminist Review* 30: 61–88.

—— (2003) *Feminism Without Borders: Decolonizing Theory, Practicing Solidarity.* Durham; London: Duke University Press'

Mojab, Shahrzad (1988) "'Muslim" Women and 'Western' Feminists: The Debate on Particulars and Universals." *Monthly Review* 50 (7): 19.

—— (2001) "Theorizing the Politics of 'Islamic Feminism'." *Feminist Review* 69 (1): 124–146.

—— (2006) "Gender, Political Islam, and Imperialism." In *The New Imperialists; Ideologies of Empire,* edited by C. Mooers. Oxford: Oneworld.

Moussa, Janine (2011) "The Rightful Place of Gender Equality Within Islam." *openDemocracy,* February 24. http://www.opendemocracy. net/5050/janine-moussa/rightful-place-of-gender-equality-within-islam.

Mufti, Aamir R. (2004) "Critical Secularism: A Reintroduction for Perilous Times." *boundary 2* 31 (2): 1–9.

—— (2013) "Why I Am Not a Postsecularist." *boundary 2* 40 (1): 7–19.

—— (2014) "Talal Asad on 'Violence, Law, and Humanitarianism': A Response." A Public Seminar on Humanitarian Violence by Critical Inquiry, 16 May, Chicago. http://criticalinquiry.uchicago.edu/ talal_asad_on_violence_law_and_humanitarianism_a_response/.

Mumtaz, Khawar and Mumtaz, Samiya K. (2012) "Women's Rights and the Punjab Peasant Movement." (Revised paper) *South Asian Journal* 35: 138–150. http://sa.indiaenvironmentportal.org.in/files/file/Punjab%20peasant%20 movement.pdf.

Mumtaz, Khawar and Shaheed, Farida (1981) *Invisible Workers: Piecework Labour Amongst Women in Lahore.* Islamabad: Women's Division of the Government of Pakistan.

—— (1987) *Women of Pakistan: Two Steps Forward, One Step Back.* London: Zed Books.

Mumtaz, Zubia, Salway, Sarah, Nykiforuk, Candace, Bhatti, Afshan, Ataullahjan, Anushka, and Ayyalasomayajula, Bharati (2013) "The Role of Social Geography on Lady Health Workers' Mobility and Effectiveness in Pakistan." *Social Science & Medicine* 91: 48–57.

Mushtaq, Faiza (2010) "A Controversial Role Model for Pakistani Women." *South Asia Multidisciplinary Academic Journal* [Online] 4. http://samaj.revues.org/index3030.html.

Naqvi, Haider Ali, Huma, Shafqat, and Kazim, Syed Faraz (2011) "Suicide Bombing: A Geopolitical Perspective." *Journal of Pakistan Medical Association.* http://www.jpma.org.pk/full_article_text.php?article_id=2540.

Narayan, Uma (1998) "Essence of Culture and a Sense of History: A Feminist Critique of Cultural Essentialism." *Hypatia* 13 (2): 86–106.

National Emergency Action Plan for Polio Eradication (NEAP) 2016–2017, Government of Pakistan.

Nesiah, Vasuki (2013) "Feminism as Counter-terrorism: The Seduction of Power." In *Gender, National Security, and Counter-Terrorism: Human Rights Perspectives,* edited by M.L. Satterthwaite and J.C. Huckerby. London: Routledge.

Noorani, Ahmad (2012) "HRW Presented One-sided View on Balochistan to US panel." *The News*, February 21. https://www.thenews.com.pk/archive/print/620382-hrw-presented-one-sided-view-on-balochistan-to-us-panel.

O'Hanlon, Rosalind, and Washbrook, David (1992) "After Orientalism: Culture, Criticism and Politics in the Third World." *Comparative Studies in Society and History* 34 (1): 141–167.

Offenhauer, Priscilla (2005) "Women in Islamic Societies: A Selected Review of Social Scientific Literature." A Report prepared by the Federal Research Division, Library of Congress under an Interagency Agreement with the Office an Interagency Agreement with the Office of the Director of National Intelligence/National Intelligence Council (ODNI/ADDNIA/NIC) and Central Intelligence Agency/Directorate of Science & Technology, November. https://www.loc.gov/rr/frd/pdf-files/Women_Islamic_Societies.pdf.

Ong, Aihwa (2003) "State Versus Islam: Malay Families, Women's Bodies and the Body Politic in Malaysia." In *Feminist Postcolonial Theory; A Reader*, edited by R. Lewis and S. Mills. New York: Routledge.

Oppel Jr., Richard A. and Shah, Pir Zubari (2009) "In Pakistan, Radio Amplifies Terror of Taliban." *New York Times,* January 24. http://www.nytimes.com/2009/01/25/world/asia/25swat.html.

Pakistan Labour Force Survey (2014–2015) Thirty-third Issue, Statistics Division, Federal Bureau of Statistics, Government of Pakistan. http://www.pbs.gov.pk/content/labour-force-survey-2014-15-annual-report.

Papanek, Hanna (1971) "Purdah in Pakistan; Seclusion and Modern Occupations for Women." *Journal of Marriage and Family* 33 (3): 517–530.

—— (1973) "Men, Women, and Work: Reflections on the Two-Person Career." *American Journal of Sociology* 78 (4): 852–872.

PLD (1994) Ms. Shehla Zia v. WAPDA. *The All Pakistan Legal Decisions* published by P.L.D. Publishers, Lahore, Supreme Court 693. https://www.elaw.org/content/pakistan-zia-v-wapda-p-l-d-1994-supreme-court-693.

Pratt, Nicola (2013a) "Weaponising Feminism for the "War on Terror",

Versus Employing Strategic Silence." *Critical Studies on Terrorism* 6 (2): 327–331.

—— (2013b) "A Response to Afiya Zia's Call for Prioritising Gender." *Critical Studies on Terrorism* 6 (2): 334–335.

Puar, Jasbir K. (2007) *Terrorist Assemblages: Homonationalism in Queer Times*. Durham, NC: Duke University Press.

Quraishi, Asifa (2011) "What if Sharia Weren't the Enemy: Rethinking International Women's Rights Advocacy on Islamic Law." *Columbia Journal of Gender and Law* 22 (1): 173–249.

Rahim, Lily Zubaidah (Ed.) (2013) *Muslim Secular Democracy: Voices from Within*. Palgrave Macmillan.

Rahman, Fazlur (1982) *Islam and Modernity: Transformation of an Intellectual Tradition*. Chicago: University of Chicago Press.

Rashid, Ahmed (2000) *Taliban: Islam, Oil and the New Great Game in Central Asia*. London; New York: I.B. Tauris.

—— (2003) *Jihad; The Rise of Militant Islam in Central Asia*. UK: Penguin.

Rashid, Tahmina (2006) *Contested Representation: Punjabi Women in Feminist Debate in Pakistan*. Karachi: Oxford University Press.

Razack, Sherene H. (2008) *Casting Out: The Eviction of Muslims from Western Law and Politics*. University of Toronto Press.

Rehman, Masood (2011) "Backlog of Over 1.35m Cases 'Haunts' the Judiciary." *Pakistan Today*, August 30. http://www.pakistantoday.com. pk/ 2011/08/08/national/backlog-of-over-1-35m-cases-%e2%80%98 haunts %e2%80%99-the-judiciary/.

Rehman, Zia Ur (2016) "Winds of Change." *The News on Sunday*, March 27. http://tns.thenews.com.pk/winds-change/#.WVLZCIVLY7A.

Reilly, Niamh (2011) "Rethinking the Interplay of Feminism and Secularism in a Neo-secular Age." *Feminist Review* 97 (1): 5–31.

Roald, Anne Sophie (1998) "Feminist Reinterpretation of Islamic Sources: Muslim Feminist Theology in the Light of the Christian Tradition of Feminist Thought." In *Women and Islamization: Contemporary Dimensions of Discourse on Gender Relations*, edited by Ask, Karin and M. Tjomsland. Oxford; New York: Berghahn.

Rose, Nikolas (1999) *Powers of Freedom: Reframing Political Thought*. Cambridge: Cambridge University Press.

Rouse, Shahnaz (1992) "Discourses on Gender in Pakistan." In *Religion and Political Conflict in South Asia: India, Pakistan, and Sri Lanka*, edited by D. Allen. Westport, Connecticut: Greenwood Press.

Rowbotham, Sheila (1975) *Hidden from History: 300 Years of Women's Oppression and the Fight Against It*. Pluto Press.

Roy, Olivier (2004) *Globalised Islam: The Search for a New Ummah*. UK: C. Hurst & Co. Publishers Ltd.

—— (2007) *Secularism Confronts Islam*. New York: Columbia University Press.

Sa'dawi, Nawal El (translated and edited by Sherif Hetata) (1980) *The Hidden Face of Eve: Women in the Arab World*. London: Zed Books.

Sahi, Aoun (2012) "Dawa, Jihad, Charity or All?" *The News on Sunday*, April 15 (last accessed December 2015).

Saigol, Rubina (2010) "Ownership or Death: Women and Tenant Struggle in Pakistani Punjab." Monograph. New Delhi: Rupa & Co.

—— (2011) "Women's Empowerment in Pakistan: A Scoping Study." GEP/USAID. Aurat Foundation Publication.

—— (2013) *The Pakistan Project: A Feminist Perspective on Nation and Identity*. New Delhi: Women Unlimited.

Sarkar, Sumit (2000a) "The Decline of the Subaltern in Subaltern Studies." *In Mapping Subaltern Studies and the Postcolonial*, edited by V. Chaturvedi. London: Verso.

—— (2000b) "Orientalism Revisited: Saidian Frameworks in the Writing of Modern Indian History." *In Mapping Subaltern Studies and the Postcolonial*, edited by V. Chaturvedi. London: Verso.

Sarkar, Tanika (2002) *Hindu Wife, Hindu Nation: Community, Religion, and Cultural Nationalism*. Bloomington: Indiana University Press.

Sathar, Zeba Ayesha, and Kazi, Shahnaz (2000) "Women's Autonomy in the Context of Rural Pakistan." *Pakistan Development Review* 39 (2): 89–110.

Schuler, Dana (2006) "The Uses and Misuses of the Gender-related Development Index and Gender Empowerment Measure: a Review of the Literature." *Journal of Human Development* 7 (2): 161–181.

Schwartz, Stephen (2007) "Moderate Islam and Its Muslim Enemies." *American Thinker* [online], July 20. http://www.americanthinker.com/articles/2007/07/moderate_islam_and_its_muslim.html.

Scott, Joan Wallace (2001) "Fantasy Echo: History and the Construction of Identity." *Critical Inquiry* 27(2): 284–384.

—— (2008) *The Politics of the Veil*. New Jersey: Princeton University Press.

Shah, Aqil (2011) "Security, Soldiers, and the State." In *The Future of Pakistan*, edited by S. P. Cohen. Washington: Brookings Institution Press.

Shah, Nafisa (2016) *Honour and Violence: Gender, Power and Law in Southern Pakistan*. New York; Oxford: Berghahn.

Shah, Saeed (2011) "CIA Organised Fake Vaccination Drive to Get Osama bin Laden's Family DNA." *The Guardian*, July 11. https://www.theguardian.com/world/2011/jul/11/cia-fake-vaccinations-osama-bin-ladens-dna.

Shaheed, Farida (1998) "Engagements of Culture, Customs and Law: Women's Lives and Activism." In *Shaping Women's Lives: Law, Practices and Strategies in Pakistan*, edited by F. Shaheed, S. A.Warraich, C. Balchin, and A. Gazdar. Lahore, Pakistan: Shirkat Gah.

—— (1999) "The Other Side of the Discourse; Women's Experiences of Identity, Religion, and Activism in Pakistan." In *Resisting the Sacred and Secular: Women's Activism and Politicised Religion in South Asia*, edited by A. Basu and P. Jeffery. India: Kali.

—— (2002) "Women's Experiences of Identity, Religion and Activism in

Pakistan." In *The Post-Colonial State and Social Transformation in India and Pakistan*, edited by S.M. Naseem and K. Nadvi. Karachi: Oxford University Press.

—— (2010) "Contested Identities: Gendered Politics, Gendered Religion in Pakistan." *Third World Quarterly* 31 (6): 851–867.

Shaikh, Farzana (2011) "A Review; 'Secularizing Islamists? Jamaat-i-Islami and Jama`at-ud-Da`wa in Urban Pakistan by Humeira Iqtidar." *International Affairs* 87 (6): 1557–1559.

Shehabuddin, Elora (2011) "Gender and the Figure of the "Moderate Muslim": Feminism in the Twenty-First Century." In *The Question of Gender: Joan W. Scott's Critical Feminism*, edited by J. Butler and E. Weed. Bloomington: Indiana University Press.

Shehrbano, Afiya (2010) "Unveiling Freedoms." *The News International*, May 9. https://www.thenews.com.pk/print/87575-unveiling-freedoms.

Sholkamy, Hania (2011) "Creating Conservatism or Emancipating Subjects? On the Narrative of Islamic Observance in Egypt." *IDS Bulletin* 42 (1): 47–55.

Siddiqui, Niloufer (2010) "Gender Ideology and the Jamaat-e-Islami." *Current Trends in Islamist Ideology* 10, August 17. http://www.current-trends.org/research/detail/gender-ideology-and-the-jamaat-e-islami.

Siddiqui, Taha (2013) "5 Female Teachers Killed: Pakistan Aid work Imperiled." *Christian Science Monitor,* January 2. http://www.csmonitor.com/World/Asia-South-Central/2013/0102/5-female-teachers-killed-Pakistan-aid-work-imperiled/(page)/2.

Sinha, Mrinalini (2011) "Historically Speaking: Gender and Citizenship in Colonial India." In *The Question of Gender: Joan W. Scott's Critical Feminism*, edited by J. Butler and E. Weed. Bloomington: Indiana University Press.

Sonbol, Amira El-Azhary (Ed.) (1996) *Women, Family, and Divorce Laws in Islamic History.* Syracuse, NY: Syracuse University Press.

Spivak, Gayatri C. (1988) "Can the Subaltern Speak?" In *Marxism and the Interpretation of Culture,* edited by C. Nelson and L. Grossberg. Urbana: University of Illinois Press.

—— (1992) "Acting Bits/Identity Talk." *Critical Inquiry* 18 (4): 770–803.

—— (1999) *A Critique of Postcolonial Reason: Toward a History of the Vanishing Present.* Cambridge, Mass: Harvard University Press.

—— (2000) "The New Subaltern: A Silent Interview by Gayatri Chakravorty Spivak." *In Mapping Subaltern Studies and the Postcolonial,* edited by V. Chaturvedi. London: Verso.

—— (2010) "In Response: Looking Back, Looking Forward." In *Can the Subaltern Speak? Reflections on the History of an Idea,* edited by R.C. Morris. Columbia University Press.

Spivak, Gayatri C., and Zia, Afiya Shehrbano (2013) "Faith and Feminism in Pakistan: Afiya Zia and Gayatri Spivak In Conversation." Presented at the Center for Place, Culture, and Politics, New York, CUNY Graduate Center, February 25. http://pcp.gc.cuny.edu/2013/03/video-afiya-zia-and-gayatri-spivak-in-conversation-faith-and-feminism-in-pakistan/.

Stowasser, Barbara (1998) "Gender Issues in Contemporary Qur'anic Interpretation." In *Islam, Gender, and Social Change*, edited by Y.Y. Haddad and J.L Esposito. New York: Oxford University Press.

Syed, Jawad (2010) "An Historical Perspective on Islamic Modesty and its Implications for Female Employment." *Equality, Diversity and Inclusion: An International Journal* 29 (2): 150–166.

Tadros, Mariz (Ed.) (2011) "Gender, Rights and Religion at the Crossroads." *IDS Bulletin* 42 (1).

—— (2011) "The Muslim Brotherhood's Gender Agenda: Reformed or Reframed?" *IDS Bulletin* 42 (1): 88–98.

Taylor, Charles (2007) *A Secular Age*. Cambridge, MA: The Belknap Press of Harvard University Press.

Tharoor, Ishaan (2007) "The Original Insurgent." *Time.com*, April 19. http://www.time.com/time/magazine/article/0,9171,1612380,00.html.

The Express Tribune (2012) "No Female Speakers at Jamaat e Islami's Hijab Day Rally." September 4. http://tribune.com.pk/story/431238/no-female-speakers-at-jamaat-e-islamis-hijab-day-rally/).

The Express Tribune (2012) "There's No Shame in Wearing a Hijab." September 16. http://tribune.com.pk/story/437401/celebrating-culture-theres-no-shame-in-wearing-a-hijab/.

The Express Tribune (2012) "If Malala Survives, We Will Target Her Again: Taliban." October 9. http://tribune.com.pk/story/449070/national-peace-award-winner-malala-yousufzai-injured-in-firing-incident/.

The Express Tribune (2012) "Taliban Says its Attack on Malala Justified." October 16. http://tribune.com.pk/story/452331/taliban-says-its-attack-on-malala-justified/.

The Express Tribune (2012) "The TTP's 'Defence' of the Attack on Malala." October 17. http://tribune.com.pk/story/452910/the-ttps-defence-of-the-attack-on-malala/.

The Express Tribune (2013) "Controversial Remarks: Army Demands Apology." November 17. http://tribune.com.pk/story/630232/controversial-remarks-army-demands-apology-from-munawar-hassan/.

The Nation (2010) "Certain Clauses of WPA 'Repugnant': FSC." December 23. http://www.nation.com.pk/pakistan-news-newspaper-daily-english-online/Politics/23-Dec-2010/Certain-clauses-of-WPA-repugnant-FSC.

The News International (2010) "Unique Rally to Demand Dr. Aafia's Release." August 21. http://www.thenews.com.pk/TodaysPrintDetail.aspx?ID=311&Cat=4&dt=1/5/2011.

The News International (2012) "Bullet Successfully Removed from Malala." October 10. http://www.thenews.com.pk/article-70908-Bullet-successfully-removed-from-Malala.

The News International (2012) "Malik Announces Rs100m Bounty on TTP Spokesman." October 17. http://www.thenews.com.pk/Todays-News-13-18224-Malik-announces-Rs100m-bounty-on-TTP-spokesman.

Tohid, Owais (2010) "Swat Paradiso in Black and White." *Daily Times*,

March 20 (last accessed December 2015).

Tohidi, Nayareh (2005) "Transnational Feminism: A Range of Disciplinary Perspectives." Roundtable conference, UCLA, USA.

Toor, Saadia (2012) "Imperialist Feminism Redux." *Dialectical Anthropology* 36 (3–4): 147–160.

—— (2011) "Gender, Sexuality, and Islam under the Shadow of Empire." *The Scholar and Feminist Online* 9 (3).

Tucker, Judith E. (1986) *Women in Nineteenth-Century Egypt*. Cairo; Egypt: American University in Cairo Press.

Tusan, Michelle (2002) "Gender, Patriarchy, and Colonialism in Nineteenth-Century India." *H-Women, H-Net Reviews*. http://www.hnet.org/reviews /showrev.php?id=7036.

Ud Din, Iftikhar, Mumtaz, Zubia, and Ataullahjan, Anushka (2012) "How the Taliban Undermined Community Healthcare in Swat, Pakistan." *British Medical Journal* (BMJ) 2012; 344:e2093, March 21. http://www.bmj.com/content/344/bmj.e2093.

USAID (2008) "Evaluation Of The Access To Contemporary Markets For Homebound Women Embroiderers Project." A Report. April. MSI: Washington. http://pdf.usaid.gov/pdf_docs/PDACL798.pdf.

USAID (2010) "Religion, Conflict And Peacebuilding." A Report from a Roll Out Event, March 8. Under the aegis of the US Agency for International Development and including, the Bureau for Democracy, Conflict and Humanitarian Assistance, the Office of Conflict Management and Mitigation.

Yadlin, Rivka (2006) "Female Martyrdom: The Ultimate Embodiment of Islamic Existence?" In 'Female Suicide Bombers; Dying for Equality?' Memorandum 84, edited by Y. Schweitzer. Jafee Centre for Strategic Studies: Tel Aviv University. http://www.inss.org.il/uploadimages/Import/ (FILE)1188302013.pdf.

Yasmeen, Samina (2013) "Democracy for Muslims: Javed Ahmed Ghamdi." In *Muslim Secular Democracy: Voices from Within*, edited by L.Z. Rahim. Palgrave Macmillan.

Wadud, Amina (2006) *Inside the Gender Jihad: Women's Reform in Islam*. Oxford: Oneworld.

Walsh, Declan (2011) "Raymond Davis Trial Underway in Pakistan." *The Guardian*, February 25. http://www.theguardian.com/world/ 2011/feb/25/raymond-davis-trial-starts-pakistan.

Warraich, Sohail Akbar, and Balchin, Cassandra (1998) "Confusion Worse Confounded: A Critique Of Divorce Law And Legal Practice In Pakistan." In *Shaping Women's Lives: Law, Practices and Strategies in Pakistan*, edited by F. Shaheed, S.A. Warraich, C. Balchin, and A. Gazdar. Lahore: Shirkat Gah.

Warren, Alan (2000) *Waziristan, the Faqir of Ipi, and the Indian Army: the North West Frontier Revolt of 1936–37*. Oxford: Oxford University Press.

Wee, Vivenne, and Shaheed, Farida (2008) "Women Empowering Themselves: A Framework That Interrogates and Transforms." The

Research Programme Consortium on 'Women's Empowerment in Muslim Contexts (WEMC); Gender, Poverty and Democratisation From the Inside Out.' Southeast Asia Research Centre, Hong Kong University (funded by DFID). http://r4d.dfid.gov.uk/Output/180051/Default.aspx.

Winter, Bronwyn (2013) "Secularism and Religious Freedom; Challenging the "Postsecular"." In *Muslim Secular Democracy: Voices Within*, edited by L.Z. Rahim. Palgrave Macmillan.

Woodhull, Winifred (2003) "Unveiling Algeria." In *Feminist Postcolonial Theory; A Reader,* edited by R. Lewis and S. Mills. New York: Routledge.

Yusufzai, Rahimullah (2010) "And Now, Women Suicide Bombers." *The News International*, December 29. https://www.thenews.com.pk/archive/print/276980-and-now-women-suicide-bombers.

Zafar, Fareeha (1991) *Finding Our Way: Readings on Women in Pakistan.* Lahore: ASR Resource Centre.

Zaidi, S. Akbar (1999) *Issues in Pakistan's Economy.* Karachi: Oxford University Press.

—— (2002) "The Dismal State of Social Sciences in Pakistan." *Economic and Political Weekly* 37 (35) August 31–September 6: 3644–3661.

—— (2005) "State, Military and Social Transition: Improbable Future of Democracy in Pakistan." *Economic and Political Weekly* 40 (49) December 3–9: 5173–5181.

—— (2011) *Military, Civil Society and Democratisation in Pakistan.* Lahore: Vanguard.

—— (2012a) "The Power of Land." *Dawn*, August 13. http://dawn.com/news/741775/the-power-of-land.

—— (2012b) "Contesting Notions of Pakistan." *Economic and Political Weekly* 47 (45) November 10–17: 32–39.

Zain, Ali (2015) "4 Terrorist Groups That Condemned APS Terror Attack." *Daily Pakistan*, December 16. https://en.dailypakistan.com.pk/top-lists/4-terrorist-groups-that-condemned-aps-terror-attack.

Zia, Afiya Shehrbano (1994) *Sex Crime in the Islamic Context; Rape, Class and Gender in Pakistan.* Lahore: ASR Resource Centre.

—— (2008) "A State of Suspended Disbelief." *Economic and Political Weekly* 43 (23) June 7–13: 69–71.

—— (2009a) "The Reinvention of Feminism in Pakistan." *Feminist Review* 91 (1): 29–46.

—— (2009b) "Faith-based Challenges to the Women's Movement in Pakistan." In *Contesting Feminisms: Gender and Islam in Asia*, edited by H.A. Ghosh. New York: SUNY Press.

—— (2009c) *Challenges to Secular Feminism: a Critique of Islamic Feminism and Revivalism.* Centre of South Asian Studies, Occasional Paper 29. University of Cambridge.

—— (2011a) "Donor-driven Islam?" *openDemocracy*, January 21. http://www.opendemocracy.net/5050/afiya-shehrbano-/donor-driven-islam.

—— (2011b) "Two Million Dollars: A Patriarchal Bargain."

openDemocracy, March 29. http://www.opendemocracy.net/5050/afiya-shehrbano-zia/two-million-dollars-patriarchal-bargain.

—— (2011c) "Female Suicide Bombings in Pakistan: What's In It For Women?" *openDemocracy*, October 4. http://www.opendemocracy.net/5050/afiya-shehrbano-zia/female-suicide-bombings-in-pakistan-whats-in-it-for-women.

—— (2013a) "Redefining Faith and Freedoms: the "War on Terror" and Pakistani Women." *Critical Studies on Terrorism* 6 (2): 323–326.

—— (2013b) "A Response to Nicola Pratt's Call for "Strategic Silence." *Critical Studies on Terrorism* 6 (2): 332–333.

—— (2013c) "Rights-based vs Faith-based Development in Pakistan." In *Development Challenges in Pakistan*, edited by S.G. Khattak and A. Weiss. Kumarian Press.

—— (2014a) "Being Malala." *openDemocracy*, October 13. https://www.opendemocracy.net/5050/afiya-shehrbano-zia/being-malala.

—— (2014b) "Fear of Liberal Politics." *The News*, March 14. https://www.thenews.com.pk/print/88457-fear-of-liberal-politics.

—— (2017) "The Secular Myth." *Dawn*, May 24. https://www.dawn.com/news/1334995/the-secular-myth

Zia, Amir (2013) "False Fault Lines." *The News*, May 6. http://www.thenews.com.pk/Todays-News-9-175638-False-fault-lines.

Zia, Shahla (1998) "Some Experiences of the Women's Movement: Strategies for Success." In *Shaping Women's Lives: Law, Practices and Strategies in Pakistan*, edited by F. Shaheed, S. A. Warraich, C. Balchin, and A. Gazdar. Lahore, Pakistan: Shirkat Gah.

Index

Note: Entries for Pakistan and Secular/Secularise are too numerous to be indexed for any gain.

About the Author

Afiya S. Zia is the author of *Sex Crime in the Islamic Context* (1994, ASR) and has contributed essays to several edited volumes including, *Contesting Feminisms: Gender and Islam in Asia* (SUNY Press, 2015) and, *Voicing Demands* (Zed Books, 2014). Her peer-reviewed essays have been carried in *Feminist Review* and the *International Feminist Journal of Politics*. She teaches at Habib University, Karachi and at the University of Toronto, Canada and is an active member of Women's Action Forum, Pakistan.